The Museum
Educator's Manual

The Museum Educator's Manual

Educators Share Successful Techniques

ANNA JOHNSON, KIMBERLY A. HUBER,
NANCY CUTLER, MELISSA BINGMANN, AND TIM GROVE

A Division of

ROWMAN & LITTLEFIELD PUBLISHERS, INC.

Lanham • New York • Toronto • Plymouth, UK

AltaMira Press
A division of Rowman & Littlefield Publishers, Inc.
A wholly owned subsidary of The Rowman & Littlefield Publishing Group, Inc.
4501 Forbes Boulevard, Suite 200, Lanham, MD 20706
www.altamirapress.com

Estover Road, Plymouth PL6 7PY, United Kingdom

Copyright © 2009 by AltaMira Press

British Library Cataloguing in Publication Information Available

Library of Congress Cataloging-in-Publication Data

The museum educator's manual : educators share successful techniques / Anna Johnson ... [et al.].
    p. cm. -- (American Association for State and Local History book series)
  Includes bibliographical references and index.
  ISBN-13: 978-0-7591-1166-0 (cloth : alk. paper)
  ISBN-10: 0-7591-1166-9 (cloth : alk. paper)
  ISBN-13: 978-0-7591-1167-7 (pbk. : alk. paper)
  ISBN-10: 0-7591-1167-7 (pbk. : alk. paper)
 1. Museums--Educational aspects--Handbooks, manuals, etc. 2. Museums--Educational aspects--Case studies. I. Johnson, Anna.

  AM7.M866 2008
  069'.15--dc22

                                        2008031383

Printed in the United States of America

∞™ The paper used in this publication meets the minimum requirements of American National Standard for Information Sciences—Permanence of Paper for Printed Library Materials, ANSI/NISO Z39.48-1992.

Contents

Acknowledgments

Authors receive the credit for writing books, but ultimately many people assist with research, editing, publishing, and support, including family and friends. We acknowledge the following people for their useful comments and suggestions: Melinda Adams, Connie Ainsworth, John Akers, Paul Ashton, Amy Bartow-Melia, Mary Anna Bastin, Kathy Boyer, Heidi Brinig, Michael Casebier, Christine Castle, Jane Clark, Cynthia Copeland, Jerri Copenhaver, Clare Cuddy, Bryan Curd, Tim Cutler, Barbara Decker, Amy Douglass, Theresa Esterlund, Alan Gartenhaus, Carolyn Gilman, Ann Grimes, Bill J. Harrison, Ann Lane Hedlund, Bob Huber, Briana Huffman, Gretchen Jennings, Richard Johnson, Maureen Kerr, Kayla Kolar, Bob and Patsy Kovalesky, Kathleen Love, MaryLynn Mack, Patrick Martin, Linda McCleary, Jeanne Moe, Melissa Moore, Susan Moore, Howard Morrison, Debbie Mueller, Janice O'Donnell, Rob Price, Kristen Pumo, Marliese Reeves, Blake Reid, Wayne Rice, David Schaller, Beverly Sheppard, Alissa Simon, Patricia Smith, Kathleen Socolofsky, Scott Solliday, Laura Stone, Laurie Kilgour Walsh, Larry R. Warner, Jannelle Warren-Findley, GladysAnn Wells, and Chad Wollerton.

Many thanks go to all of the museum professionals who responded to an inquiry we disseminated in the summer of 2007 on "What is the role of a museum educator?" and "What do museum educators do?" A selection of their thoughtful responses introduces our chapters. Included in this group is the George Washington University Graduate Museum Education Program class of 2008, which was just beginning its classwork.

As authors we have benefited from the colleagues at organizations that have informed and shaped our experiences and allowed us to share our forms and textboxes to benefit others in the profession. We thank our friends at the following organizations: American Association for State and Local History, American Association of Museums, Arizona Museum of Natural History (formerly Mesa Southwest Museum), Arizona State Library, Archives and Public Records Agency, Central Arizona Museum Association, Bureau of Land Management, City of Tempe, Deer Valley Rock Art Center, Desert Botanical Garden, Fort Necessity National Battlefield, Gilbert Historical Museum, The Heard Museum, Indiana University–Purdue University Indianapolis, Museum Association of Arizona, Museum Educator's Council of Arizona, Museum of Northern Arizona, Providence Children's Museum, Rhode Island Historical Society, Sirrine House, Smithsonian Institution, and Tempe Historical Museum.

Special thanks go to Larry R. Warner for his illustrations and to AltaMira Press and our editor, Serena Leigh Krombach, for her guidance throughout the review and writing process. Also instrumental to this publication were Christopher Anzalone, Marissa Marro Parks, Jehanne Schweitzer, and Claire Rojstaczer.

Introduction

KIMBERLY A. HUBER

> Experts on professions maintain that a profession communicates formally through its writings. Moreover, a profession determines its autonomy to the extent that it controls its own knowledge base. In essence, writing for professional publication is integral to the development of a profession. Writing meant for fellow practitioners constitutes the discourse requisite for advancing any field of endeavor. When a profession must rely on the literature from other fields, describing and analyzing its own concerns and approaches proceed haphazardly at best. A profession's identity and vitality spring from a shared command of its history, theory, and practice as continually updated and refined through a vigorous professional literature.[1]

Ever since *Museums for a New Century* was published in 1984, education and its role within museums has increasingly become a significant professional concern. Additional publications, such as *Excellence and Equity: Education and the Public Dimensions of Museums* (1992) and *The Educational Role of the Museum* (1999) have reinforced the need for creativity, excellence, and accountability in museum educational programs. *The Museum Educator's Manual: Educators Share Successful Techniques* will address the role museums and museum educators play from an experience-based perspective. Each author contributes key themes and case studies that provide practical examples that can be immediately applied to everyday work.

The Museum Educator's Manual is ideally suited for museum educators, volunteers, and students of museum studies. It will help organizations develop strategies that work to improve the effectiveness of educational activities within all types of museums. This manual might also be relevant to teachers—public, private, charter, and homeschool, or anyone who takes students to museums for tours and educational activities—to understand and plan how schools, parents, and museums can best work together. The authors believe it would be a useful resource for directors and other museum professionals, as well as for future

museum managers or program planners, to better understand the responsibilities that fall under museum education departments.

The Museum Educator's Manual is also a good complement to AltaMira's Museum Manual series: *The Manual of Museum Exhibitions*, *The Manual of Museum Management*, and *The Manual of Museum Planning*. This book is valuable to the field because it offers practical help to new museum educators, educators who don't have a lot of formal training and expertise, or people who work in rural and small to midsize museums. Using this manual's sample forms, checklists, and model programs will enhance professional development. It can serve as an excellent reference guide for any museum library. Academic and public libraries with museum studies materials may also wish to add *The Museum Educator's Manual* to their collections.

INTENDED AUDIENCE

The Museum Educator's Manual is written for a variety of practitioners working in all types of museums—art, history, anthropology, and science—as well as zoos and botanical gardens. Beginning and mid-level museum education professionals and volunteers or those interested in pursuing a museum career will find this handbook relevant. This all-in-one museum education resource provides helpful information on training and management, programs and outreach, and working with others. In this handbook, the authors write from the voice of experience as educators. They provide tips and suggestions based on their successes that any museum educator can implement. Each author brings specific expertise to her or his chosen chapters, and collectively they have worked in the profession for nearly eighty years.

This manual can also be an excellent teaching tool for museum studies and art history students in colleges and universities. Museum studies students can use it to prepare them for internships and the workplace. Most present-day museum educators come out of content specialty disciplines like history, anthropology, or art history, whereas others have formal training in schools of education. Although the number of universities offering graduate degrees in museum studies has greatly expanded in the past ten years, these students often do not have the opportunity to explore the depth of the practical knowledge presented in *The Museum Educator's Manual*. The few museum education classes that are available to them focus on theory, leaving them lacking in useful planning tools. This manual will enable universities to expand course materials for educators. Students can learn about a variety of museum education–related topics from this one resource manual. University professors often bring practical application into graduate courses by inviting experienced practitioners into their classrooms to speak to students. *The Museum Educator's Manual* will enhance this tradition by introducing five practitioners directly into their curricula via this publication, as the authors draw from their own experiences to provide practical and cost-effective strategies. Following the chapters, an appendix includes action templates and tips to use and adapt, along with reference notes.

ABOUT CHAPTER TOPICS AND GROUPINGS

Chapter topics were selected for *The Museum Educator's Manual* because they were typical issues most museum educators face or will soon encounter. In them the authors define terms, offer suggestions, and provide examples. Sidebars often provide case studies from outside the chapter author's experiences. In 2007 we asked a wide variety of museum professionals from around the country and museum education students at George Washington University two questions: "What is the role of a museum educator?" and "What do museum educators do?" We have included

their responses as a prelude to each chapter. Following the chapters are forms and tips to help novice educators plan and prepare for their tasks. We offer these sample forms to serve as a starting point for those who need assistance. We encourage and expect that educators will take what we have presented and adapt the forms and textbox information to better suit their museum, mission, and program. Forms can and should be re-purposed so educators are not constantly reinventing materials and ideas. For example, teacher pre- and postvisit packets might be modified and used for Elderhostel or Scout programs. The information prepared for a changing exhibit handout might be used to train the docents who give tours of the area. Use your creativity and reuse your materials and ideas as often as possible.

Chapters have been grouped in a way we believe will be useful to museum educators: Training and Management, Programs and Outreach, and Working with Others. We recognize that this book can serve as a reference manual for educators, who may read chapters as needed, whereas students and beginning educators may find it helpful to read each chapter in order. Regardless of how you read *The Museum Educator's Manual*, we recommend that you begin with the Introduction and Chapter 1 to help you better understand the themes, purpose, format, target audiences, and theoretical framework for this text. Each chapter will also include endnotes relevant to the information presented. A preview of the chapters follows to help readers determine the best way for them to use this book.

PART I: TRAINING AND MANAGEMENT

In Chapter 1, "Museum Education and Museum Educators," Johnson, in cooperation with the other authors, defines museum education for the purposes of this book and talks about the role of the educator within the museum setting. This chapter discusses several different aspects of museum education and who is responsible for it. Some of the questions to be answered in the chapter include the following: What is museum education? What comprises a museum education program? What is the role of the education program within the museum? and What does a museum educator do? This overview will lead to a discussion about job qualifications, skills, personality types, and responsibilities. A strategic planning form is included in the appendix.

In Chapter 2, "Working with Volunteers," Cutler highlights the unique and successful "team approach" to volunteer management at the Desert Botanical Garden. Cutler shares her insights into this management style both as a volunteer and as a manager, focusing on volunteer recruitment, retention, and recognition. The appendix includes a questionnaire to assist in recruiting volunteers, which can help the museum professional place each person in the appropriate position.

Chapter 3, "Docent Training Guidelines," recognizes the key role that docents play in their interaction with museum visitors. They may be the only museum representative the visitor encounters, so building their people and tour skills is essential according to Johnson. She draws on her 25 years of museum experience to discuss docents' roles and necessary skills. Sample techniques and exercises to use in docent training are found at the end of the book.

Chapter 4, "Building Effective Tours: Taming Wild Docents," builds on Johnson's docent experiences from the previous chapter. In it she shares her successful tour techniques and provides tips for guides to adapt their tours to the needs of a variety of visitors. In part 1 of this chapter Johnson focuses on creating flexible tours using transitions. Part 2 details the logistics to consider when establishing a tour program. A transition exercise is just one of the items included as part of this chapter.

PART II: PROGRAMS AND OUTREACH

Chapter 5, "Professional Development for Teachers," moves beyond in-house training. Bingmann specializes in developing workshops for teachers. The chapter presents several philosophical approaches to professional development for teachers, provides models for structuring meaningful programs, and discusses options for participation incentives through partnerships with universities and state departments of education. Identifying, recruiting, and training content providers are other major topics of this section. The author supplies an overview of organizations that specialize in professional development for teachers and suggests ways that museums can learn from and partner with these well-established programs. She also provides an analysis of what makes these programs successful. A list of teachers' professional development organizations is provided in this section.

In Chapter 6, "Families and More: Intergenerational Learning," Bingmann, Grove, and Johnson explore successful methods of facilitating interaction among intergenerational groups. Two recent research efforts in this area and children's museums provide useful

guidance. The authors discuss various approaches to family learning including hands-on learning galleries, specific labels within exhibitions, and printed family guides. They also draw comparisons between home-school audiences and family programming. The chapter includes an example of a successful teen program.

In Chapter 7, "Reaching Out into the Community," programs with schools, traveling history trunks, and Master Arts Parents are three types of outreach programs discussed by Cutler. She has developed traveling trunks that target third and fourth graders for a small history museum in Arizona, in collaboration with a teacher's advisory board from local schools. She participated as a volunteer in the Art Masterpiece outreach program of the Phoenix Art Museum. She writes about the potential for developing similar volunteer outreach programs for any museum, from her perspective as a volunteer. Cutler weighs the pros and cons of outreach and suggests ways to involve people from the target audience in the project's development. A sample teacher's advisory council survey and a model for an innovative outreach project are included.

Because most museum education programs include more than tours, in Chapter 8, "Planning and Managing Museum Programs and Special Events," Huber and Johnson list the reasons to have programs, how to plan them, and things to consider during the planning process. A sample event-planning time line/checklist is included in the appendix, along with other program organization forms.

In Chapter 9, "Education Online," Grove points out that although the Internet is still a young technology, it has already transformed the museum world in many ways. Most museums have an online presence, and while the early stages of Web efforts for museums focused on marketing and online collections, future efforts will focus more on education. Grove believes that educators should play an important role in website development, including a leading role in online exhibitions and educational Web activities. It is important for educators to understand how the medium is unique, what its strengths and limitations are, and how people use the medium. This chapter also briefly touches on electronic field trips. Grove includes discussion questions for help in developing online activities.

In Chapter 10, "Evaluation," Cutler again draws from her experiences at the Desert Botanical Garden to demonstrate how evaluation is a vital component of successful museum programs. In evaluation it is important to know what the goal of the program is as well as the who, what, where, when, and some suggestions for how. Cutler also shares suggestions for how to use the evaluation results. The appendix includes sample evaluation forms.

PART III: WORKING WITH OTHERS

Chapter 11, "Financing Museum Education Programs," suggests that although internal funding is common for many museum education programs it can be supplemented by self-supporting programs and event program fees. However Huber's emphasis is on external funding in the form of grants (private, public, corporate), sponsors, gifts, and bequests. She addresses when to seek outside funding and some unusual sources. A textbox within this chapter offers "Tips for Making Successful Funding Requests."

In Chapter 12, "Educators on Exhibition Teams," Grove highlights the key ways that educators can contribute to exhibition development. Educators bring knowledge of learning theory and can help curators shape content for all types of visitors. They should be advocates for both physical and intellectual accessibility and should be a strong voice for evaluation at various stages. While every exhibition team is different, the educator's role on the team should be clearly defined. Cutler contributes a sidebar that is based on her experiences with exhibits as part of the education department at the Desert Botanical Garden. There, education was integrated with exhibit development and evaluation. Grove's textbox adds ideas for discussion when educators work on exhibition teams.

Huber brings a unique collaborative perspective to museum education in Chapter 13, "Collaboration." Her background in mediation and experiences building collaborations between museums, libraries, archives, and other cultural institutions throughout Arizona inform her viewpoints on the subject. She shares some ideas about internal and external collaborators and answers: What is collaboration? Why should museum educators collaborate? What are the pros and cons? and With whom should they collaborate? She has developed "Keys to Successful Collaboration" and offers them in a textbox.

BIBLIOGRAPHY

Finally a suggested bibliography will include each author's list of must-have museum education reference books and articles that will help to build your museum's library and enhance professional development. Bibliographic resources will be divided by chapters.

CONCLUSION

Certainly other books have covered docents and their training, grantsmanship, exhibits, events, and evaluation; however, none has taken our wide-ranging approach using personal examples and ready-to-use forms and checklists. Previous works have specifically focused on limited topics. What makes *The Museum Educator's Manual* truly unique is that it takes these topics, along with several more, and compiles them into one comprehensive resource that is written with the museum educator in mind.

It is our intention that *The Museum Educator's Manual: Educators Share Successful Techniques* will support the important role of educators and educational programming in museums. Use our strategies in combination with your own to effectively interpret museum collections for visitors of all ages and manage the critical issues of human and material resources. The manual can provide a practical foundation for the daily operations of your museum's education department, essential for accountability in public, private, and government organizations. Revise the forms to create your own keys to success. Then pass them along to future generations of museum professionals.

NOTE

1. Carol B. Stapp with Joanne S. Hirsch, eds., *Writing for Professional Publications: Advancing the Museum Profession through Self-Development* (Washington, D.C.: American Association of Museums Technical Information Service, 1995), 9.

TRAINING AND MANAGEMENT

Illustration by Larry R. Warner

CHAPTER 1

Museum Education and Museum Educators

ANNA JOHNSON

> Museum educators are responsible for making the museum experience meaningful to all visitors. Where the curator is responsible for the integrity of the subject, and the designer for creating a dynamic environment, the educator strives to present the material in appropriate ways so that everyone can come away with a higher level of understanding.
>
> —*Rebekah Y. Brockway, exhibit designer, National Air and Space Museum, Smithsonian Institution*

While attending a social function, someone I don't know comes up to me, we introduce ourselves, and the person asks, "What do you do?" I answer that I'm a museum educator at a local history museum. "Oh," comes the reply, followed by the questions I always dread, "What does that mean, and what exactly do you do?" I only dislike the questions because it is so hard to briefly explain to someone all the different activities that are included in my job. I'm most likely talking to a person who until a few moments ago didn't even know there were educators in museums.

On behalf of educators everywhere, this chapter tackles these questions and provides insight into an educator's perspective and the essential skills required to be an educator, as well as descriptions of ways to prepare to become a museum educator (the sidebars in the chapter share each of the author's paths to their careers in museum education). The jobs in the museum education field are varied, and the descriptions include different applications in order to show that museum educators do much more than just work with school groups, docents, and teachers. The answer still may not be succinct, but it is helpful to acknowledge the breadth of work in the field.

DEFINITION OF MUSEUM EDUCATION

Museum education is complex and diverse and enables museums to connect with their audiences in ways that help visitors take away a richer, more meaningful experience. The diversity of the field is evident in the variety of responsibilities museum educators assume and the range of educational training these professionals bring to the discipline. Throughout *The Museum Educator's Manual* the authors celebrate the array of activities museum educators initiate as well as identify those common threads that bind the field. In 1985 in the book *The Good Guide* museum education was described as "a relatively new field of study."[1] It was considered a new field in that museum staffing had started to include dedicated educators who created special activities for the public. Since then the field has grown by leaps and bounds, but there is still not one agreed on definition for museum education.

Education represents, for visitors and educators alike, different preconceived applications such as traditional teaching and learning for some, and for others divergent forms of learning such as Falk and Dierking's free-choice learning as described in *Learning in Museums*, or constructivism, as defined in *Museums: Places of Learning*. In *Museum and Gallery Education*, Hanneke de Man, curator of interpretation, describes her museum and also speaks to the breadth of museum education: "Education is now understood in the wide sense of any museum activity pursued with a view to conveying knowledge or experience to the public. This definition includes exhibitions, implying that a vision of education is in fact a vision of the museum's purpose as a whole."[2] This description allows for great variety and diversity in programming, and permits a broad definition of education including learning, entertainment, recreation, and more. Staying away from the term "education" specifically limits a predisposition to a specific learning style and allows one to think about a greater variety of applications. It also further emphasizes the connection between the purpose of the museum and the direction of the education program. Exhibitions, education, and the purpose of the museum, as well as the visitor and their experience at the museum, encompass the public programming package. Museum education programs and exhibitions are end products of a combination of the mission of the museum and the work of all of the staff. Consider how much better that end product is when Education and Exhibition Departments are intertwined. Ironically, museum education has become so vital that some institutions have eliminated education departments, and instead have restructured the organization to emphasize the idea that education is so integral to museums that educators need to have a presence in all museum divisions rather than be separated from curatorial, administrative, and research activity.

In addition, the visitor of today has become more sophisticated and is often seeking more knowledge and depth of information. Museum education provides many forms, structures, and applications to aid in that presentation of information, for example, classes, tours, and interactives. Out of these ideas we present the following definition for museum education:

Museum education is understood in the broadest sense as any museum activity pursued with a view of facilitating knowledge or experiences for public audiences. The vision of education is in fact a vision of the museum's mission and purpose as a whole. Education and exhibitions are related and should be mutually inclusive.

CHANGING ROLE OF MUSEUM EDUCATION

It is also true that the role of museum education is constantly changing and evolving. The status of education within museums has shifted because museums themselves have progressed toward more involvement with the public. Originally many museums were privately owned or existed solely to care for specific collections. Now museums are open to the public, and their ability to provide audiences with individualized, meaningful experiences is paramount to their success.

The field of museum education has grown as a profession in recent years because of the support and definition provided by the American Association of Museums (AAM) Education Committee (EdCom). In 1990 EdCom first articulated guidelines in its *Statement on Professional Standards for Museum Education*.[3] In 1992 AAM's Museum Education Task Force published *Excellence and Equity: Education and the Public Dimension of Museums*,[4] which put front and center the importance of education in the museum. This was endorsed by the Institute of Museum and Library Services, which began requiring detailed education services descriptions in its grant applications (EdCom).

MUSEUM EDUCATION STANDARDS

In 2005 EdCom developed *Excellence in Practice: Museum Education Principles and Standards*.[5] These principles and standards are organized into three functional areas that relate to museum education:

accessibility, accountability, and advocacy. Below are listed the Professional Standards for Museum Educators, with the appropriate subtopics:

Accessibility
1. Focus on Audiences and Community
2. Diversity of Perspectives

Accountability
3. Excellence in Content and Methodology

Advocacy
4. Advocacy for Audiences
5. Advocacy of Education
6. Dedication to Learning

This working definition of museum education, along with an understanding of standards, is intended to lead the field forward in developing museums where visitors acquire perceptual skills that will enable them to uncover new relationships on their own. Also these techniques will provide ways for the visitors to think, to explore, to marvel, and to inquire. It also defines a broader base for museum educators to work within.

THE WORK OF A MUSEUM EDUCATOR

Working in a new museum and challenged to develop the education program from scratch, I sought to understand what comprised the activities of other museum education programs. During the course of attending conferences (national, regional, and local) in the early 1990s, I asked various educators what types of activities were considered the responsibility of the education department at their museum, and what duties they carried out on a regular basis. I categorized the answers, as I was looking for the bigger picture rather than exact details of job positions.[6]

The categories of activities include:

DOCENT TRAINING The training of people who lead tours, which includes overseeing their continuing education, scheduling, and maintaining motivation.

TOURS Bringing information to the visitors in a user-friendly way so they will leave with new learning experiences and have an enjoyable visit as well. Included here is the development of the tours and special activities presented by docents in the exhibit halls and for special audiences/events.

TEACHER TRAINING The trainings are offered in a variety of formats. They provide instruction and resources in the areas of the museum's content specialty and familiarize teachers with museums and what they offer, and can also be an excellent way to get the community involved with the museum. Just think of the future generations that will know about your museum because of information generated from a single teacher.

SCHOOL PROGRAMS The development of age-appropriate tours and special activities both in the exhibit halls and off-site at schools. Programs that are coordinated with the curriculum in schools often bring teachers and their classes back to the museum year after year. Included also is handling and repairing materials sent to schools (i.e., traveling trunks), teacher contact, coordinating with schools, booking school tours, and evaluating effectiveness of tours and/or trunks. This also includes homeschooled children.

SPECIAL PROGRAMS AND EVENTS These specialized programs are targeted to particular audiences and/or are often offered at set times of the year. Running events includes planning, organizing, and coordinating with many people to run the event as well as often requiring licenses, vendors, contracts, and entertainment. Exhibit openings, holiday events, or informational events are a few examples. Events can include thousands of visitors in a compressed period of time of just a few hours.

MUSEUM THEATER Includes living history as well as performances, object theater, vignettes, and reenactments. It often involves presenting historical characters in costume, and the techniques are all intended to bring the visitor closer to history, culture, or art. It is dependent on detailed research, creation of costumes, and extensive theatrical training on the part of the character. Living history can be presented in first person (representing a specific person set in a time period and not recognizing today's time), or third person (set in a time period, but able to talk back and forth between time periods).

CLASSES/WORKSHOPS These special programs include lectures, performances, classes, and workshops. Often they are targeted to different audiences by age, interest, or cultural diversity. The topics should (ideally) link to exhibits in the museum and add depth to the information presented in the exhibit halls. Running these types of programs requires coordination, keeping in contact with presenters and performers, as well as writing contracts, room setups, and scheduling around other programs and activities. There is also the visitor sign-up and class registration. Lifelong learning is an important goal for many adults, and these types of programs often serve that need. Elderhostels are another growing component of the extension of lifelong learning.

NEWSLETTER/PUBLICATIONS Developing a staff (paid or volunteer) to write and compile the newsletter or other publications; also includes layout, printing, including photographs, folding, and mailing. In addition, institutions can create special brochures or gallery guides for their exhibits. In some cases, museums regularly publish books on various exhibit topics.

EVALUATION This includes assessment of programs and exhibits for their effectiveness. When the goals and objectives for a program or exhibit are clear, it is easier to evaluate and determine if an activity/program/exhibit is accomplishing what it set out to do. Therefore setting goals and objectives becomes an important part of successful evaluation.

PROGRAM DEVELOPMENT Involves areas of new development, expansion of existing programs, budgeting, and also grant writing or other fund-raising.

INTERPRETIVE PLANNING Emphasizes the development of educational elements within each exhibit. This includes defining the teaching points or goals and objectives of an exhibit, what the message is to the public, and mechanisms to involve the public directly with the topic. Hands-on or interactive elements and written materials such as pamphlets are some ways to engage the public. Success involves coordination from the beginning of the development of an exhibit between the curator, educator, exhibit developer, and other staff members, and especially support from the director. In order to be the most effective, educational elements need to be an integral part of the exhibit development and not added on at the end of the project.

COMPUTER-BASED PROGRAMS Developing online programs, classes, and activities to be used in school classrooms or by those who cannot visit the museum, and also programs for computer stations in the exhibit hall, keeping always in mind the learning goals and objectives of the project.

MARKETING Often this is included as one of the functions of an education department. At larger museums, this is generally separated from education. It includes marketing of programs including exhibits and special activities and keeping the museum visible in the community.

Note: None of the people I interviewed mentioned research specifically, yet the authors find it is an inherent part of the work of the educator. Content is at the core of exhibitions and program development. Educators, through research, seek to create interesting formats and curriculum materials to engage their audiences.

No one educator or education department that I talked to performed all of these activities. However, each educator prioritized aspects of the education program by considering strengths, interests, and institutional goals. Choosing an approach is often based on available resources, staffing, the community the museum serves, the interests of patrons, and potential funding. Because of the great variety of activities, museum educators work in a multifaceted world that requires creativity, multitasking, intense involvement with people (staff, volunteers, visitors), and fluctuating responsibilities. The challenges are exciting and stimulating; however, the pressure can cause burnout.

ESSENTIAL SKILLS FOR MUSEUM EDUCATORS

The duties of a museum educator take many forms. The following identifies some of the applications of an educator's skills: *training* others to be accurate and reflect the knowledge of the discipline of the

---

Nancy's Story

I came into museum education (unexpectedly) through the back door. My education degree is in child development, and I had taught preschool for several years. I have always enjoyed teaching, but was never tempted to do so in a public school classroom. After visiting the Desert Botanical Garden one autumn day I signed up as a volunteer and became a docent. I was also very active working with various children's programs and volunteer trainings. I discovered that the interactive (experiential) learning promoted in this museum was the way that I truly enjoyed helping people learn. I felt a familiarity that I recognized from working with preschoolers in making concepts real for them. I enjoyed working with the creative education staff and volunteers on all aspects of interpretation, learning new things on every visit,

and sharing the Garden's fascinating science stories with visitors of all ages. When a new staff position became available to manage the docent program I was excited to become an official member of the education team. Training docents to provide enticing and interactive learning opportunities for visitors young and old became my passion. I attended as many professional development opportunities as I could to learn as much as possible about interpretation techniques in order to provide the best to our docents. Coming in from the back, I had to work hard to stay current, and it fed my passion all the more. Working with happy, enthusiastic volunteers who enjoy sharing excitement in learning about the desert with visitors, along with stretching my own abilities, has been my great reward.

—Nancy Cutler

museum; *creating* public programming from tours to large events; *evaluating* the public and staff reaction to the programming; *organizing* tour schedules and registration; *managing* personnel (staff and volunteer) at tours, events, and activities; *facilitating* the visitor experience and the expectations of the staff; *troubleshooting* when things are not running smoothly; and *communicating* the programs accurately so people will want to visit the institution and participate in the programming. Museum educators must also think and act strategically and think reflectively. Looking over these skills can help in creating a job description for an educator. They need a background in education or a content discipline that emphasizes applied research for public audiences, experience conceptualizing and creating educational programming, the ability to communicate clearly both orally and in writing, and skills dealing with people, organizing, and multitasking. Creativity, enthusiasm, and a love of learning are also key elements.

THE ROLES OF EDUCATION AND INTERPRETATION

Because the visitor's experience is primary in the educator's mind, educators often ask such questions as "Why are we doing this?" or "What is the purpose or point?" and "Who is the audience?" These questions are not meant as a challenge to researchers, exhibit developers, or administrators, but they are evidence of strategic thinking and clarification. Educators *translate* researched content and exhibits into activities, presentations, tours, and various other creative formats. Creating a dialogue between curators and educators can be very helpful. The discussions that follow in these situations can aid the educators and curators as they develop, explain, and clarify the exhibits for the visitors. These discussions will enable the educator to do a more thorough job and make the intended purpose of the exhibit clear to the visitor. If these outcomes are not made clear to the educators they are left on their own to figure it out or guess at what was intended. What can happen is that the exhibit had one purpose and/or goal, but the educators developed another because the conclusions were not shared or were not clear in the beginning. The result is that the educators then set the focus to be emphasized in the programming to the public and it could be quite different than that originally intended. To avoid this, educators must ask questions about (and sometimes challenge) purpose statements and mission statements. Consideration of audience is not always on the minds of other staff, making the role of educator as visitor advocate an essential function in all museums. Placing the visitor's experience above all else is the essence of museum education.

In order for educators to continually improve the learning environment in museums, they need flexibility and the freedom to take risks as they develop new programming. It is incumbent on educators to keep their supervisors informed, present the museum's message, and encourage supervisors to visit and comment on the education programs. Involvement and support from supervisors, including ongoing communication, is vital for the institution and for the education program. Inherent in program development must be an element that will allow educators to sell ideas not only to the public, but internally to museum directors, board members, and colleagues as well. Goal setting, planning, and budgeting are essential to communicating new ideas, but even more significant is the ability to be observant, intuitive, and reflective about past experiences to know what will attract and be of value to the array of audiences museums serve.

THE IMPORTANCE OF STRATEGIC PLANNING

Educators often head a department, manage staff, and are involved in strategic planning for both their department and the museum. It is essential for these leaders to continually assess what is currently going on in the museum and to evaluate existing programs to see how well they meet institutional goals by identifying the specific tasks required, who is doing what, the intensity of staff time involved, who the audience is, and the program cost, and then considering if the program may need to be revamped, to be continued as it is, or to be terminated. In a small museum it can be a struggle to define exactly what your job is. Figure 1.1 can be used either to look at the department as a whole, or by one educator seeking to clarify their job duties. (See Sample Form 1.1 in the appendix for the full form.)

First, on the left list all the activities that you or your department currently do or participate in. Be sure to list all the little duties subsumed under the title; for example, under tours, you would list taking reservations, training docents, and scheduling, as in the example. Then define exactly who is currently doing the work. Fill in the rest as best you can. Take this form to your supervisor and give him or her a copy, and now you have a format to discuss your job and further define for both you and your supervisor exactly what your duties are. A department head would fill this in for all activities in the department, and could use other information and meetings with staff to determine program viability and set goals for the next year. This form is one way to develop strategic plans.

Perhaps a program requires too many staff or too much staff time compared to its ability to meet institutional goals, or it has not been consistently successful with the visitors. It is good to use a variety of assess-ments, including some form of evaluations, comments from docents, staff input, your own observations, and statistics, to draw your conclusions.

When a program is successful, it is just as important to try to determine what it is that makes it so popular. What are the educational techniques that are working? Looking for things like wayfinding (how the visitor is drawn through the exhibit), pace of learning that is going on in the exhibit (for example, an area with an interactive, then a quiet space with some pictures, then a docent with a cart). Where do the visitors spend the most time, do they seem to get frustrated, are they motivated to continue, are they excited by their experience, are they sharing information with others around them, and what evidence of learning is observed? Do visitors prefer tours all the time? Is always using written material the best way to go? What roles do light and color play in exhibits? These are just a few examples of the issues that educators can address and use their expertise to define.

In the end, the purpose of the education department is learning. Learning in museums is an informal style of learning where individuals choose where, when, and what (if anything) to learn, as opposed to the formal or structured teaching that often takes place in classrooms. This learning takes place in the context of the museum's focus and discipline—history, nature, art—within its buildings, its exhibits, its objects on display, and its mission. The job of the museum educator is to design programs within those contexts that *entice* visitors to want to learn, to participate, to whet their appetites for wanting to know more. Making the learn-

Strategic Planning					
Current Activities	Person to do task and time required:	Audience:	Budget:	Expansion possible only with additional resources:	Needs to be eliminated:
Tours: Reservations Confirmation Sched. Doc. Mail Info. Write Guide Docent Trng.					
4th Grade Program:					

Figure 1.1. Strategic Planning: Example of How to Define Current Activities
See Sample Form 1.1 for a complete copy of form.

Melissa's Story

My first undergraduate major was nutrition and exercise science. About the same time I learned that I would need to complete a zoology course that would require me to dissect a dead, furless cat, I was in the dentist's office, reading a magazine article on unusual careers that featured a museum curator who spent the night in a museum as part of an overnight program she developed. At that very moment, childhood memories of my fourth-grade teacher reading aloud *From the Mixed-Up Files of Mrs. Basil E. Frankweiler* by E. L. Konigsburg, picnics with my family in Valley Forge Park, and trips to Independence Hall and the Betsy Ross House surged through my brain, and I began my quest to work in a history museum. I enrolled in a graduate program in applied history that had the option of specializing in museums, archives, or preservation. Just as sure as I was that I wanted to work in a history museum, I was oblivious to the different types of museum jobs. My first internship was in collections, which eventually led to a full-time position in museum education that was much more suited to my personality. The positive experiences I had as a child at museums and historic sites inspired my ongoing passion for the study of the past. I am thoroughly convinced of the power of museums and historic sites to instill a lifelong appreciation for history.

—Melissa Bingmann

ing enjoyable and rewarding is the task at hand. Education departments are coming into their own within the museum structure; however, communication, coordination, and collaboration between all other departments is essential to make the efforts successful.

CONCLUSION

The future of museum education must involve continual assessment and discussion about exactly what does take place in exhibit halls, historic sites, gardens, science centers, and other types of museums. Educators can learn much from the effective techniques used in classrooms, but they must go beyond that in the museum setting. Museums are a place where informal learning takes place, where people learn *if* they want to and *when* they want to. This intrinsic learning is internal, and people choose what to do based on not just intellectually interesting information, but also based on emotional decisions such as feeling connected to the topic in some way. Tracking what a visitor has learned is difficult because many of these visitors may not even recognize what they have learned until days, weeks, months, or even years later when a situation may cause them to recall with detail their museum visit. Today, little is known or even understood about delayed learning.

It behooves all educators to keep current with the literature; frequently discuss with other educators what they experience (and educators are always willing to share information and techniques); work to define, explain, and describe the educational experiences happening in their museum; support research at their institution and others to help define museum educational experiences; constantly create new educational experiences at their institution; and share their success stories. Joining professional organizations (on the local, state, and national levels), participating in the programs, attending conferences, and networking are all behaviors museum educators can use to keep current with the field and participate in conversations that will shape the future. In this way all educators can work together to advance the profession of museum education. Education is the responsibility of everyone, but truly museum educators are experts in the ways people learn, and in developing materials and activities so visitors will be engaged. Educators need to step forward, define and discuss education, document it, and sustain an ongoing conversation. It is our hope that this book will serve as part of that dialogue.

NOTES

1. Alison L. Grinder and E. Sue McCoy, *The Good Guide: A Sourcebook for Interpreters, Docents and Tour Guides* (Scottsdale, Ariz.: Ironwood Publishing, 1985), 16.
2. Hanneke de Man, "Case Study 1: Developing and Revising an Education Policy," in *Museum and Gallery Education: A Manual of Good Practice*, ed. Hazel Moffat and Vicky Woollard (Walnut Creek, Calif.: AltaMira Press, 1999), 24.
3. 1990 EDCOM: Statement on Professional Standards for Museum Education, www.edcom.org/about/standards.shtml (October 2007).
4. *Excellence and Equity: Education and the Public Dimension of Museums* (Washington, D.C.: American Association of Museums, 1992).
5. Museum Education Principles and Standards. To look up entire document go to www.edcom.org (October 2007).
6. *Note:* Information was informally collected by speaking primarily with educators at history museums. This list is not necessarily complete, but it does give insight into how varied education programs and educator duties at museums can be.

CHAPTER 2

Working with Volunteers

Nancy Cutler

Museum educators use their understanding of how visitors of different ages and backgrounds experience and learn in museums to:
- advocate for visitors in program and museum planning processes,
- create their own ways to facilitate enjoyable learning, and
- train frontline staff in ways to enhance positive museum experiences.

—*Ellen Rosenthal, President/CEO, Conner Prairie*

Each person who donates their time and talents to any organization needs to feel they are contributing something of value; that their contributions are appreciated; and their time is never wasted.

What is a volunteer? It is a person who freely chooses to donate their time and talents without remuneration. There are many models for volunteer programs and countless resources to advise in developing and maintaining a program. The experiences drawn from for this chapter include years of working as a volunteer, as well as managing teams of volunteers. My volunteer experiences varied from helping with my daughter's Girl Scout troop to chairing a statewide committee of volunteers who planned the annual state conference for the Museum Association of Arizona. In this chapter I will relate my experiences with a very successful model.

As a museum educator at the Desert Botanical Garden I managed and trained volunteers, primarily for the large docent program, but also cosupervised the general volunteer training for other departments. The volunteer management approach I experienced, learned, and helped to promote there is based on a "team approach" Kathleen Socolofsky developed when she was the director of education at the Garden.[1]

Let's do a little exercise to help recognize some of the features of a volunteer, writing answers to the following questions. Putting into words your own desires and requirements for volunteering will help to understand the needs and requirements for *managing* volunteers. Decide on a hypothetical or potential place where *you* might choose to be a volunteer. What do you enjoy? (A few ideas might include helping in a classroom, working in some aspect of a museum or a library, delivering meals on wheels, or ushering at theater performances.)

Name your volunteer venue.

What is your motive for choosing to volunteer at this place?

What would entice you to actively pursue volunteering here? (*Would it be the people to work with . . . the atmosphere . . . the training . . . the opportunity to work alone or to socialize? Or some other benefit, e.g., seeing theater productions?*)

What might be your personal rewards for volunteering here? (*What will you personally get out of your time and activity here? Perhaps new friends, new skills, etc.*)

How many hours per week (or month) could you *commit* to this activity?

What skills do you have that you can share as a volunteer here? (*For example: Are you a people person? Do you have specific computer skills? Are you good at organizing things? Do you enjoy working with children? Are you an art or history buff? Do you have retail experience? Do you know another language?*)

In order to volunteer at this venue, you will want to know:

- What are the specific needs of the venue?
- What is the structure of volunteers and staff?
- Is there training to orient and inform you?
- Are the volunteers really appreciated?

Keeping these points in mind we can then look at designing and managing a volunteer program, in this case, based on the team approach. Whether the program has only one or two volunteers or a huge group of 500 or more, you can build a structure that will meet the needs of your organization and those of volunteers, where each person who donates their time and talents feels they are valued. In this chapter we will discuss why people volunteer, and how the "Three R's of Any Volunteer Program" are interrelated.

WHY DO PEOPLE VOLUNTEER?

Why do people choose to share their time, talents, and energy for NO financial remuneration? According to psychologist Mihály Csikszentmihályi,[2] people are motivated to engage in an activity for some type of reward. Rewards can be *extrinsic* such as financial incentives, good grades, prizes, or "pats on the head" (recognition). Or the rewards can be *intrinsic*—some internal satisfaction (it feels good), such as having fun, learning something interesting, extending their abilities, having a thrill, or making others feel good.

For people who volunteer, those rewards, according to many sources, take the forms of:

- *Service*: giving service to the community—being involved and/or giving back.
- *Social Rewards*: meeting new people with similar interests—making new friends.
- *Affiliation*: an interest in the organization's mission such as art, history, science, nature, etc., and an interest in learning more about the discipline.
- *Skills*: continuing to use their skills, but in a new environment, or learning new skills.
- *Power*: usually the power is directed toward furthering the mission of the organization. (Beware of the individual who sees the power as a way to further mainly their *own* interests.)

Volunteers are used in nearly every aspect of the museum, including serving as docents and school guides; providing computer help—from data entry to creating programs; holding temporary or regular office jobs and administrative positions; and assisting with outreach, collections or archives, special events, greeting, recruiting new members, exhibit construction or development, evaluations for various programs, and fund-raising. Members of the board of trustees are also volunteers. Where there is a need and a niche a volunteer *may* fit. How do you know if volunteers could help in your institution?

THE "THREE R'S" OF ANY VOLUNTEER PROGRAM

Recruitment = getting volunteers
Recognition = showing appreciation
Retention = keeping volunteers

All three aspects are intimately connected as we shall see. But how do we get from these labels to a good volunteer program?

Obviously, not all volunteer venues are identical and people are different, but the process of recruiting, recognizing, and retaining volunteers is fundamentally the same. Creating a good volunteer environment and experience can result in rewarding life experiences for both the volunteer *and* the volunteer supervisor. I have many wonderful friends among the volunteers that I have worked with, trained, and supervised. Make no mistake: The care and feeding of volunteers *takes time and attention* and is essential for bonding the volunteer's commitment to your institution. Thinking that all you need to do is recruit a volunteer and point them at a problem without further supervision is a mistake. Consider how lost and ineffective you might feel if you were put in that position without knowing what was expected.

RECRUITING

The first thing to do, before any recruiting can begin, is to *assess your needs*—Do I need a volunteer (or several volunteers)? Why? Where and how will I use them?

Why you might need volunteers:

- You have too much work and not enough time.
- You might be missing opportunities due to lack of time or experience—for example, creating and producing a newsletter.
- A need for skills you do not possess—perhaps photography or some computer skills, like creating a database or a website.
- Ongoing projects—such as mailing jobs, office work, interpretation, retail, library, membership, or fund-raising.
- Special projects—a special exhibit installation, or a large project, such as cleanup or painting, data in-

put, or organizing something, such as photographs.
- Special events—which might require help with everything from greeting or passing out items like posters, prizes, or food, to planning and running an event and/or supervising other volunteers.

Another way to determine if there is a need for volunteers is to list all the tasks you do (or should do, or would like to do) for a period of days—say a week, or for a year. You can also look at your job description and your responsibilities. Then determine if any of those tasks or responsibilities could be delegated and perhaps expanded using a dedicated volunteer. However, do not expect a volunteer to take over all the tasks you hate. According to Susan Ellis,[3] organizations should not recruit volunteers just because they cannot afford to hire paid staff. A museum should view volunteers as people who bring special gifts and talents to enhance existing programs and jobs. Look at volunteers, then, as a talented resource to enhance or grow your institutional objectives.

So, you have some jobs that volunteers could do to help the institution. The next questions are: How do I find volunteers? How will I use them? How will I train these wonderful people? And how will I keep them once they are trained? Before you can actually recruit anyone you need to be able to advertise the tasks, duties, and skills that are required. The key to success is to match the skills and interests of the volunteer to the job. How is that best achieved?

1. First, do a "needs assessment." (See Sample Form 2.1 in the appendix.)
2. Then, define the program or project. What is its objective?
3. Then create a job description. (See Sample Form 2.2.)

The Job Description

The job description is one of your best tools for creating a successful volunteer program. It gives you concrete tasks that both you and the potential volunteer can recognize and understand, and helps both of you to match skills and interests to the task. The job description should come from the needs assessment for the position you are wishing to fill. According to Patricia Smith, former volunteer administrator at the Desert Botanical Garden, a needs assessment is exceptionally helpful for "getting what you want by knowing what you need." The consequent job description is the same as the job description would be for a paid position.

Whether paid or unpaid, people need to know what is expected of them, and if they are meeting those expectations. The job description is not only a recruiting tool, but also a part of the evaluation tool and a point of reference if a disagreement occurs. It also helps ensure job consistency and that the position contributes to the goals and mission of the institution.

Key elements of a job description include:

JOB TITLE A specific title for each volunteer position. A title helps to define the position and gives it purpose and importance. For example, docent, horticulture or collections aide, sales assistant, library aide.

JOB DESCRIPTION Briefly describe the position and the volunteer activities. For example, provide themed, accurate, fun, guided tours and interactive experiences for visitors of all ages.

JOB OBJECTIVE The result expected when this job is successful. For example, docents will help visitors engage in fun and educational experiences focused on the museum's collection of (desert plants and animals or Tempe History, or contemporary art, etc.).

PLACE OF WORK Where the activity will take place, such as in the library, in the museum galleries, etc.

QUALIFICATIONS What type of person are you looking for? List the essential *skills* necessary prior to the required training. For example, it is helpful if someone wishing to be a docent in a history museum likes history and people. Through the needs assessment, consider what are the bare minimum skills needed for someone to do this task. For example, a docent should like interacting with people and be able to learn and share accurate information with enthusiasm to visitors.

STAFF SUPERVISOR (MANAGER) It is important that every volunteer understand who their supervisor is and vice versa. Sometimes a staff person is not comfortable working with volunteers, and consequently the volunteers are ignored. Clarifying who is in charge and to whom the volunteer reports builds structure and accountability into the program. The staff person listed as the supervisor should also be involved in the needs assessment and the creation of the job description for that job. "Participation in the design of the position" [including the needs assessment and job description] "helps the prospective supervisor think through the working situation and empowers them as a supervisor," says Anna Johnson.

DUTIES AND RESPONSIBILITIES OF THE JOB Define *exactly* what you expect the volunteer to do and be responsible for—such as "lead tour groups through the museum and involve visitors in activities per the training"; requires mobility, public speaking, learning (local history), working comfortably within a day team structure, assisting in care and use of supplies and materials, participation in _____ number of continuing education courses per year.

TRAINING REQUIREMENTS Describe all of the training required and how it will be provided so all requirements are clear up front. For example, Orientation class (3 hours), Content classes (___ hours), Interpretive techniques (___ hours), or Collections management (__ hours).

TIME COMMITMENT Length of time required and frequency—for example, 4 hours per week on a regular day, during the regular interpretive season (October–May) and when able, as needed for . . ., or "lead 20-minute tours and stay with group for 1 hour, flexible times, usually at least twice a week."

NOTES Any additional information. (See Sample Form 2.2 in the appendix.)

Now we can begin recruiting!

How Do I Find Volunteers?

There are several places to look for appropriate people. Think about the audience you are trying to recruit for the jobs needed (age, interests) and try to target that audience—what publications does that audience read, organizations do they belong to, and so forth? Consider the following:

- Word of mouth is more effective than any other method, and your best recruiters are your current volunteers. Current volunteers know the institution, its management style, and how volunteers are treated. They also know when they can use more help. For example, museums can always use more docents to be available more hours and reach more visitors. Docents, by their nature, like to interact with other people and in the process will often recruit new volunteers to join them in their passionate commitment to the museum.
- An open house or volunteer fair can be effective, especially if you have fun demonstrations (by current volunteers) of the jobs you are looking to fill and offer door prizes. Food is always a helpful enticement, too. Advertise the fun to be had by attending your fair. Then sell the volunteering benefits at the fair.
- Place a volunteer recruitment brochure in strategic places, and share it at events or presentations.
- Advertise among your membership. They are members of your organization for a reason! Let them know the benefits of also being a volunteer.

- Advertise on your website and anywhere your target volunteer base is likely to see the ad; for example, newspapers. Free PSAs (public service announcements) on radio and TV can also be helpful.
- Advertise at the local volunteer center (this can be a great resource) or in targeted news media. For example, if you need help with schoolchildren, advertise through the local school board's retired teacher magazines or newsletters, or for summer help advertise in schoolteacher newsletters in winter or early spring.
- Retirees and senior centers.
- High schools and colleges that require community service (usually good for specific, short-term projects).
- Teens can also be wonderful volunteers, especially if they are motivated and love learning and responsibility. Teen programs require additional supervision and teen types of enticements that make the job fun and rewarding for their interests. The team approach system works well for this group, too.
- Colleges may have museums studies students looking for experience for résumés. Interns can be paid or unpaid. Often internships are a requirement for a class or degree, and interns are motivated to have in-the-field experiences. Interns, whether paid or unpaid, should have a job description and a specific learning objective as part of their participation. They should not be given insignificant busy work with little benefit to them.
- Many large companies have employee volunteer incentive programs. Check the websites of companies in your area for volunteer incentive programs or community service opportunities, or contact them and inquire.

The Next Steps—Getting to Know Each Other

VOLUNTEER APPLICATION FORM When you have recruits who have shown interest, the next step is a volunteer application form, which will give some basic information about the applicant, such as vital statistics (name, contact information, and emergency contact), availability (days available—mornings, afternoons, evenings, and seasonal availability), employment, interests and skills, possibly references (criminal convictions), and the signature with the date. (See Sample Forms 2.3 and 2.4 in the appendix.) On this application you can ask any information you wish to (legally) learn in a general sense about a potential volunteer's interests, abilities, and skills.

Teen Volunteers

Teen volunteer programs can be a great asset to your public programs. During the summer I ran a weekly family day at the museum, which was extremely well attended. On this day we played with history using games, puzzles, activities, speakers, and many other formats. In the summer many of my senior docents left the area or were unavailable. So I used the teens to supplement needed staffing, and this became very popular.

First, students were interviewed in order to be placed in the program. We regarded anyone from age 13 to 19 as a teen. My preference was 14 years of age and up; 16 was a good age because they could drive themselves to the museum.

Next, I did a training just for them and asked some of my senior docents to join in if possible. This was a two-hour training with clear instructions handed out in a written packet, and included scheduling. My one comment here is do not get discouraged if you are doing a teen training and find they look bored, disinterested, or sleepy! They always looked this way, but at the end of the time, I passed out the sign-up sheets, and they signed up and always came doing their best.

The program included their working on the special program day either morning or afternoon and coming to a meeting every Friday morning just for them. The Friday morning meeting was for discussions about their experiences, career development, and program development. They went behind the scenes of the museum and met with each curator on the different Fridays. In addition, these teens helped design a special program at the end of the summer focused on teens and family. They picked the theme, split up the duties, and developed different activities for visitors to do in the hall. Then these teens ran the activities themselves at the actual program. The teens also often developed some of their projects in the photo archive or working with the exhibits coordinator. Through the years there were many different programs: Some were theatrical, others used artifacts and tried to match them to current-day examples or to determine in which decade a variety of styles were popular, or used games to emphasize information in the exhibits (such as a baseball quiz show, hangman adaptation), and so forth. For my part, I always supplied a disc jockey, so there was music and dancing, and provided a mechanism to encourage visitors to go through the exhibit hall, trying everything and then getting a prize. (The Prize Map [punch card] from one teen event is shown in the figure.)

I also found it easier to have an intern oversee this program during the summer. The teens did a great job in the hall in general, but they did need to know someone was around in case they had questions. There were also a few rules, such as siblings or best friends will not be assigned to the same activity at the same time, friends are welcome but not to hang around your activity all day, no younger siblings may accompany a teen who is directing activities in the exhibit hall.

Providing T-shirts and/or name tags which indicated they were official was important. Without some designation of their status, the public would not listen to them. The teens and the senior docents worked together extremely well and enjoyed each other's company.

—Anna Johnson

Prize Map
Developed at Tempe Historical Museum

INTERVIEW The application information is a starting point for the next step, an interview to help match volunteer interests and skills with the positions available. A personal interview, where you get to know the volunteer and vice versa, is a very important step (just as for paid staff) for assessing and placing a volunteer. It is a good idea to have a set form to follow for each interview. (See Sample Form 2.5 in the appendix.)

Interview questions can help with volunteer placement and should also cover the following:

- Go over the job description, the training courses, schedule of the courses, and the costs (if applicable).

- It is important to share the mission, vision, and goals of the institution with the applicant. It gives them the big picture.
- In your questions to the applicant look for the following:
  - Why is he or she interested in volunteering with you?
  - Ability to make the time commitment needed to volunteer and to attend the training.
  - Commonalities with your program's needs. Help the volunteer see where he or she would enjoy working, and learning.
- Have the applicant give two references—one personal and one professional.

- Let the applicant know that working with children and some other jobs require a background check (and no felony convictions).
- Make sure you have answered all the questions the applicant may have.
- If it is not a good fit that fact needs to be politely admitted. You can direct the applicant to other resources, such as the local volunteer center, for them to find a volunteer situation that is a better fit and will provide rewarding rather than frustrating experiences for both the volunteer and the institution.

Matching a volunteer's skills and interests with a specific assignment that utilizes those skills and interests will result in a successful placement. From a successful personal interview, recruits will have a better idea of how they can fit with the volunteer program. Also, "recruits who do not feel they can meet the needs of the institution or their own personal needs will often realize this before they have invested valuable time and energy in hours of training," says Anna Johnson. If the institution clearly presents its needs from the beginning of the recruiting process, then recruits will *usually* realize early on whether or not this volunteer position fits. Occasionally, a person might think he or she would be good at something they have never done before—for example, giving tours—later to realize they are too nervous to talk in public. On the whole, the personal interview is a real value in this process as you and the potential volunteer are getting to know each other.

How Will I Organize and Use the Volunteers?

There are probably as many ways to organize a volunteer program as there are programs. As your volunteer program grows and attains a group, having some type of structure is important for volunteers to know where and how they fit into the organization. They will feel a better sense of belonging, and therefore stay longer.

The most successful structure I have seen is used at the Desert Botanical Garden. The Garden has used the "team approach" for more than twenty years, and in 2008 supports over 1,000 volunteers in a wide array of programs and projects. This large volunteer program began in the 1980s as a small core of dedicated people, mainly docents and horticulture aides; and under the nurturing care of Volunteer Administrator Patricia Smith, it has successfully grown and expanded into every department of the Garden. This "team approach" is especially useful for the ongoing tasks needed daily, weekly, or seasonally, such as docent interpretation, library helpers, fund-raising, collections management, special events, or seasonal projects. It is based on the idea that every department that uses volunteers is responsible for managing its own team, rather than having a single volunteer coordinator who is responsible for the impossible task of managing all volunteers. This style of management is effective regardless of the number of volunteers in your institution. It works with a small group and can grow from a small group into a huge volunteer program and still be efficient, as has been demonstrated at the Desert Botanical Garden. We will explain how, in this system, volunteers become specialists in the department (or departments) where they choose to volunteer and are real assets to that department. This fulfills the volunteers' requirement of feeling useful and gives them a reason to continue volunteering (retention).

A TEAM APPROACH   The benefits of this style of management are that teams are locally managed, cared for, and appreciated as smaller specialized groups. Individuals can be known on a personal level by the staff they work with as well as the other volunteers on their team. The specialized training and continuing education are done by the staff they will be working with. This, too, provides more opportunities for staff and volunteers to get to know each other, which engenders a sense of belonging and bonding to the department, the institution, and to other like-minded volunteers. This bonding encourages volunteers to stay in the organization for long periods of time, usually several years. Small turnover means a more stable organization that volunteers and staff can count on.

At the Garden there is a central volunteer administrator/coordinator who is responsible for recruiting, interviewing, and placing the volunteers in their respective venues, for overseeing their initial orientation and training, and for supporting the volunteer management teams. How does it work? Each department partners a staff liaison with a volunteer chair (liaison), and they jointly manage their team of volunteers. The volunteer administrator works with the liaison team to ensure a quality experience for the volunteers and consistency across all the Garden departments using volunteers.

Not all staff, however, are suited to or interested in managing a volunteer, never mind a whole team of them. The key is to find one person in the department who is willing, give them training on how this team approach works and how it can benefit their department and the volunteer program as a whole, and provide support for their efforts. Over time the team takes on a stable life of its own and will sustain itself. However, in order for the volunteer program to stay connected with the mission and goals of the institution (rather than veering off on its own mission), there *must* be the staff manager/liaison working with the volunteer chair/liaison to set the policies and guidelines for what volunteers are doing. An experienced volunteer as the chair/liaison to the team of volunteers is especially helpful in maintaining the continuity of the team with a new staff liaison. For this system of volunteer management to work well you need a volunteer coordinator who will champion the project, and the support of the director as well as the department supervisors.

Figure 2.1 presents a model of this structure. Bold boxes show departments with paid staff. Nonbold boxes show volunteer groups that those departments supervise.

Figure 2.2 presents an example of an extended structure from Figure 2.1, representing specifically the docent program (listed under Education) at the Garden. Volunteer teams for the other departments are structured in basically the same way. Consistency of structure across departments avoids volunteer teams being treated differently (some better than others) in different departments and across a variety of managers. If you have several volunteers in one department this following model should work for you and it will accommodate growing your team of volunteers. You can even start small with a team of two or more volunteers on a single day (which provides the social interaction that is a draw for many) or with one or more people on any regular day of the week, or as needed for your jobs.

The idea in this model is to begin to bring qualified, experienced, and trained volunteers into leadership positions (such as day captains or docent chair) to handle the coordination of the team (whether small or large) and allow the leaders to coordinate the ongoing tasks. The structure of the docent program at the Garden (as a model for any program) consists of:

EDUCATION STAFF LIAISON The "interpretive programs manager" oversees all aspects of the docent program and coordinates with other departments needing interpretive assistance—say for a special event, and for

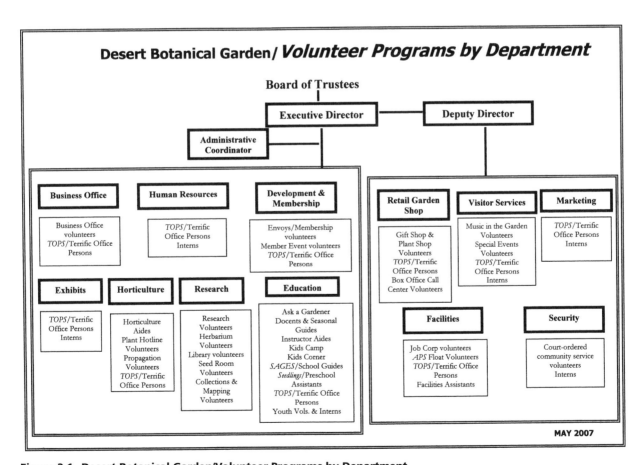

Figure 2.1. Desert Botanical Garden/Volunteer Programs by Department
Written by Patricia Smith, volunteer training manager, and used by permission of Desert Botanical Garden, Phoenix, Arizona, all rights reserved.

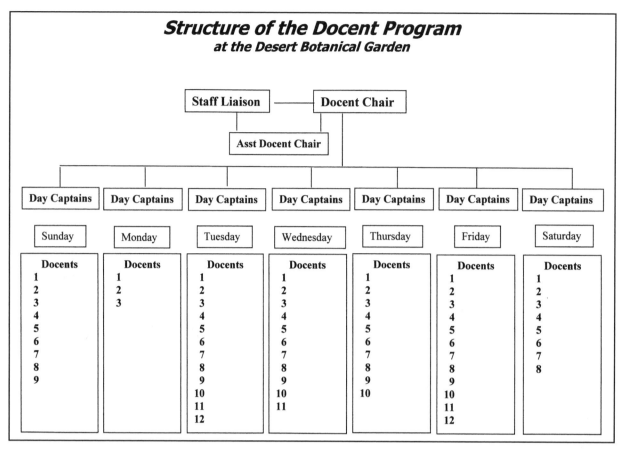

Figure 2.2. Structure of the Docent Program at the Desert Botanical Garden
Created by Nancy Cutler

the special or ongoing needs within the education department.

DOCENT CHAIR The volunteer side of the liaison team is responsible for communication between volunteers and staff and vice versa. The interpretive programs manager (staff) could ask the docent chair to contact docents for specific special assignments. The docent chair also organizes the day captain meetings, especially the seasonal kickoff meeting in the fall; and the staff liaison is a team participant.

ASSISTANT DOCENT CHAIR The assistant works with the docent chair and also has responsibility for managing the huge quantity of hands-on items used in this docent program.

DAY CAPTAINS Each day team has a pair of co–day captains. Their basic job is to support their day team members, encourage them to bond with the team and to the institution, and see that the advertised tours and hands-on activities are staffed for the required hours. Day captains are also an avenue of communication through the docent chair or directly to staff of issues, problems, or good ideas occurring on their day. There are day captains' meetings three times a year—at the

beginning of the regular interpretive season, at midseason, and at the end of the season. These meetings and their timing are important for purposes of communication.

The *kickoff meeting* at the beginning of the season shares new information for the season that day captains carry from staff and share with their team. At the *midseason* and *end-of-the-year* meetings day captains evaluate what is going well on each of their days, and discuss any ongoing problems or issues that have not surfaced to staff. And group brainstorming addresses how they can work to improve any problem issues. Recognizing and acknowledging what is working well is as important as identifying problems that need attention. This helps give a sense of balance to the evaluations and puts it into a bigger picture, rather than focusing only on the negative aspects.

DAY TEAMS OF DOCENTS Between 5 and 20 docents (including at least one of the day captains) begin arriving at the Garden's Interpretive Headquarters (docent room) around 8:30–9:30, or 10:00–10:30 on their chosen regular day to volunteer. Publicly advertised start times on the trail determine arrival times. However, "flex" arrival times are encouraged for some docents in order to extend interpretive coverage on the trails into the afternoon. Docents do a little socializing with other team members when they arrive and sign up on the "Docent Daily Tasks Schedule" (see Sample Form 2.6 in the appendix) for the interpretive tasks they choose to do for their four-hour commitment. These consist of tours of the Garden, staffing one of the 15+ hands-on discovery stations, or floating on the Garden trails with a basket of hands-on items to do impromptu minipresentations with visitors. At the end of their shift or at lunch break, many of them will stay and have lunch together and socialize.

This team system has the advantage of always having an available point person (day captain or docent chair person) docents can look to for help, coordination, communication, or advice, and, in fact, builds teams that are strong, cohesive, and reliant on all members, and that stay together for years. They have, actually, created little cooperative communities of interdependence within their teams—knowing the strengths, weaknesses, and preferences of their team members. Some bonds that were created persisted beyond the Garden volunteer program, such as the Wednesday docents "book bunch" that began as a book club and evolved into more of a social activities group outside the Garden; and the Tuesday docents "hiking gang" or the school guides "Golfing Gals." People who work/volunteer together often find like-minded friends regardless of how the group is structured. This team approach system, however, facilitates an effective social "community of practice" within the team by providing a comfortable structure and flexibility within the structure for independence, personalization, and cooperation.[4]

How Will I Train These Wonderful People?

How much training is required? The degree of training is dependent on the task at hand, and always begins with an orientation.

ORIENTATION Orientation should include the following:

- Some type of orientation to your institution, including a physical orientation tour. (As a potential volunteer, consider how it would increase your comfort level and interest to have a behind-the-scenes tour.)
- A look at the volunteer opportunities available, and a chance to meet some of the staff—especially staff they could be working with.

- An introduction to the institution, including:

  ○ the mission of the institution,
  ○ the goals and objectives of the programs where they may choose to volunteer, and
  ○ the expectations of the institution.

A good orientation starts volunteers off on a positive foot and begins to form a comfort level with the organization that you hope will be like a second home for each person. These are the beginning stages of commitment and retention.

CONTENT TRAINING The more volunteers understand about why your institution matters, the more committed they will be to the institution, and the more effective they will be in their volunteer endeavors. Today's volunteers have a love of learning that helps keep them lively and growing. The content information of your museum is essential for some positions, such as docents or collections, and will give any volunteer a more rounded view and appreciation of your collection and mission.

SPECIALIZED TRAINING Any volunteer position will require some degree of specialized training, whether it is aimed at caring for your valuable collection, learning interpretive techniques, or understanding the system you use for folding and mailing your newsletters. Whatever the training requires volunteers to do should be clearly described and modeled for them in the course of the training so there is no guesswork on their part. Modeling is a very effective procedure for getting the specifics of your activity across to new volunteers. Then allow them to adapt the model to their own personality and style. This is especially effective with docents, as will be discussed in Chapters 3 and 4 on training docents. Independence and individuality within the framework of the procedures for the job give volunteers a sense of ownership and strengthen their commitment.

In many organizations the orientation, content training, and the specialized training are together within the same class. This is efficient if you are training a group for only one specialty project, which may be docents, gift shop/retail help, and so forth. At the Garden, with the team approach, we found it to be more efficient, and the content more consistent, by doing a general orientation for all volunteers, teaching the general content to all volunteers, and then separating specialized (or methods) trainings done by the staff, who are the experts in the department of the volunteers' chosen specialty. Experienced volunteer mentors in each department help continue and reinforce the specialized training and integrate new volunteers into the team. The point to recognize is that all three types of training need to be covered in whatever system works best for your organization.

CONTINUING EDUCATION Continuing education provides a variety of benefits that go beyond just extended learning. In a good volunteer program your volunteers will be passionate about what they are doing to help the institution. Having, on a somewhat regular basis, new learning opportunities that are related to the museum and that feed their passion is rewarding and inspiring, and shows that the institution values their passion and commitment. Continuing education fosters social interaction and bonding among fellow passionate participants, and an intermingling of volunteers from different days or different departments. This is especially effective when they are involved in an activity or workshop designed for them to interact with one another. Ongoing programs of continuing education can also provide opportunities for leadership roles in planning and arranging the presentations or field trips. Trained, trusted volunteers, guided by staff, can do the planning, research to find speakers and workshop presenters, and even set up the schedules and arrangements, making those volunteers more involved and committed to your institution.

Some examples of possible and popular continuing education offerings might include:

- Field trips to similar institutions, either locally or internationally; these are very popular.
- Walks with an expert—"behind the scenes" tours by some expert on your staff, another institution's staff, or someone from a related field at a local college or university that will pique the interest and enhance the knowledge of the participants.
- Luncheon lectures or "brown bag lunch bunch" talks by some respected specialist.
- An off-season offering of a series of lectures or fascinating presentations or workshops will keep volunteers around and engaged during what would otherwise be down time.
- Hands-on workshop-type presentations that fill a morning or afternoon are always popular.

Finding presenters to fulfill these workshops, tours, and lectures is relatively easy and fun to scout. A good place to start looking is the staff at your own or a similar institution. Also check with local colleges or universities that have staff or even graduate students who might

> **Textbox 2.1**
>
> Becoming active in local, state, and national professional associations for museum professionals is an unbeatable way to make contacts that will be valuable in innumerable ways.

present some of their graduate work—which is often new in the field. Check at professional societies related to your discipline whether it is history, art, science, nature, or whatever it may be; there are likely related organizations in your own or nearby communities.

Training classes at the Garden are a mix of lecture, reading, discussion, and hands-on labs. The educators recognize they are training volunteers who come with a variety of learning styles, many of whom have not been in a classroom in many years. A variety of teaching methods is built into each training session in an effort to connect with all volunteers, to make the learning meaningful, useful, fun, and as interesting as possible.

RETENTION: HOW WILL WE KEEP THEM ONCE THEY ARE TRAINED?

Keeping volunteers depends mostly on their commitment to your organization. How do you build that commitment? First, recognize why people volunteer—and specifically why your volunteers are working in your institution. The list on page 16 (Why Do People Volunteer?) can be used as a guideline to build those aspects of the volunteer experience into your program. Next, understand the importance of communication to help each person feel a valued part of the team.

Three main elements of retention in my experience consist of:

- Learning/growing opportunities that are interesting and continuing—*opportunities to use or stretch their skills in a new environment, or learning new skills, and social rewards.*
- Opportunities to do meaningful work—*giving service to the community, and the power to do so.*
- Bonding with staff and volunteers and to your institution. People who share experiences, such as training and working together, frequently form friendships that engender a sense of belonging to a community—*affiliation and social rewards.*

Building the Team

Some methods to help make volunteers feel a part of the team that they are affiliated with for social interaction and bonding include the following:

ORIENTATION AND TRAINING Sessions are informative and fun and begin building social/work teams. For example, in a large class, new volunteers are placed into small teams (where they can get to know each other) with experienced specially trained volunteers as team leaders who act as mentors and help with new training, assimilation, and bonding.

CONTINUING EDUCATION AND REFRESHER COURSES It feeds their passion and commitment and provides inspiration for personal growth.

POTLUCKS Food creates a comfortable social environment and is included in all meetings and training sessions at the Garden. It is usually provided by the team members via a sign-up sheet. In early trainings it forms the beginnings of doing your part for your team and the larger group. No one wants to let the group down. Bringing food to share (either created or purchased) is an easy step.

LEADERSHIP OPPORTUNITIES All teams need leaders and organizers, whether they are out front or behind the scenes. Many volunteers are skilled, educated, and experienced from the business world. Recognize the skills, abilities, and commitment of trained volunteers, and provide opportunities for their growth by offering additional training for positions of leadership, such as day captains, chair (liaison) positions, advisors, mentors, coordinators, team leaders, consultants, instructors, exhibit development, or whatever suits your organization's needs. With training for whatever the task, volunteers can grow and provide services for other volunteers and the organization. A quote from General George Patton, "Never tell people how to do things. Tell them what to do and they will surprise you with their ingenuity," is very apropos. With training on the goals and objectives of the job at hand as well as the general goals and objectives of the institution (along with a modicum of supervision), allowing these skilled leaders to be creative in how they handle the job not only relieves you of having to do the work, but often results in really excellent creative solutions.

Notice that although they may be working independently, volunteers are always under the guidance of staff. In leadership positions they work side-by-side with paid staff to enhance the work and goals of the institution (rather than splintering off into entities on their own, doing projects that are not coordinated with the needs of the institution). Beware, though, that there is a fine line between not enough supervision and micromanaging, which no one appreciates. Learn your volunteers' abilities, guide them, and trust them, and you will find that *leadership builds ownership*.

Communication

Regular communication with all volunteers is an important part of keeping them connected to your institution. No one wants to feel "left out," but it is *so* very easy to miss contacting every individual. It seems somehow to happen that the same individual misses several communications, which leaves them feeling left out and unwanted.

Some important communication tools include:

- Clearly defined expectations within the structures of a job description, policies and procedures, trainings, as well as in the actions of other volunteers, particularly those in leadership positions, let volunteers know exactly what is expected and contribute to their comfort level. (An important expectation is the commitment of their valuable time—time to learn in the training classes, and time to "give back" via the team of their choice.)

- A volunteer handbook in some form is the easiest, most efficient and consistent method for communicating expectations and everyday information such as policies, logistics (for example, recording volunteer hours; see Sample Form 2.7 in the appendix), safety policies, code of ethics, a required dress code (if applicable), training requirements, and a general overview of volunteer opportunities. It also becomes a handy reference resource.

- A monthly or quarterly volunteer newsletter can share on a regular basis, with the entire group (even those who only volunteer occasionally), announcements of upcoming events of the institution, upcoming volunteer opportunities and trainings, and a calendar of those events, also fun stories from other volunteers (for example amusing happenings in the museum), and an article on some aspect of the museum or a fact or feature related to the museum (for example the Garden newsletter often features the splendor of a different plant available in the gift shop, and also an occasional feature on something fascinating going on in the research department). This communication gives all volunteers the opportunity to be kept "in the loop."

- Volunteer team leaders or day captains who coordinate and "nurture" their team members also have the responsibility of keeping each member informed.

- Daily recognition: "Recognition is more than awards and ceremonies," says Patricia Smith, volunteer administrator at the Desert Botanical Garden. A positive and sincere "thank-you" to a volunteer as they leave for the day goes a long way to showing your personal appreciation. Another way of showing appreciation is in every meeting, training, and continuing education class to make it a policy to connect how volunteers' tasks are related to the larger picture. This reinforces to them that their role is continuing to contribute and that their work is meaningful.

- Clear instructions make it easy to understand and follow through—you are much more likely to get what you are asking of people if their instructions are clear and easy to follow. This is where physical modeling is also helpful for many. For example, training for using a computer cash register—clearly written, *brief* step-by-step instructions for easy reference, then modeling and (possibly) supervised practice.
- Formal and informal evaluation sessions provide valuable feedback in both directions:
  - Formal evaluations are usually done at the end of a class, training, or event. It is helpful to have a written evaluation from each participant (see Chapter 10, "Evaluation," for more information) and also a group discussion of team leaders to share those evaluations as well as their own feedback. This discussion often inspires some brainstorming as members feed off of others' thoughts or insights and keeps everyone aware of the situation.
  - Informal evaluations can happen in a relatively social session, such as a regular luncheon meeting, and provide important feedback from volunteers and volunteer leaders to the staff. As an example, garden docents have monthly luncheon meetings with the docent (staff) coordinator to share, as a team, what has been going well and what problems may have cropped up since the last meeting or have not been resolved since that meeting. These group sharing sessions have been very successful—especially when they *begin* with the positive side of events—What's new or fun that has happened today or recently? A docent will usually share something from the day, and this begins a kind of brainstorming session where others may have something to add or something else to share. From there, often without the question even being asked, something that needs attention or is not working so well will come out of the positive discussion. This method helps keep the session from beginning on a negative note and degenerating into something where docents go away

with a negative sentiment. It helps keep the "bad" in balance with the good. These informal evaluation sessions are extremely valuable for getting feedback that might not otherwise come out and for learning about minor problems before they become major issues. This process can work easily with any group that has an informal gathering, and again, food makes it a social event.

- Always do what you say you will do! Promote and model a relationship they can trust.
- Don't air dirty laundry. A word of caution: People generally want a positive experience in their volunteer endeavors. They are there to do good work, socialize with staff and other volunteers, and to think of themselves as a part of the "happy family," all pulling together. All institutions have their politics and their conflicts. As a volunteer coordinator or leader it is your responsibility to shield volunteers from the "dirty laundry" of the daily staff conflicts. Therefore, never discuss other staff or volunteers or internal politics with or in front of a volunteer. Volunteers do not want to feel they are on a sinking or troubled ship. They will leave like rats if they have that sense.

These are many of the motivating features for keeping volunteers happy and attached to your organization. "If they love what they are doing, they will flourish, and so will the program," says Anna Johnson.

RECOGNITION

Formal Recognition

Is it important? In a word, YES! Celebrations are more important than they may seem at first glance. The celebration should put the voluntary efforts in the limelight of public recognition and include an accounting of the successes of their jobs done. Why? This recipe helps volunteers, and staff, realize what their day-to-day work accomplishes and how it fits in with the big picture and brings a sense of pride to the whole institution. Pride is an intrinsic motivator and will support retention within your institution. A celebration is fun and rewarding to all.

In this public celebration individuals should be recognized for the number of accumulated hours they have contributed, both annually and in milestones over the years. For example, 100, 500, or 1,000 hours, and so forth. This personal recognition should include some concrete award such as a nice certificate, a pin (either specially created or something that has some significance), or a very small gift of some type. A gift that holds significance or can have a story related to their position in some way is the most fun and meaningful. For example, I once gave very tiny inexpensive flashlights to the day captains at a thank-you recognition party, and thanked them for being the guiding light and leading the way for their teams. Remember, that the people holding leadership positions also need a special thank-you for their contributions. These are very easy to overlook.

The total annual hours of the volunteer group as a whole are important as well. For one thing it can be very impressive—to everyone. Also, putting a dollar amount like that used by the Points of Light Foundation to the total number of annual hours will show how many full-time paid staff those volunteer hours represent and the money they have saved the institution. The statistics can be astounding! The pride this instills in the volunteers is a minimotivator for many of them to remain a part of the team.

A celebration can be handled in many ways, but any party is usually supported by the great social attraction of food, and a theme or decorations is also a fun, festive touch. Whether the celebration is in the setting of a breakfast, brunch, luncheon, tea, dinner, or ice-cream social (use your creativity to make it fun), the ceremony needs to be carefully planned. I have used a special speaker or activity that enticed volunteers to come out for a small evening thank-you celebration. Some type of entertainment like music can be an added nicety.

Informal Recognition

Informal recognition includes the following:

- Frequent small things that say "we appreciate you being here giving your time and talents to this organization." For example, the genuine thank-you when a volunteer leaves for the day, or a bowl of candy placed out on holidays with a group *Thank-you* sign in the volunteer room. Be clever—perhaps do it with a catchy little rhyme or some appropriate clip art. Volunteers appreciate this small amount of

time you put into making them feel wanted. Not all recognition and rewards need to be costly.
- Badges. Believe it or not, something as simple as formal name badges recognizes the value you place on your volunteers as unpaid staff.
- Continuing education offerings to enhance their knowledge and skills, and feed their passions, as discussed earlier.
- At the end of the off-season we held a special little thank-you soirée to show appreciation for volunteers sharing extra time and talents for events in the off-season. This included tooting-the-horn of their accomplishments in supporting the big picture (how many visitors were reached in tours, classes, new members recruited, etc.). Make it fun and rewarding, and they will come.
- A kickoff meeting at the beginning of the season or for a special opening brings volunteers up to speed for the event and says, "You are valuable, and we want you to know what is going on before this season or event unfolds."
- Leadership roles. As discussed earlier: recognize skills, talents, ambition, and dedication to your institution. Recognizing and rewarding these is definitely motivating for these donors of time and talent, and contributes to commitment and retention.
- Evaluation. All programs need a periodic assessment to ensure they are meeting the needs of the volunteers and the goals of the organization. Inviting your volunteers to be a part of the evaluation processes for their programs shows you recognize and value their input, their ideas for any necessary solution, and their buy-in to the expectations of the group and the institution. Most volunteers are so committed to your institution they will meet or exceed the expectations, and they appreciate your willingness to continually improve their situation with their in-put. (See Chapter 10 for more information.)

When the Garden volunteer group was small, each person on the staff contributed a cooked/created dish to share at the annual recognition luncheon as their personal thank-you. The volunteers *really* appreciated that gesture on their behalf. As the Garden volunteer corps grew, the luncheon or breakfast became a catered event with the food being donated by the preferred caterers who had contracts to serve at the Garden. All staff members then held other roles in the event to participate and show their appreciation.

—Nancy Cutler

Textbox 2.3. Problem Volunteers—Should You Fire?

It should be noted that occasionally a volunteer will either outgrow his or her ability to perform the agreed-to duties or will, in some way, no longer be a good fit in your organization. Could you, should you ever *fire* a volunteer? The first line of approach should be to see if there is another place in the institution where the volunteer can contribute. If the volunteer is not working out, is being disruptive or destructive, or truly is not able to perform the assigned duties, you should reevaluate the job description with the volunteer. Try to help the volunteer come to the correct conclusion for himself. Never attack the volunteer's attitude, but calmly discuss behavior. Rarely, it is necessary for policy or behavioral or safety reasons to ask a person to leave your institution. This is never pleasant, but the overall health of the institution and the volunteer program must be your priority. If necessary, you could request security personnel or an authority figure to escort the former volunteer off the premises. Be sure to have the volunteer turn in his or her volunteer name badge.

Textbox 2.4.

It should be noted in this chapter that volunteerism is more prevalent in the United States than in other parts of the world. President Ronald Reagan recognized this wonderful spirit in Americans in this quote:

> The work of volunteer groups throughout our country represents the very heart and soul of America. They have helped make this the most compassionate, generous, and humane society that ever existed on the face of this earth. (October 16, 1973)

CONCLUSION

Recruitment, Recognition, Retention—the three R's of working with volunteers are all intimately connected. Simply stated, the structures and procedures used for recruiting good volunteers, beginning with a needs assessment and clearly communicated expectations, form the basis of the structure needed to retain them and are echoed in how you recognize them. Recognition and appreciation show your respect, and everyone thrives on it. Volunteers are donating their time and talents; they are not required to participate in activities they do not wish to. The challenge for those who need and use volunteers is to *entice* them to want to be a part of the larger team and a variety of departmental teams, to recognize their efforts appropriately and often, and to always let them know *how* their contributions matter.

Good recruitment can entice people to join your organization, and a good management structure will keep them. A "team approach" to volunteer management can help put the structures in place to grow teams of voluntary workers in your institution. Create teams of volunteers with a common interest, bonded to the institution by the work they do and the people they work with, and rewarded by those associations as well as by their ability to do meaningful work in the community, and you are motivating volunteering. Start small and help it grow.

There are many resources available on managing volunteer programs that you can turn to for additional help. A few are listed in the bibliography. The Internet or your local volunteer center can direct you to many more. The structures described in this chapter can be used as guidelines that can be modified to fit the situation in your environment. The sample forms in the appendix are models for you to modify and fit to your situation or as suggestions to help you design your own pages. Good luck!

NOTES

1. Kathleen Socolofsky, "A Team Approach to Volunteer Management," *The Public Garden* 6, no. 2 (April 1991): 12–15, 33.
2. Mihály Csikszentmihályi and Kim Hermanson, "Intrinsic Motivation in Museums: What Makes Visitors Want to Learn?" *Museum News* (May/June1995): 35–61.
3. Susan J. Ellis, *The Volunteer Recruitment (and Membership Development) Book*, 2nd edition (Philadelphia: Energize, Inc., 1996).
4. Joel O. Iverson, PhD, "Volunteers as Communities of Practice: The Docents of the Desert Botanical Garden" (Research paper for Department of Communication, Texas A&M University, College Station, Tex., 2004), 3.

CHAPTER 3

Docent Training Guidelines

ANNA JOHNSON

> I always think of museum educators as translators: people who put the highly-detailed, complex (and occasionally long-winded and convoluted) explanations that curators develop into a form that museum visitors can easily understand, appreciate, and use. They clarify without oversimplifying.
>
> —*Margaret A. Weitekamp, curator, National Air and Space Museum, Smithsonian Institution*

Why are docents being discussed separately from the volunteer chapter? Aren't they volunteers too? Docents have a critical function in the visitor's experience at museums. They are often the primary people visitors interact with, and as such play key roles in the understanding and memories visitors have of the museum. Therefore, high-quality training programs are vitally important in developing effective docents who project a good image of the museum. The title *docent* is very specific in museums to the volunteers/staff who lead tours and interact with the public. A museum volunteer program can comprise docents as well as other volunteers. Including the docent program in the volunteer program allows the docent program to meet its unique needs, remain an active part of the whole museum volunteer program, and be a valued asset of the museum.

Some museums pay their docents and do not use volunteers in this capacity or may have both paid and volunteer docents. For example, paid docents will lead tours at odd times when voluntary docents choose not to participate.

Creating a visitor experience that is positive and rewarding involves organization and attention to detail. As ambassadors of the museum, docents often set the tone for the entire visitor experience. Docents are generally caring, concerned volunteers who want to represent the museum well and who truly appreciate the training and support. Frequently, they choose to be docents because they themselves are lifelong learners and see a carefully planned and rich docent training experience as a personal growth opportunity. In addition, these volunteers are usually socially oriented individuals who are seeking opportunities to meet and interact with others. The institution's commitment to creating a supportive environment for docents results in their presenting successful museum tours and having positive and engaging interactions with the public. Successful museum tours are those in which the visitors enjoy themselves, learn new information, engage in an activity or activities, and leave wanting to know more and to return to the museum in the future.

This chapter discusses ideas for structuring a docent training program, building docent interpretive skills, continuing education, and recognizing and evaluating docents. In addition techniques used successfully in docent training including curriculum ideas for docent classes and varied activities that can be used to teach docents about museums are included.

INSTITUTIONAL COMMITMENT

In developing and managing a docent program, it is important to have a strong commitment from the organization as a whole. That includes defining the importance of docents, what a docent is, and what they do; setting institutional goals that include the docent program; and providing financial support for staff and materials for the program.

Definition of Docent

What does the word *docent* mean and where does it come from? According to the Merriam-Webster dictionary, *docent* means "a person who leads guided tours especially through a museum or art gallery," and the word is from obsolete German (now *Dozent*) and from Latin *docens*, present participle of *docere*.[1] Generally museums and libraries prefer the term *docent* to denote the volunteers/staff who lead tours or run educational activities. *Guide* is another word used for people guiding or leading tours. The dictionary defines a guide as "a person who exhibits and explains points of interest" or "something that provides a person with guiding information."[2] In addition, some institutions, often parks, use the title *interpreter* instead of docent or guide. The *Merriam-Webster's Collegiate Dictionary* defines an *interpreter* as "one who explains or expounds."[3]

Whichever title one uses, these are the people who lead tours, interact with the public on a regular basis, and represent the museum in its public programs. (Look at Chapter 2 for ideas for creating a job description for docents.) Because of this public exposure, they require specialized training in two important areas: first, to be knowledgeable about the institution and the information showcased there; and second, to know how to present this knowledge to the public. The first is more obvious than the second. However, training on methods to share information with the public is equally important.

When there are two or more locations within the organization where docents are used, for example, museum and historic sites or multiple gardens, training and scheduling docents for additional venues can be a challenge. This increases the need for flexibility when there is one docent organization. Remaining as a single docent organization increases the number of docents available for all venues and can facilitate many of the docents' moving back and forth between two or more sites depending on where the needs are and which programs they prefer. All docents should go through the general docent training, which introduces them to all sites but focuses on the main museum. Additional training should be offered at the remote site for the regular docents who are there every week. Specific docents sometimes prefer one site over the other and primarily stay at one site, but they will occasionally help at different locations. One consideration that may impact a docent's choice is the physical surroundings; for example there may be steps at the remote site, but not at the museum. When there are special programs at either site, there should always be a specific training to explain to everyone what to do so that everyone continues to work together for the museum as a whole.

Setting goals for the educational programs and the docent program is critical because those goals help set priorities and focus on what needs to be done by the docents.

DOCENT TRAINING

There are many approaches to docent training, but it is most important that the docents recognize that there is a commitment on the part of the organization to effectively train them to be knowledgeable in their presentations and their interactions with the public. The training reinforces to them how important it is that they be prepared to excel in this essential position.

Before we discuss training programs and techniques, let's define *training*. First of all, *teaching* and *training* are synonymous according to the Merriam-Webster dictionary.[4] The dictionary further states that *teach* "applies to any manner of imparting information or skill so that others may learn," while *train* "stresses instruction and drill with a specific end in view."[5] The focus of docent *training* classes is to motivate people to be good docents, develop the appropriate skills to lead tours or staff a hands-on room or touch cart, build their comfort in the physical space and in representing the institution, and increase their knowledge about the information represented in the exhibit halls. This type of *training* is somewhat like "on-the-job training," which is frequently provided by businesses to new employees.

There is great variety among training programs. Some museums meet once a week for a year for their beginning docents, while others may have one afternoon training session. The reason for this variety relates to available resources to train docents, number of docents, size of museum, types of programs being offered by museum staff to support the docent program, and on and on. It is most important that the training program be well organized, interesting to the docents, effective, and accurate.

Setting Goals

Rather than beginning by focusing on duration or time, a more productive approach to developing a docent training program is to determine what the museum's goals are for the docents as well as what it is the docents need to know in order to be successful and comfortable leading tours. Visualize, test by asking the public, or develop a committee to determine what your docents need to know and how you want them to function, and then write that down as a goal. For example, determine what are the most important elements of the tour, such as knowledge of topic, way finding, interesting stories, arousing curiosity, or making the visitor comfortable, then practice leading tours with staff or friends. Develop those important elements into a goal. The goal can be further clarified by listing individual objectives, which might include the following:

- To practice appropriate tour presentation techniques;
- To be aware of how people learn and how to apply varied teaching techniques;
- To be knowledgeable about the museum and the roles and responsibilities of the staff;
- To be informed about how to handle emergency situations (such as a fire, lost child, sick visitor);
- To learn the tour.

Preparing for Docent Class

A docent's experience usually begins in a training class. A manual presented to all potential docents on the first day of class is helpful. It makes them realize this is an important class, and it gives them a special place to keep all their docent information together. The docent manual provides the curriculum and the written information related to the topics of the class. A three-ring binder is an excellent way to organize and contain the materials. It is important to create goals and objectives for the docent training and include them in the class materials along with those for the docent program and the tour. The written material includes support information for the class and should also clearly define any requirements of the course, such as taking a test or giving a tour, so the potential docents will understand what they need to accomplish in the class.

DOCENT TRAINING PROGRAM

Rather than discuss the length of a docent training program, the focus will be on universally valuable topics. Each organization needs to determine the length of its training and what is most important for it to include. Some curriculum examples and activities will be explained and/or included in the sample forms in the appendix. Discussions about whether or not to charge a fee for the classes, interpretive skill building, and using hands-on materials are also included with ideas to add to the classes.

Topics for Docent Training Class

The following is the recommended list of topics, each with a brief description:

PHILOSOPHY OF THE EDUCATION PROGRAM AT THE MUSEUM What kind of educational experience is the museum hoping the visitor will have, and what is the role of the docent—to be a facilitator, a content provider, a greeter, security specialist, or a combination of these and other roles? The docents need to clearly understand the organizational/cultural/educational framework they function in and what will be expected of them. Going over the vision and goals of the institution and the education program as well as setting goals and objectives for the docents are important. Clarifying such points as whether docents are to memorize a presentation versus giving tours that can be adapted to each specific audience is important. Keep in mind that docents who give the exact same tour repeatedly will eventually become bored and tire of being a docent. Motivating docents to continue to participate and to do thoughtful presentations rather than just reiterating the same information as well as interacting with the visitors in their tour group is important. Defining other ways docents can contribute to the museum and be involved in the education programs, such as continuing to learn and helping develop curriculum (as suggested in Chapter 2), can be very empowering for them.

INTERPRETATION Another important part of the philosophy section is emphasis on *interpretation*. Many of the docents have long loved history, art, nature, and so forth, but do not understand interpretation. Interpretation includes discussing an object in the time and place in which it was used or lived and creating context or the background or setting of the use or lifestyle or environment. This is a difficult concept to get across in a short time, but the application is critical. Part of interpreting history is to convince the visitor of the differences between then and now. For example, on our main tour, there was a scraper. I explained in detail how it worked as we all looked it over, found the manufacturer's name on it and when it was built, and compared its use to our modern equipment such as shovels and backhoes. Then I began to discuss the purpose of the scraper, which was locally known as a *Fresno*. It was used to level fields for planting and level areas for roads and railroad beds. There was a very large photograph behind the scraper that showed the local use of deepening irrigation canals. Next I began to discuss the physical nature of using this piece of equipment, which was pulled by horses, and how dangerous this task could be. One visitor then spoke

Interpretation

One example of interpretation that I liked to use was the Star-Spangled Banner as identification, inspiration, and icon. The flag was a standard-sized garrison flag used to identify a U.S. fort during the War of 1812. You can talk about the fact that seamstress Mary Pickersgill in Baltimore sewed the flag for Fort McHenry. It was a typical flag of the day with no standard design for the star field. It has 15 stars even though there were 18 states in the Union. You can talk about flag design and when Congress set a standard U.S. flag design. As a flag at Fort McHenry it became important when during the British bombardment of the fort, an American man named Francis Scott Key, held on a British ship, was so inspired to see that flag still flying after the bombardment that he wrote a poem. You can talk about the details of the bombardment or the War of 1812 or even about inspiration and where it comes from. Key's poem was published shortly after the battle of Baltimore and became a popular patriotic song. When Congress designated the song the United States' national anthem in the 1930s, the flag became an icon because it is the subject of the song and it represents a valiant defense against enemy troops in our nation's history. You could approach talking about the flag from any of these angles or ask what the United States flag represents to your visitors, but it is really all of them put together that tell the whole story.

—Tim Grove

Textbox 3.1. Interpretation Teaching Technique

One approach used with considerable success was to bring in two curators along with the educator and have them demonstrate interpretation in the exhibit halls. It became somewhat of a game among the staff trying to stump each other, and often the class would add to the discussion or have questions. It worked as follows:

1. One curator would pick an item to be interpreted in the exhibit hall and lead the group to the object. That curator would then be the last one to interpret the object.
2. Once the item was picked, another curator would start the interpretation.
3. Each curator would interpret the object with a slightly different approach. For example, using a pitcher and bowl from a local hotel at the turn of the century: One curator would talk about the hotel and the town at the time; another curator would talk about technology at the time and what type of plumbing would be in place as well as describing a typical morning routine and use of the pitcher and bowl; the last curator would discuss who might be staying in the hotel in the early 1900s, and what traveling was like, defining local roads and their condition.
4. Then the curator who interpreted first would pick the next object and automatically be the last one to interpret it. (Presumably the last to speak could have the hardest time coming up with ideas for her interpretation.) This was not a canned or practiced presentation. The curators never knew what objects others had picked until they were participating in the interpretation presentation.
5. The curators would look far and wide in the hall to find something to stump the others. (Incidentally, no one was ever stumped, but it made for interesting artifact selections and kept the curators from getting bored with the exercise.)
6. The class was required to listen to all the presentations of each object, and then they could add their comments or ask questions.

This exercise set the stage to have discussions about basing interpretation on fact and not making up stories. It is an excellent time to emphasize that the information should be based on solid research and not hearsay.

—Anna Johnson

---

up, saying he was from Chicago and remembered as a small child (in the 1920s) when they were building roads by his house that he would hear the men scream when they were hurt, which was frequently. To be presented with the facts of a situation (how the fresno worked), to be able to connect the tangible (the scraper) with the intangible (lifestyle), and to feel connected to the examples being given through emotions (as the story that this man told unfolded, he added how it had made him cry and cover his ears to keep from hearing them), but understand that in actuality it is so much more (this was a common ex- perience across the country). Suddenly everyone on the tour began to understand that living in the 1920s was significantly different than living in 2007. I understand this kind of powerful experience does not always happen on a tour, but through research, docents can share the stories of the community and the people who lived there. These stories are also powerful.

In each class there should be some type of activity targeted at developing interpretive skills. See Textboxes 3.1 and 3.2 for techniques to use while teaching interpretation. There is also a further discussion in the interpretive skill-building section in this chapter.

INSTITUTIONAL INFORMATION In order to create individuals who are knowledgeable about the museum, docent training must include the museum's mission, history, organization chart, phone numbers, staff names, titles and duties, services available, map of the facility, hours, fees, and off-site facilities. A tour of the museum behind the scenes is essential and can cultivate a sense that docents have a role in fulfilling the mission. In addition, knowledge of the layout of the museum and the exhibit hall is important in order for the docents to be comfortable in the environment. Docents should be treated as part of the museum family, so you want to make sure they feel comfortable contacting and having access to professional staff. It is helpful if the docents will be able to meet appropriate staff members and find out what they all do. If the staff does not have time to meet with the docent class, consider videotaping all staff members explaining what they do and showcasing the area of the museum where they work. A video tour of off-site facilities is helpful if a visit is not possible. This information is useful as the docents interact with the public and encourage public involvement.

While docents primarily work with public programs, they should have a familiarity with the collections and the basic guidelines for the collection and care of artifacts. These volunteers can then speak with knowledge and pride about all that goes on at the museum, and make referrals to appropriate staff. Because they are largely in the exhibit halls, docents will be the first persons to notice damage or theft and need to feel comfortable in the role as collections stewards. By introducing docents to staff, they can immediately contact the appropriate person to report what is happening. Docents also need to become familiar with emergency procedures such as the location of fire extinguishers in case of fire and exits in case of emergency.

CONTENT INFORMATION ON THE MUSEUM SPECIALTY Whether the museum is a history, art, anthropology, or botanical site, the docents need to be grounded in the scholarship of the museum and the content embedded in exhibits. Curators who are specialists can enhance this section of the class, and it is a good way for the docents to meet staff. For example, a history museum with an emphasis on community history can have the curator of history teach an overview of state history and then a section on the history of the community. To the docents, this is an opportunity for personal growth, to develop their personal interests, and to become knowledgeable about the museum and its contents.

PRESENTATION TECHNIQUES Communication factors such as eye contact, hand and facial gestures, general appearance, use of language, voice quality, clarity of message, and confidence are important to cover with new docents. Be sure to include basics such as not talking with your back to your audience, not jangling keys or change in your pocket, and holding your hands clasped gently in front of you with your arms slightly bent, at your sides in a relaxed resting pose and not crossed across your chest.

DOCENT'S ROLE DURING A TOUR Docents need to understand that they are not in the exhibit hall as disciplinarians. When school groups come to museums, it needs to be made clear that the docent is there to share information, not manage crowd control. However, a docent can change the pace of a tour, have children sit down in some instances, or ask for assistance from a student who is being a distraction in order to better focus their tours. When leading tours for school groups, I have found that looking only at the children and not the adults will prevent adults from answering the questions instead of the students.

In addition, doing exercises with a video recorder can help everyone in the class focus on presentation techniques and improve dramatically.

Using a Video Camera for Developing Presentation Skills

When videotaping docents there are some basic rules to consider: A videotape will be provided for each person. No one will view the tape except the person being taped. During breaks, you may want to give them the opportunity to view the videotape somewhere in private in the museum. Have the class members take turns. Make sure the tapes stay in the classroom until all the class sessions are over. At the end of all the sessions, each tape will belong to the person who has been videotaped. The persons being taped will most likely see changes in themselves when they view the tape, and they will not feel threatened by anyone critiquing them. They are often harder on themselves than a trainer would be.

Activities for videotaping may include the following:

1. Have everyone go to the front of the class individually. They are to introduce themselves to the class and share information about themselves. They will be videotaped while they are doing this. Let them know they will be speaking for one minute, and no longer. You will stop them at the end of one minute, and they are to keep speaking until you stop them. When someone gives a presentation, they need to have a sense of time, and we should all be able to talk about ourselves for at least one minute.

2. Action can be effective when giving a presentation and is a way to release the nervous energy developed while speaking in front of people. Write down activities such as how to hard-boil eggs, how to plant a tomato plant, how to start a car, and so forth, on separate pieces of paper. Fold them, and put them in a bowl, box, or something everyone can draw from. Have each person in the class draw a piece of paper with an activity. Then they will each go in front of the class, not mention any of the words written on the paper, and describe the activity they have drawn using actions and words. The class meanwhile will be trying to determine what they are talking about. The talk is over when the class has guessed the right answer. This exercise will be videotaped; it is intended to show the positive aspects of action when speaking.

3. Have every person in the class choose a partner. With their partner send them into the exhibit hall/s. They are to choose an object, develop an interpretation of that object, and present it to the class together. Each of them must give half of the presentation. They will be videotaped. This activity requires that they combine their newly developed presentation skills and knowledge about the museum and its contents.

—Anna Johnson

Some techniques for leading discussions and waiting for the audience to respond can also be helpful.

MUSEUM LEARNING ENVIRONMENT Learning in a museum is often informal rather than the formal environment of a classroom with which most people are familiar. It is important to clarify the difference between formal and informal learning environments (also see Chapter 12); for example, the classroom sets specific requirements of the student, uses textbooks, and has clearly defined courses of study. Tests are used to assess how much the student learned, and the students are usually with a group of students who are all about the same age. The biggest difference is that students have to be there. In informal learning the visitors can be a group of people such as a family who are all different ages. They have made a choice to visit the museum, and there are usually varying reasons why they have come. There are no requirements for what they must learn, and the visitors go where they want, stopping longest at what holds their interest. Docents play a key role in more formal presentations at museums through their tours, but generally these situations are still not as formal as a classroom. Good discussions about the role of docents can result from these comparisons. Other points that emphasize the unique learning environment of the museum include:

- Museums serve visitors of all ages with various abilities and different knowledge levels.
- Museum exhibit halls contain constant "extra" stimuli (artifacts and photographs on display but not the focus of the tour, other visitors, noise, audio) surrounding the visitors even on guided tours.
- Museum visits can result in emotional, physical, and/or cognitive experiences.

A list called "Tools of the Trade for the Docent" is included for the docents to consider what they should be able to do and to use as a guide in preparing to lead tours (Sample Form 3.1 in the appendix).

HOW PEOPLE LEARN People learn in a variety of ways. Translated to the docents, this means they need to vary their presentation style and tempo to keep their tours interesting and accessible to people by targeting a variety of learning styles (see Chapter 6). People learn primarily through visual, auditory, or kinesthetic methods of processing information. Everyone learns through all three of these methods, but generally each person has their preferred style. In general, the more education one has, the more often visual learning (the written word) is preferred. Auditory learning is vocal instruction as opposed to the written word. Kinesthetic learning includes movement and touching or actually

Group Management

Managing groups of people, whether the group consists of adults or children or is mixed, can be a little intimidating for a new docent. Following are some tips to help.

Tours: moving a group along halls or in a gallery

- Wait until everyone arrives before beginning.
- With more than two people on your tour do not talk while walking.
- At stops leave room for other visitors to pass.
- Have visitors collect around you so they can all see and hear easily.

One way to do this is to walk past where you ask the group to stop. Then step back to (the middle of the group) in front of the object or exhibit you will be discussing.

Folks with disabilities: What can you do to help them? The solutions are usually fairly obvious.

- A wheelchair should be brought to the front of the group so the person can see.
- Your tour introduction should invite anyone who may be hard-of-hearing to position themselves near the tour guide. You may not know there is a hard-of-hearing person on your tour unless you ask either in the introduction or during your preintroduction welcome. If they can read lips you will want to be sure to face the hard-of-hearing person and speak clearly. If someone asks a question, please repeat the question before you answer so everyone can hear it and the deaf person can read your lips.
- A blind person should also be brought to the front. You can be a bit more descriptive in your presentation to help a blind person "see" what you are talking about. It is usually a good idea to let the sighted person with the blind person help you help them to handle any items they can touch. Another trick is to have each person in the group share an observation about the object. That way everyone is involved in looking at the object carefully. (Adults often must be coaxed into participating—you sometimes have to "sell the idea" to them a little and invite them to participate.) Then you can share some factual information about their observations; especially good are "gee-whiz" facts. Ask if anyone has questions, and then answer the questions. This gives the docent the opportunity to share even more content information on a level at which the visitor has demonstrated curiosity. (These interactive strategies work whether or not there is a blind visitor.)

Children: Children are *not* little adults. Nature has made the nervous systems of little growing people wiggly and craving stimulation so they will learn! And learn they will, whether or not it is directed! Therefore, it can be difficult, especially for very young people, to be still and to listen passively. The trick is to direct their learning along the lines we desire.

Some tips for managing groups of young students include:

- When eager little hands are everywhere, ask each child to personally take a giant step back or form a big semicircle around the front of the docent so everyone can see. You or the chaperone may need to physically help them to do this.
- If necessary, ask children to sit on the ground (cross-legged) in a semicircle to get them to control themselves. A very busy group could even be asked to sit on their hands, or to fold them in their laps.
- The best defense is to give them things to do along with (or in place of) things not to do.
- Assure them that *if* they can be patient they will get to see everything they want to, and you will answer their questions if they will help by sitting, not touching, and waiting for a turn.
- Engage little bodies and minds by getting them to be a part of the discussion. Ask them, in turn and when called on, to tell about one part of what they see or notice about the object or exhibit. For example, looking at a cactus one might say it is tall, another that it looks prickly, and another that it is green, and so on. You can also ask questions for them to compare and contrast with other things with which they are familiar. The idea its to get them to be involved and to direct their physical stimulation requirement. Be sure all children have an opportunity to share an observation or a comparison, even if they must wait until the next stop. Engage as many as possible at each stop on your tour.
- You might even get them to move about as part of the demonstration. For example, if you are discussing churning butter, show them the process, and then ask them to do the motion and pretend they are churning. The physical exercise is also a kinesthetic learning experience. Children learn more kinesthetically than most adults. If a discussion of an art piece focuses on lines, shapes, and textures, have young children stand up, make a line, and follow the docent leader to the next stop. The docent can have them walk in a straight line, a curvy line, a jagged line, and be sure to explain what is going on.
- Show children respect and insist that they show it to you. They can and should learn museum manners. If a single student is misbehaving you can do things like stop talking and just look at the student. Soon everyone will be looking at the student. A continually disruptive student might be given some responsibility and made a helper. There are many tricks such as these that can be effective, especially if the students know that you understand, from your behavior, they are different from adults. Brainstorm some ideas with your docents that might be effective.
- You might invite one child at a time to come up and choose an item they would like to know about.

Remember—When you engage eager little hands, eyes, and ears, they will go away with more understanding. You *will* have had an impact.

—Nancy Cutler

trying to do something—interaction. Family learning and (informal) free-choice learning has become very popular in museums. This includes setting up learning experiences to include people of different ages in the same activity and allowing the visitor to choose their preferred approach. A good reference for this is *Lessons without Limit* by John Falk and Lynn Dierking.[6] The class curriculum should also reflect a variety of presentation styles, so that you are modeling for the docents how to reach different visitors and docents. *Frames of Mind: The Theory of Multiple Intelligences* by Dr. Howard Gardner is a valuable reference. Gardner's theory of multiple intelligences has been embraced by many museum educators. It describes eight intelligences—linguistic, musical, logical-mathematical, spatial, bodily-kinesthetic, naturalist, interpersonal, and intrapersonal—that are all ways of perceiving, interpreting, and organizing information.[7] The point for museum education programs is to create tours, activities, and presentations that appeal to learners' multiple intelligences, so they will be inclined to choose and learn from them.

SPECIAL ACCOMMODATIONS AVAILABLE Information about how to respond to people with disabilities and what the museum offers to them should be incorporated into the basic docent class so all the docents will be knowledgeable. Docents should know the types of accommodations the institution offers such as wheelchairs, sign interpreters, audio and audio-described tours, tactiles (touch items), printed scripts of videos, closed captioning, and foreign language tours. If there is a wheelchair lift or other device, make sure the docents know how to operate it and where the key or button is. Excerpts from the Americans with Disabilities Act can be helpful to include in their notebook.

SCHEDULING, LOGISTICS, AND DOCENT CONCERNS New docents always want to know how they will be scheduled to lead tours, if they should contact the group coming in, how much time they should allow for leading a tour, whom they call if they can't make it, what is the appropriate dress, where they can put their purse and/or jacket, where to sign in, what happens if they are late, where they meet the tour, and how many will be in each group. Logistics need to be determined at each institution, and they always need to be clarified to the docents. (See Chapter 4 for tour information.) How to schedule the docents and how to remind them of their commitment is always a concern. Some examples of schedules have been included to give an idea of ways to set up a schedule and to inform the docents about the timing and duties for that activity

at the same time. (See Sample Forms 3.2 and 3.3 in the appendix.)

TEACHING A TOUR AND BECOMING FAMILIAR WITH THE EXHIBIT HALLS If possible, have some type of standard tour, such as an introduction to the main exhibit hall, and have every docent learn this tour. Modeling this tour is a good way to share an organizational format for a tour that could then be carried over into the development of tours in other galleries. A format for a tour "using transitions" is explained in detail in Chapter 4.

ACCOUNTABILITY It is important to hold the docents accountable for what they are learning. I found using the following techniques a successful way to build the confidence of docents:

Test. One measure of progress can be determined by giving a take-home test at the end of the course. Give the docents about a week to complete the test before turning it in for grading. Encourage them to talk to each other and to contact staff and/or other docents as they fill in the answers. The questions should be varied and could include true-false, matching, multiple choice, and an essay. Emphasize all of the class objectives in various questions on the test. If they don't know an answer then by researching it they will learn. The test is really a *confidence builder*. Completing and passing the test proves to them that they have certainly learned something. It will also encourage them to use the materials in the docent manual. Once they realize they have increased their competency and knowledge, they will be more comfortable leading tours. *Note:* I never had anyone fail this test in 12 years, but I did have plenty of people come in and ask for help. I was happy to help them, show them where in their notebook the answers were located, who on the staff to talk to about their question, or how to figure out the answer.

Tour. Tour skills should also be assessed, and the second requirement is that the class gives a complete tour to the staff and visitors as part of their graduation. The members of the docent class are encouraged to personally invite their family and friends to graduation so these special people in their lives can see what they have been learning and accomplishing. The tour is taught through transitions, a brief statement to move the tour from one location to the next (explained in Chapter 4). The docents sign up for which transitions they will present at graduation. For example, if there are 16 transitions in the tour, each person would do one or more depending on how big the class is. If there are eight in the class they would each sign up for two transitions. The first part of graduation includes gathering everyone in front of the exhibit hall, welcoming everyone, introducing the class, and explaining that these future docents will direct us through the exhibit hall by giving the tour they have just learned in class. The class members may struggle or state some unusual information as they give this tour. *However, never criticize or correct anyone at this time.* Afterward they will reflect on their mistakes and correct them. The purpose of this exercise is to let them know they can lead a tour, and that it isn't so difficult to speak in front of people. After the tour, pass out their tests, answer any questions about the tests, and then pass out their rewards for having completed the class such as diplomas (certificates), a museum pin, and a docent name tag with their name on it. Then enjoy a little celebration with some cake and punch. (*Note:* Docent name tags can be made with just the person's first name.) The exercise of giving the tour as part of the graduation really helps the docents focus on the tour and helps them gain confidence. Giving a tour to your own family and/or friends can be intimidating. These are clearly the people who will tell you what they honestly think. The first tour is the most intimidating. After this graduation exercise, the docents generally have no qualms about leading tours, and they do a great job.

Graduation

Graduation was an important element of our docent class. It was the culmination of what the docents had learned, their first public tour, and recognition of them for what they had accomplished. The graduation experience prepared the docents in a positive way to transition from the classroom experience to actually leading tours. (On average more than 90 percent of the people who took my classes went on to become successful docents.) In order to graduate, one had to attend the classes (a person could not miss more than one class), pass the written test, and lead a portion of the tour at graduation.

—Anna Johnson

Class Curriculum

The curriculum or course of study for a docent training program needs to reflect:

1. The primary goals of the class.
2. Training in the content of the exhibits and collections.
3. Techniques for sharing the information.
4. Interaction among class members so they get to know one another and to build some rapport and bond.

5. Pertinent information about the facility.
6. Having fun at what you do! If the class isn't fun, why would people continue with the program?

In your classes you should actually be modeling to the docents what you want them to do. Your classes should be interesting and frequently change the pace of learning. Do not assume that because you are teaching adults you should only lecture to them. If you train them only through lectures, their tours will reflect this, resulting in tours that are in actuality little more than lectures in the galleries. You need to engage them in activities and cause them to reflect on the information you are sharing as you develop their ability to interpret the exhibits rather than lecture about them. Listening to a lecture is passive, and often for adults (docents as well as visitors) a chance to nod off. So what can you do? Change the pace of learning: Have different speakers, tour the exhibit halls, have the class actually do activities, play games, and involve the class members in the process of learning. This makes the learning interesting and also models how they can interact with visitors. This model gives them "permission" to do more than lecture on their tours. For example, here is one session:

> History of institution by museum director—15 minutes
> Main hall tour led by educator—20 minutes
> Meet exhibits curator and go into galleries with him while he explains how exhibits are designed and built—25 minutes
> Lecture on history of Arizona to 1912 by curator of history—50 minutes
> History game—10 minutes

As you look at this two-hour class, you can see that the learning pace changes frequently through speakers and activities. The class sits, and then moves about. Note the time listed for each activity. It helps to keep the class on time, and clarify to presenters how long they are to speak. A full class curriculum is included on Sample Form 3.4 in the appendix.

Class Activities

Think creatively as you develop your course curriculum and always keep your goals and objectives in mind. Be focused on what you need to accomplish in the class, that is, what it is you want the docents to do after they graduate, and make sure your activities emphasize these needs and are not just interesting without adding anything to the training.

Using Analogies

What is an analogy? An analogy states a correspondence in some respect between things that are otherwise dissimilar, often using the word "like."

To Do—Brainstorm some analogies for your collection. For example:

- Cactus spines are *like* fur or clothing—both help shelter the skin from drying wind.
- Small leaves on plants are *like* loose summer clothing—they allow air to circulate and keep plants cooler.
- In cross-section, a moist cactus is like a vegetable—*like* a potato or a melon.
- Wooly barrel cactus with wool on the top is *like* the hair on your head—it helps protect from sunburn.

The point of this activity is to help interpreters make the *unfamiliar* more familiar and recognizable for visitors.

—Nancy Cutler

Whether or Not to Charge a Fee

Another point to consider is whether or not to charge a fee for the docent training. The institution is committing financial and human resources to docent training and expects to have a return on this investment. If someone is only taking the class for his own education, then other programs are better suited. Another reason for charging includes ensuring some commitment to the training. Instead of charging a fee, a physical commitment can be required such as spending so many hours giving tours in the main exhibit hall. There are several reasons to do this rather than charge a fee:

- This somewhat "forces the issue" and does not allow someone to take the course and not lead tours. It also emphasizes that the goal of training is to lead tours, not just to receive training for training's sake.
- Leading tours IS payback for the investment made by the organization. (If they chose to not be a docent, they were asked to return the notebook.)
- If a person is afraid of giving tours, they know from the beginning what is expected.
- If someone did their 10 hours and truly did not like being a docent, they were able to transfer to another area of the museum and not feel like they had not done their part or that they were letting the museum down.

However, there are museums that charge a fee for docent training, and these museums also have success with that process. Some institutions use a job description/contract at the beginning of class to make sure that expectations are clear. Another option could be refundable deposits, which are returned after the docent completes a certain number of tours. So it is up to your institution and what works best in your situation.

Docent Training Using Primary Sources

I think it is important in docent training to talk about the research process. How do we know what we know? Whether it is science or history, docents need to understand how curators or scientists reach conclusions based on evidence. When I trained docents to work in the Hands On History Room at the National Museum of American History, I always included activities using primary sources. We analyzed photographs of families in front of sod houses, we explored objects and documents related to an eighteenth-century Delaware family, we tried different ways to gin cotton, and we listened to oral histories about life on a rice plantation. As a result of our discussions, the docents gained a better understanding of the various types of information that different historical sources reveal, which they in turn were able to explain to visitors.

—Tim Grove

Interpretive Skill Building

Using interpretation in tours is important, and, yet it is often overlooked in docent training classes. Freeman Tilden describes interpretation as "an educational activity which aims to reveal meanings and relationships through the use of original objects, by firsthand experience, and by illustrative media, rather than simply to communicate factual information."[8] Tilden also defined six principles, listed briefly below:

1. Any interpretation that does not somehow relate what is being displayed or described to something within the personality or experience of the visitor will be sterile.
2. Information, as such, is not interpretation.
3. Interpretation is an art, which combines many arts.
4. The chief aim of interpretation is not instruction, but provocation.
5. Interpretation should aim to present a whole rather than a part.
6. Interpretation addressed to children should not be a dilution of the presentation to adults, but should follow a fundamentally different approach.[9]

It is important to teach interpretation as part of your docent classes. There are several good books written about what it is, including *Personal Interpreta-*

What is interpretation? Because interpretation is such a key element of presenting history, each class session should have some discussion or activity related to interpretation. This is an introductory activity to interpretation and levels of interpreting.

First, show the students an oil lamp and simply state that this is what was used for light before electricity. Then put it down and point out that we could leave it there and everyone would understand the point; however, we could go back and look more closely. Then pick up the oil lamp, take it apart, and put it back together, explaining the details of using an oil lamp for light including cleaning, filling, and lighting it. Then walk over and turn the light switch off and on to compare the use of the lamp with modern light. Now everyone has a better idea of the time and energy the oil lamp took versus the light switch.

—Anna Johnson

To Do

- Have several mysterious looking items available for groups of trainees to handle and look at very carefully.
- Divide trainees into groups of 2 to 4 and give each group one of the mystery items.
- Give groups 10 minutes to carefully look at their items. Ask them not to identify the items, but instead, to
   1. Record all their observations as a group. Compare and contrast with things that are familiar. Encourage them to use their senses for the observations.
   2. List at least three curiosity questions about the item.
- After ten minutes,
   1. Return attention of the entire group and have each group show their item to the class, share their observations, and ask their curiosity questions.
   2. Discuss with the class the observations and answer their questions. Tell what the item is and why it is valuable—What its story is. People are usually fascinated to learn about these unusual objects.
   3. Discuss throughout the activity how these techniques can be used with visitors to involve them in observation and discussion of items in your collection.

The point of this exercise is for docents to experience that making simple observations is a very easy and powerful way to get people involved with the object(s) being interpreted and to stimulate their curiosity. It then invites visitors' questions and gives docents opportunities to share their factual information on a level that connects with visitors' interest or curiosity. This interactive approach also helps limit the amount of information that is required to be shared.

—Nancy Cutler

tion by Lisa Brochu and Tim Merriman.[10] Included in these books are many excellent examples of ways to do interpretation in science centers, parks, and other like facilities. It is my view that there is not enough time spent in docent classes on interpretive skill building. Interpretation is often used in the sense of ordering and laying out a tour. There is the big overriding idea or interpretation for the tour such as the development of a city. The idea is that the city will be interpreted through the exhibit and the tour. Then there are the themes that make up the big interpretation such as economy, diversity, politics, social environment, and infrastructure. When someone leads a tour, the interpretation is guided by all of this, but it is actually happening more directly on the theme layer. Making all of these ideas real includes lots of little story examples, which are in and of themselves interpretation. This is where I think the docent can shine. It is not enough to raise questions; encourage visitors to reach for answers (using stories with unusual endings). What are the questions that should be asked? (What do the stories add to the tour/exhibit?) What about historical significance? (Is this an important thing to know? Why?) Does it always have to be logical? (Is the truth always logical?) Interpretive skill building is the complement to developing the docent's knowledge of the subject (see Textbox 3.3). It provides the tools that will help the docents maintain the attention of the visitor, use the artifacts in their story, and apply their content knowledge in a museum tour (see Textbox 3.4).

Using volunteers to tell the stories often raises the concern that the stories that are told on the tour are more exaggerated than what actually happened and may not be based on fact. For this reason especially, I think it is extremely important to spend some time in the training classes teaching interpretive skills, and the importance and relevance of the facts. I have added some of the exercises I used in my classes to help my docents begin to see the power of interpretation on a personal level as well as in a tour. Also consider using games, interactives, and other ways to aid the visitors to experience interpretation on their own (see Textbox 3.5). Docents can still lead the activity (see Chapter 6). Irrespective of the type of museum one works in, interpretation is at the heart of what is presented, and this needs to be portrayed to the public not only through exhibits, but also through tours and public programs in general.

Using Hands-on Materials

Because the quality of interaction with the public is part of this discussion, using hands-on materials effectively should be covered. Many docents are not totally comfortable with using hands-on materials. Reasons for this include:

1. Passing the object focuses the visitor on the object rather than on the one leading the discussion (docent).
2. The docent feels loss of control over the discussion because the students/visitors are not as tuned in to what is being said as they are thinking about the object as they touch it.

Textbox 3.5. Using Universal Concepts

These are human concepts that everyone can identify and relate to on an emotional or sensory level across all cultures. Give a couple of examples, then have the class brainstorm a list such as the following:

Love	Heavy/Light
Hate	Light/Dark
Fear	Hard/Soft
Safety	Rough/Smooth
Joy	Survival
Anger	Smiles
Sorrow	Fast/Slow
Hunger	Beauty
Thirst	Art
Hot/Cold	Humor
Warm	Time

Follow up by sharing a couple of examples (planned ahead) using a universal concept within an interpretive sentence and contrasting the impact felt when the universal concept is left out.

The *point of this exercise* is that using universal concepts in your interpretation helps visitors emotionally identify with how the objects or concepts are important/valuable to people. It helps the discussion have more impact on the visitor. Think of and collect universal concepts you can use in your interpretation.

—Nancy Cutler

To counteract these concerns, do some activities involving passing of objects in the docent training, and have the docents explain how it helped them to actually see, touch, and hold the object. Once the docents think about the value of passing objects and actually experience that value, they are more likely to include hands-on activities in their presentations.

Another issue is that allowing some objects to be touched and not others creates a mixed message. Usually in a museum this is not a big issue, as most objects that need protection are in cases. However, in historic homes and gardens the situation can be a little different. If the docent prefaces the use of hands-on objects by explaining that what the visitor will be looking at are artifacts that cannot be touched but that the docent will occasionally pass special objects for the visitor to inspect more closely, the issue can be clear from the beginning.

MAINTAINING A CONTINUING COMMITMENT TO THE DOCENT PROGRAM

Once the docent program is developed and operational, then retaining and motivating docents, maintaining presentations with accurate information, and supporting their needs become major concerns. The following topics will help identify successful techniques and suggest points to consider.

Docent Needs

How do docents organize themselves for tours when there is more than one docent involved? Establishing a type of hierarchy among the docents can be helpful when staff is not available to help with organization for tours (see Chapter 2). Whatever system you use, it must make the best use of your staff and docents as well as represent your organization in a consistent, positive way.

Keeping docents informed about new exhibits and able to lead tours in these areas is always a concern. One solution is to arrange a minitraining, on the day before a new exhibit opens, with the following components:

1. All the docents are invited to come in to see the exhibit so they are familiar with it and able to prepare to lead tours through it.
2. Set a meeting for the docents with the lead curator on any new exhibit. The curator can better inform the docents about the exhibit and its goals, and provide them with more detailed information.

3. After this presentation the docents can discuss with the educator ways to lead tours through the exhibit.
4. Docents should receive a packet of written material on the content of the exhibit.

It is essential that docents be informed about what is happening in exhibit halls and not be surprised by changes when they come in to lead tours.

Docent Meetings

Docents usually work either alone or with only two or three other docents at a time. Even when they are working at the same time, they are generally each leading a tour and not able to visit with each other. Having a room for the docents to gather, visit, eat lunch, and so forth, is very important. However, often they are so busy leading tours that there is no chance for them to relax and socialize among themselves. Having regular meetings is a good way to create opportunities for socialization as well as continuing education and problem-solving sessions. Every museum needs to look at its own calendar and determine when docents are generally around and most active and then schedule their meetings accordingly.

These meetings may include a variety of activities for learning, program evaluation, and continuing education opportunities. For example:

- Visit other institutions, tour other facilities, meet their staff, and learn more about the general locale.
- Discuss successes and problem tours and how to deal with them. These meetings become a time of sharing by everyone, which is also empowering to the whole group.
- Present new programs that are being developed. The docents could try out the program and discuss ways to improve it before it is presented to the public.
- Bring in guest speakers such as guest curators, interpretive specialists such as storytellers, and others who could help improve the docents' knowledge base and/or touring techniques.
- Train the docents for an upcoming school/special program.
- Brainstorm new ideas for programs, tours, activities, and exhibits.
- Always include a year-end wrap-up celebration.

Docents love these meetings, and their enthusiasm for the museum and their interest in and motivation for what they are doing often increases. It is also an excellent opportunity for them to get to know one another better, develop new friendships, and be more comfortable when working together. Regular meetings help keep docents connected (bonded) to your institution and encourage them to stay involved rather than drifting away.

Continuing Education

From time to time, it will be necessary to run special trainings perhaps for an educational program, summer programs, and/or special activity/cart docents. These trainings are generally more concise, focused, and shorter than the general introductory training. This list may help to determine what should be included:

1. What is the purpose of the training? As a result of the training, what do you want the docents to know/do? For special trainings, you may have teens or others who have come in just for this program or the season (summer). In this case you need to introduce them to the institution as well as the program and its purpose. Choose from below what is appropriate to your situation.
   a. To introduce institution and its importance in community.
   b. To be knowledgeable about the institution.
   c. To be welcoming.
   d. To involve visitors in the exhibit/activity.
   e. To lead school tours, a special program, or a touch cart presentation.
2. How long should the training be?
   a. Two hours maximum.
   b. Recognize that your training is focused on a special program, and stay focused on that outcome.
3. Conducting training:
   a. Create a packet of written information, and be sure to include goals for presentation. (See "Awesome Arizona Architecture," Sample Form 3.5 in the appendix.)
   b. Have everyone introduce themselves and say why they want to participate in this program. (This gives insight into motivation.)
   c. Model greeting, welcoming, and interacting with the public.
   d. Set expectations of doing a good job, being on time, etc.
   e. Include scheduling information, and address how early to be there before the start of the program as well as setup and teardown explanations.

Interpreting Slavery at the John Brown House, Providence, Rhode Island

Local scholars, community advocates, and Rhode Island Historical Society staff sought to improve the interpretation of slavery at the John Brown House in 2003. A major part of the initiative was to determine why docents tended to shy away from the topic. Through written surveys and informal conversations, we learned that the primary reason John Brown's role in the slave trade was not emphasized was that docents did not feel they knew enough about Rhode Island and the slave trade or its relationship to John Brown. Several docents stated that they discussed John Brown's ardent support to keep the slave trade legal when they contrasted him to his brother Moses Brown, a Quaker who was staunchly against the slave trade, in the "Moses Brown room." Staff determined that continuing education was necessary to make sure all docents understood that a discussion of the slave trade was a required part of all tours, to provide examples of period rooms and artifacts that could be used to prompt discussion of slavery and the slave trade throughout the entire tour (rather than solely in the "Moses Brown room"), and to increase confidence in their ability to intelligently discuss the topic through intensive historical content training (lecture and analysis of primary source material). In addition, we provided an overview of a forthcoming gallery exhibit that would focus on slavery and enable them to show visitors some of the documents that historians used to research the Browns' involvement in the slave trade, views on slavery, and John Brown's ownership of enslaved people. In the course of developing the continuing education classes, we paid particular attention to training in interpretive techniques to tell the story of slavery and the slave trade. Prior to this initiative, the John Brown House docent training largely consisted of lectures and a detailed walk-through of the house with the curator, focused on decorative arts. The resultant continuing education program not only expanded docents' understanding of the significance of the slave trade in Rhode Island, but was the first step in revising the entire docent training program to include interpretive skill-building activities in addition to traditional lectures and the walk-through.

—Melissa Bingmann

f. Include dress code information.

g. Be specific about what happens where, and be sure to show the class the area where they will be located.

h. Inform them about the location of bathrooms, drinking fountains, and so on—as they will be asked by visitors.

i. Have name badges for them, or explain where the badges will be when they come in.

j. Supply them with information about your organization.

k. Think about what you most want the docents to accomplish and make sure that it is covered in the training.

4. How to bring people up to speed who were not at training:

a. Run a second training.

b. Have them come in and observe a tour/program and also pick up a copy of the information packet.

c. Videotape one of the docents, and have others come in and view this tape as well as picking up the information packet. (Actually, videotaping docents during a presentation they do extremely well can raise the overall quality of other presentations. It is also fun for the docents, and emphasizes to them how important it is they continue to deliver a good and accurate presentation.) This videotape can also be used by other docents to refresh their knowledge and focus just before they do a presentation.

d. *Note:* In order to include all this information, discuss the most important topics and pass out printed information on other topics such as dress code, locations, etc.

In addition to the docent meetings, it is good to make special continuing education classes available for docents. These include special speakers targeted at motivating docents and developing their skills (often for cost reasons held jointly with other museums) and talks and presentations related to different exhibits that are also offered to the public. Continuing education classes fill a niche for docents desiring personal growth, as well as keeping them current on what they need to know. Some museums require that docents attend so many continuing education classes per year; others do not have this requirement.

Scheduling

Many docents like to volunteer at a set time each week, and yet most scheduling is done by request of incoming groups. For a small museum, there is a delicate balance between being busy enough for the docents to feel productive and of value, and yet not so busy that everyone is overwhelmed. In the beginning, schedule docents for specific tours, then as visitation grows, begin to schedule docents in at set times on the busiest week/weekend days, for example from 10 a.m. to noon and/or 10 a.m. to 2 p.m. on Saturdays. (*Note:* Keep records of which days of the week most of the visitors come, and when during the day it is particularly busy, so the times scheduled for docents are the best choices.)

"Ask Me"

Tours can be offered at set times that are advertised. However, other tours will still be available by reservation. When there are no tours scheduled, such as on Saturday afternoons, docents can float in the gallery wearing "Ask Me" tags and visit with guests on a one-to-one basis. Sometimes docents walk with visitors giving them a minitour, other times they just answer specific questions. This one-on-one interaction provides a much friendlier, more personal, and more welcoming feel to the museum. This structure also allows docents who want to volunteer at set times each week an opportunity to be involved at the museum.

The "Ask Me" badges and format can be used for special presentations, touch carts, hands-on carts, or for more informal visits with the guests, such as having a docent on the floor to answer questions about an exhibit, or to lead a special activity. The "Ask Me" badge is intended to indicate to visitors that the docent is approachable and willing to answer questions. I found this worked particularly well with teenagers who were not always accepted by adults as being knowledgeable. The presence of the badge indicated that they were officially representing the museum and trained for the presentation/cart/activity they were leading.

However, this format can be a difficult situation for both the docents and also some visitors. Some docents aren't comfortable walking up to complete strangers and asking them to come and see their activity. Visitors often tend to say no; they are not interested when approached and seem somewhat uncomfortable with being asked to join. They may feel afraid of being trapped in a long, uninteresting presentation. To develop this into a more effective technique for the docents, it may be helpful to develop guidelines. For example, if a docent starts a casual conversation with visitors about where they are from, the museum and their visit, then a connection is made with the visitor who will then be

When to Schedule Docents

For example, I found that in the winter our busiest time was from noon to 2 p.m., but during the summer, the busiest time was from 10 a.m. to noon. Our busiest days were Thursday and Saturday. So, my first scheduling of docents was on Thursday and Saturday from 10 a.m. to 2 p.m.

—Anna Johnson

Portable Interpretive Carts

Guiding tours and staffing portable interpretive carts require different approaches, and thus not all docents are necessarily suited for both. Tour docents often relish captivating an audience with their knowledge, and tours tend to emphasize one-way communication. The cart interpretation is usually more exploratory and intimate. Most cart programs rely strongly on inquiry and offer an opportunity for more exchange between docent and visitors. Younger visitors are often drawn to carts if they include a tactile opportunity. Carts require more flexibility and can be visitor-directed. With tours, the docent is in charge. One of the most successful carts I've worked with was a cart about cotton gins at the National Museum of American History. Visitors could feel the raw cotton, feed it into the gin, turn the crank, and see the process at work. Tour docents would bring their groups over to the gin while on a tour because it provided a moment of activity within a mostly passive experience.

—Tim Grove

more likely to join the docent's presentation. Guidelines could include the following:

- Wear a tag that says "Ask Me." This will encourage people to approach you and make it more comfortable for you to approach them. (Inform the docents where they can get their tags.)
- Start an interaction with a smile and a friendly, nonthreatening opening question such as "How are you today?" Develop a rapport with the visitors, finding out perhaps where they are from or their experiences at the museum. Then use an open-ended question such as "We live in a desert—where do you think our water comes from?" to move them into your activity. Because the visitors have gotten to know the docent, they are generally more receptive to participating in an activity. Once the docent gets people started interacting with the activity, then others will be more willing to approach and get involved.
- Develop the visitors' confidence as observers and participants by asking them for their opinions or reactions and listening carefully to their responses.
- Speak clearly and simply without using technical terms and show a reassuring sense of humor.
- Allow the conversation to go in the direction visitors want rather than doing a canned and prewritten presentation. Canned presentations can make visitors feel trapped, as they do not want to interrupt the presentation to either ask a question or to leave.
- Respond to questions with enthusiasm and interest, and be honest when you don't know an answer.

This list was adapted from an article in *The Docent Educator* publication written by Hilary Inwood.[11]

Docents find they enjoy this special interaction with the visitors and are often amazed at how much they learn from the visitors.

RECOGNITION

Regardless of how a program is structured, recognition for the docents is a very important component. Recognition takes many forms (see Chapter 2). It is also very important to docents for the educator to be out in the exhibit halls with them, working with them, listening to them, and complimenting them when they do a good job. Also, asking docents to participate in program development, building quality programs, evaluating programs, having interesting presentations for the docents, and being open to new ideas are ways to help docents stay motivated and develop as supporters of the institution. While these are not often listed as part of recognition, they are in fact an important part of a good program and give the docents a sense of accomplishment and pride about what they are doing. The more obvious types of recognition include a docent appreciation daytime/evening program with service awards and invitations to special events at the museum.

Evaluation

How do you evaluate docents in an effective manner, and yet not appear overzealous to them? That is the question. Here are some suggestions:

- The educator should lead tours in the docent class (modeling what is expected of docents), and even ask the docents to evaluate the educator's tour. This shows not only that the institution believes in evaluation but also that the staff and volunteers participate.
- Discuss evaluation in the docent class; have docents use a form to evaluate the educator, and then supply forms for the docents. Have them ask other docents to evaluate them from time to time. (See Sample Form 3.6 in the appendix.)
- Listen to their presentations unannounced and standing off to the side or obscured so that you are not actually seen by the docents. (This will prevent them from getting nervous about your presence, and you will have a better sense of their style.) This is a technique that can be used occasionally and casually, but never as the primary method of evaluation. If there is something to discuss with

the docent, make your presence known before their presentation is over.

- Conduct occasional formal evaluations. Make sure the docent knows you will be evaluating them. Be visible, and then go over your comments privately with the docent as soon as possible after the program. Select one thing to evaluate that you both agree on in advance.
- Occasionally join a docent, with their permission, as they manage a tour. Jointly lead the tour, and "model" for the docent what you think should be done. Do not do this as a correction, but as assistance. Try to emphasize the positive.
- Sometimes just walking through areas where presentations are going on and looking at the reactions of the visitors can give you a good idea of how the tour is being received.
- Ask docents what they thought of their presentations. Were they satisfied with their presentation, was there something missing that would help them do a better job? Docents often respond with informative and helpful answers.
- Visitor evaluations often identify excellent presentations and will also allude to areas that might need more work.
- Develop an evaluation form for the docent training class. The evaluation can be helpful in documenting positive reactions to the class and its effectiveness. It can also elicit many good comments about how to improve the class. Implement those ideas when possible. If a form is developed asking for ways to improve something, it becomes meaningful only when ideas received are actually considered and used. Not all ideas can be used, but when reasonable and appropriate they should be. Using the ideas underscores the institution's commitment to developing and maintaining a good program and listening to its docents. A form used for docent training evaluation can be found as Sample Form 3.7 in the appendix.
- Have the docents fill out an evaluation form after each tour/day at the museum. This helps create some insight into the tours, how prepared docents were for curriculum programs, and ideas for future visits. It is difficult to create an institutional memory about groups, and this is one way to start that record. If, for example, the same group comes late every year, it is helpful to know this in advance. It is necessary to prepare for their being on time, but the docents can be apprised of the usual lateness and can build some extra time into touring that day so the group can still be served and the docents will not

be inconvenienced. The evaluations can be kept in a log and could be referred to year after year.

- Each special program should have its own evaluation.

Basically, wherever there is a need to develop more information is a good place to do some type of evaluation. Determine who the questions are best asked of: the docents, the visitors, the students, the staff, or the general public. Then develop the questions according to what information is needed (see Chapter 10).

CONCLUSION

This chapter covers the importance of institutional support for docent programs including staff and materials, identifies and details topics and activities to include in the classes, and concludes with an emphasis on the importance of continuing commitment and support for the docent program and what that might look like. Hopefully the information in this chapter will be helpful as you organize or reorganize your docent program. Docents are a critical part of what museums do, and when they are well trained, treated with respect, given opportunities for growth, listened to, and involved in programming everyone profits. Most of all, have fun in those trainings, tours, and programs! It benefits everyone!

NOTES

1. *Merriam-Webster's Collegiate Dictionary*, 11th edition (Springfield, Mass.: Merriam-Webster, Inc., 2003).
2. *Merriam-Webster's Collegiate Dictionary*.
3. *Merriam-Webster's Collegiate Dictionary*.
4. *Merriam-Webster's Collegiate Dictionary*.
5. *Merriam-Webster's Collegiate Dictionary*.
6. John H. Falk and Lynn D. Dierking, *Lessons without Limit: How Free-Choice Learning Is Transforming Education* (Walnut Creek, Calif.: AltaMira Press, 2002).
7. Howard Gardner, *Frames of Mind: The Theory of Multiple Intelligences*, 10th edition (New York: Basic Books, 1993).
8. Freeman Tilden, *Interpreting Our Heritage*, 3rd edition (Chapel Hill: University of North Carolina Press, 1977), 8.
9. Tilden, *Interpreting Our Heritage*, 9.
10. Lisa Brochu and Tim Merriman, *Personal Interpretation: Connecting Your Audience to Heritage Resources* (Singapore: National Association for Interpretation, 2002).
11. Hilary Inwood, "The 'Ask Me' Program," *Minds in Motion: The Docent Educator* 4, no. 4 (Summer 1995): 4–5, 20.

CHAPTER 4

Building Effective Tours

Taming Wild Docents

ANNA JOHNSON

> **A museum educator is a facilitator of learning who builds on collections, locations, and history to inspire and excite visitors of all ages. As audience advocates, museum educators recognize and address visitor needs and expectations all the while making museum content accessible, providing context and building meaning.**
>
> —*Sheri J. Levinsky, curator of interpretation and education, The Intrepid Sea, Air, and Space Museum*

When you go on a tour, can you believe what your guide or docent is telling you? According to an article appearing in the *Arizona Republic* on June 3, 2007, "That's a concern of some Philadelphia hospitality officials, who worry the city's most valuable asset—its history—is being tarnished by unreliable tour guides who mix up dates and spice up biographies of famous founders like Benjamin Franklin and George Washington."[1] In my opinion, this is a critical issue for not only historic cities, but also for every museum/park/garden that uses docents or guides.

This chapter discusses touring from the perspective that there is much more to a tour than merely standing up and talking. The docent is a resource of information, and institutions lose credibility with the public if the docents are not knowledgeable about the museum and the exhibits. Likewise docents can struggle, tell made-up stories, and misinform the public if they are not given good information and direction about touring—docents gone wild! In order for docents to be engaging, interesting, and personable, they also need to be comfortable with what they are doing. Memorizing a tour and then giving the exact same tour over and over again can result in the docents' losing interest, becoming bored, and eventually giving up leading tours or "going wild" with stories.

Tours are generally docent- or staff-led through an exhibit hall, museum, garden, or historic site with a focused, concise theme that is presented to the visitors in an interesting and informative way. The tour needs to be flexible enough for the docents to respond to different age groups, be presented at various levels of interest, and allow for diverse presentations. This chapter discusses a specific format for a tour that allows for flexibility so that the docent can respond to varying age groups and levels of questions. How to teach this format to the docents is also described. The point is that training (see Chapter 3) combined with a flexible tour format can go a long way to prevent the "docent gone wild" scenario. In addition to the format for a tour in Part 1, this chapter discusses logistical matters to consider when starting development of and operating a tour program, included in Part 2.

PART 1: CREATING FLEXIBLE TOURS USING TRANSITIONS

Transitions can be a powerful device to create cohesiveness in the tour and also allow for presentation flexibility. Transitions are defined in *Merriam-Webster's Collegiate Dictionary* as "movement, development, or evolution from one form, stage, or style to another."[2] In a tour, transitions are the lead-in to the next location and concept of the tour—almost like a topic sentence.

Creating a Tour with Transitions

GOALS A tour needs to be cohesive and ultimately result in a complete thought. In the very beginning, it is important to establish goals or teaching points for a tour. These identify the purpose of the tour and the main information that will be presented. It is generally good to keep the number of concepts to three and not more than five. The reason for limiting the purpose is to keep the tour focused in order to have a clear and concise presentation.

TOUR DEVELOPMENT After determining the goals, it is a good idea to go to the area/exhibit where the tour will be presented and walk through the area. It is often helpful to have several people (no more than five) work together to develop the tour. Educators, curators, docents, and other interested individuals can make a good team, which will be referred to from here on as the development team. Content experts, such as the curator and educators, are the key people to involve in this discussion. The development team will need to review the goals of the tour including what informa-tion the tour needs to convey (tour focus), and then choose the locations in the exhibit area where the tour will stop. Each stopping point on the tour needs to tie in with the purpose of the tour as defined in the goals. The topic at each location that ties in with the focus of the tour needs to be clarified in this process. Transitions will be developed from the identification of the topic at each stop and will be tied in with the goals and focus of the tour. For example, the focus of the tour is the history of the town, and one goal of the

tour is "To give a brief overview of the town's history in an interesting and effective manner." One transition, emphasizing a detail of the history, is, "Over here we will see how the town has grown." The transitions tell the story in the briefest of forms.

IDENTIFYING LOGICAL STOPPING POINTS Working with the development team and keeping in mind the fo-cus/goals of the tour, visit the exhibit area and identify logical stopping places where discussions about the focus of the tour can occur. These locations should ideally have some pertinent object, setting, or person's story that will illuminate a specific point/s related to the focus. Talk about each stop as a team and discuss the pros and cons of that location and the information that can be conveyed there. At first, do not have any restrictions on location choices. After going through the entire area in which the tour is to be given, take a break and come together for another meeting in a day or two or a week. During that time each member of the team should be considering their preferred choices of stops and why, including topics and the order of the stops. The stops chosen should be the ones considered by the team most important to the topic with the best visual support. Visual support is the object that will be the focus of the story at this location. Objects are critical as they are what museums have to tell the story, and they are credible and real for the visitors. Consider then objects that are particularly significant, interesting, or dramatic that will grab the visitors' at-tention. At the next meeting, the team should review its choices for stops and determine which ones will be most effective for the focus of the tour as well as the length of time it will take to communicate the in-formation (that is, to tell the story). Setting the order of the locations also needs to be accomplished at this same time.

SETTING THE ORDER OF THE TOUR STOPS The consid-erations in determining the order include having the tour move smoothly and efficiently, and following a progression in the development of the information. Make sure to record the objects and supporting in-formation the group feels are important to include at each of the selected stops, as well as the basic con-cept represented. This information will make it much easier to develop the actual transitions.

Next write the transitions. They should be simple statements and/or questions that are easy to remem-ber and say. It is helpful if they create anticipation or expectation about the next location such as this one used in the Tempe Historical Museum, "Let's look at the water feature and see how water was diverted."

Remember, each transition should highlight an important point relative to the topic of the tour.

DESIGNING THE TOUR Once the goals, basic concepts, and layout (stopping points) of the tour are determined, and the transitions are defined, the actual tour needs to be developed. There are basically three divisions within a tour:

- the welcome and introduction
- the main body
- the conclusion

Welcome and Introduction. In the starting location, the welcome can begin as the tour group members assemble. The docent can move through the group, greeting them and asking where they are from, what they hope to see today, and other questions to get to know them better. When the tour officially begins, the docent should introduce himself/herself and his/her role as docent/guide, the purpose (goal) and length of time of the tour, general information about topics in other galleries, and the location of the gift shop and restrooms. Greeting the public in a warm and friendly manner will help visitors feel more comfortable and excited about the tour.

The introduction will introduce the tour topic, a brief orientation to the hall, and the movement of the tour through the space. (Consider that if the visitors know where they are going, they will not feel so lost and be more open to thinking about the information in the tour.) *Note:* If the group has been divided into smaller groups, it is very important to tell the group that they will all receive the complete tour. Students, especially as part of school tours, are often concerned about missing out on something when groups are split.

The introduction and conclusion fit into the transition format at the beginning and end of the tour. For example, a tour could start, "Welcome, my name is Jane Doe, and I would like to welcome you to the XYZ museum." In the introduction the docent can go on to discuss the tour, where they will go, and what the tour is about, as well as getting to know the visitors. Then the next transition will actually start the exhibit content part of the tour. For example, it could be something as simple as, "Please follow me into the exhibit hall as we begin our tour."

Main Body. The docent can include either expansive information or just a few items under each transition depending on the interest and knowledge of the visitors, and then transition on to the next location.

Using transitions also allows the docent flexibility in presentation style at each location. Hands-on and interactive devices fit very comfortably into this format. When transitions are questions or pique the visitor's curiosity, they encourage the visitors to move to the next location. A brief tour could be given using only the transitions, and it would still be cohesive and have a clear focus. If a docent cannot think of what to say in one area, he/she can transition on to the next location and the continuity will not be lost. Transitions also encourage connections between concepts; for example, "As we look at this urban setting, what has happened to all the agriculture we discussed earlier?" The items identified at the locations by the development team are important to include under each transition. These will give the docents ideas of what to focus on and then describe in more detail at each stop. However, the docent can pick and choose between the information judging by the interest of the group and their familiarity with the information. The transition will carry the main point, so the focus remains constant.

Conclusion. The conclusion is an important final step in the tour, during which the main points can be reiterated. The conclusion should be brief and reemphasize the primary goal, such as, "Before our tour of the town's history concludes, let's discuss what we saw. You can see how the town has changed from an agricultural community to a very modern city today. You are now familiar with the primary interactive features in the exhibit hall. I hope you will explore them at your leisure. Are there any questions?" If the docent stays in the hall with the tour for awhile, this is a good time to reiterate their availability to the visitors. The docent should always conclude the tour with a thank-you to the visitors and include a comment about hoping to see them at the museum in the future. Suggesting that the visitors stop in the gift shop is another good idea, and this is also a good time to pass out evaluation forms for the visitors to fill out.

VALUE OF TRANSITIONS The idea behind using transitions in tours is to emphasize for the docent the "pull" of the tour and making connections from one area to the next. Once the docent becomes comfortable with using transitions, he or she can relax and respond to and interact with the visitors.

In addition, transitions will provide a consistency of information presented to the visitors. Many museums spend a great deal of time educating their docents on the knowledge of their museum such as art, history, and botany. However, these same museums then allow the docents to develop their own tours with little

This tour using transitions was used in a workshop. Even though you are not in the room, it gives a good idea about the flow of transitions and their flexibility. Remember the transitions are bolded.

Transition:	**Welcome**
	Make visitors welcome and comfortable. Move among them before tour starts finding out where they are from and what they hope to see on the tour, tell them it is good to see them today, or you are glad they came for a tour, etc.
Transition:	**Introduction**
	Name of tour leader
	Topic of tour: to discuss amenities of meeting room
	Purpose of tour: to help visitors be more comfortable in meeting
	Length of tour: 5 minutes
	For example: Welcome, my name is Anna Johnson, and I will be your guide today as we tour this room. This will be an "eyes only" tour, so please stay seated and follow with your eyes as we discuss this room. The tour will be about 5 minutes long.
Transition:	**This is a versatile room.**
	Uses of room
Transition:	**We find something very welcoming in the room.**
	Table with food and coffee
	Could explain what the food is
	Could define when lunch will come, etc.
Transition:	**As we look around, what do we realize?**
	This is an older building.
	This building was once a nice home.
	Could tell some house history if the group is interested.
Transition:	**What is missing in this room that we all would like to know is available?**
	Restrooms; explain where they are located.
Transition:	**Why does the house seem so busy?**
	There are several organizations located in this building.
	Could discuss the organizations and what they do or not.
Transition:	**Conclusion**
	Hopefully you will be more comfortable in our meeting now that you know more about this room and what is available. Thank you for participating in the tour today.

guidance. Many of these people enjoy learning the information, but they do not know how to translate that knowledge into an effective and consistent tour. This format using transitions will work for them as well. It will give them a plan, general goal for their tour, and then they can find the locations to talk from on their own. It will be easy for them to develop topic sentences or transitions to move from one location to another. The advantage for the inexperienced tour developer is that this is a physical experience (picking locations) as well as an intellectual one. The concepts are easier to grasp and develop when in the actual setting (see Textbox 4.1).

The transition format has also been helpful in keeping tours on time. When a docent goes into great detail, giving them set times to be at certain stopping points in the tour can help. It is also advantageous for the museum when the docents welcome the visitors, introduce the topic, and conclude the tour with a brief summary. The transition format also emphasizes that process. The welcome and conclusion are considered as part of the transitions.

TEACHING TRANSITIONS The tour using transitions would be taught in the docent training class, but the procedure for teaching it to docents is explained in this chapter along with how to create transitions. When a tour is being developed, the transitions need to be ordered and assigned a location in the exhibit/historic home. Under each transition the different topics that can be discussed should be listed. The flexibility in the presentation is that the docent can choose which of the topics to discuss as well as using objects, stories, and questioning techniques. This type of format allows the docents to give the "same" tour over and over again without becoming bored. It also allows them to focus on areas or topics they are particularly interested in and still share information on the other areas as well.

It is this author's opinion that it is very helpful to teach one tour to the docents in the introductory training program. This introduces them to the whole process and has them using transitions and experiencing the success. The lessons described below are given in a series of classes, not all at once. When teaching a tour using transitions:

1. Take the class on the tour and model the complete tour. Do not say anything about transitions before this; just let the members experience the tour itself.
2. Explain what transitions are. Give each class member a copy of the tour with the transitions indicated and bolded on the paper. Include under the transitions, in regular type, the topics that could be discussed under each transition. (Examples are taken from the Tempe Historical Museum tour.) For example:

   Transition: How did this change?—Because it is not that way today.

   Redevelopment (topics)
   - Renewed interest in history through city being one hundred years old in 1971 and country two hundred years old in 1976
   - Mill Avenue Merchants Association (MAMA) Festival to promote downtown area and merchants
   - New City Hall built in 1970
   - Refurbishing of buildings downtown

3. Go through the transitions with the class. Read each transition on the paper handout as they go through the tour, but do not talk about the rest of the information, which should be included elsewhere in the class.
4. Take the class again to the location where the tour begins (include the welcome/introduction and conclusion as transitions). Have the class follow along on their handouts as you lead them to each stop, and then repeat the correct transition. The first concept the class must begin to understand is where to be located when using each transition.
5. Again, take the class back to the beginning location for the tour. Have the class read aloud the transition. Then have the class, as a group, determine where to go next. Continue on with this process for the entire tour. This will emphasize how important it is for them to know where to go.
6. Again, take the class to the beginning location, and call on someone and have them present the welcome and introduction. Then call on someone else to do the next transition and lead the class to that spot. Call on people randomly, but make sure everyone in the class is asked to do at least one transition.

7. Have each member of the class select a partner in the class, and send them into the hall to practice the transitions together. They may memorize the transitions, carry the sheets handed out in class, or copy them onto note cards.
8. Model the full tour again, using the transitions, and also filling in the information. If the tours are timed, ask the docents to time the tour and to evaluate the presenter.
9. Have an experienced docent come in and lead the tour, so the class can see someone else do the tour.
10. Now send the future docents into the hall with their partners, and have them practice the full tour. They are also welcome to practice on their own.

This will be the tour that is given at graduation, and each new docent will give at least one transition with the supporting information as part of the graduation tour (see Chapter 3). The docents sign up at the last class, so they come to graduation knowing what they will be doing and prepared for their presentation. In addition to learning the tour, they will have been exposed to information about the history during the classes (see Chapter 3).

Conclusion

Once the docents have learned the tour, they have also learned the format for tours. The welcome and introduction will have many consistencies from one tour to the next, as will the conclusion. The docents will understand how well the process works for them, and with the guidance of the goal for a tour in another location such as a changing gallery, they can then develop their own tours.

PART 2: TOUR LOGISTICS

While the tour itself is very important, the organization required for taking reservations and handling confirmations, and guidelines for tours are also key to the success of a tour program. Many museums have developed very successful visitor and tour management systems. The following are merely ideas/thoughts to consider in the development of tour programs and for the museum just getting started.

Reservations

A reservation involves someone contacting the museum and making an appointment to bring a group of people/students into the museum for a tour/activity/class. Reservations can be made in person, over the telephone, or via e-mail or a website, depending on what fits best with the available technology of the museum. The museum needs to be prepared to organize and record the reservation, inform a variety of people about the existence of the reservation, mail out a confirmation detailing what the visit will be about, and schedule a docent who will be prepared to lead the visitors through a successful visit. Confirmations sent to the individual(s) who made the reservation as well as others is an important part of the process. The following information identifies items to consider when developing a reservation system:

TAKING A RESERVATION Who on the staff will take the reservations? Often reservations are taken over the phone or electronically on the museum's website. A specific calendar just for tours/educational activities is important. This calendar should include all the places in the building that can be reserved (i.e., each exhibit hall, classroom, meeting room, etc.). With computers there are many ways to set up a calendar; just be sure there is *only one place the entries go*, so there are not two calendars with conflicting reservations. (A calendar used by beauty salons, with several columns for the same day and each hour broken out into 15-minute appointments, works well for this. The calendar can be purchased through an office supply store.) View Figure 4.1, "Reservation and Confirmation Checklist,"which includes a list of information to be included in reservations and confirmations.

LEAD TIME Is there a required lead time (i.e., can you take a reservation one day and run a tour the next)? Many museums require that reservations be made two weeks before the visit. This gives the museum time to schedule a docent, send out a confirmation with specific directions and information, and contact the gift shop, security guards, or whomever else they need to inform. If there is a short-run special exhibit, scheduling will have to be handled differently. In this case, the museum may want to schedule docents every day in order to handle tours. In fact, many museums with high visitation have set times they run tours and schedule docents every day to lead tours.

CONFIRMATIONS Confirmations are a good way to reinforce to the incoming group the date and time of the reservation and the specifics of the tour itself. Determining who receives a confirmation is based on who needs to have the tour information, such as the group, the docent who will be leading the tour, the gift shop to make sure it is prepared, and anyone else who might be impacted by the tour group. It is good to include other information about the museum, such as a map of how to get to the museum, museum group visitation guide-

---

Reservation and Confirmation Checklist

Reservations and confirmations generally include:

- ❑ Date of contact
- ❑ Date and time of reservation
- ❑ Cost (if there is a charge)
- ❑ Information about organization making reservation including name, address, zip, phone number, e-mail address
- ❑ Name of person making reservation and their phone number
- ❑ Number coming in group: No. of children: ____ No. of adults: ____
- ❑ Age of students coming
- ❑ Description of general tour including length of time for tour and recommended visit time
- ❑ Special instructions: Explanation of how the group will be divided. What the group/school requested for its visit, and what the museum will be doing.
- ❑ If sharing the visit with another agency, may also want to indicate that.
- ❑ Enclose map, museum brochure, special materials related to tour, bus parking information, museum guidelines
- ❑ Previsit teacher packet if school group
- ❑ Docent assigned to tour and/or contact person at museum

Tip: Write scripted guidelines about reservation procedures in a one-page format to aid the person taking calls at the museum. This will create consistency of information going out to the public.

Figure 4.1. Reservation and Confirmation Checklist
Courtesy of Anna Johnson

lines (see Sample Form 4.1 in the appendix), name tags for students, description of the museum shop and rules about students shopping, previsit teacher packets, and special bus parking instructions. Furthermore, gift shops often do very well with school groups by selling low-priced items related to exhibits.

Tour Details

As museums look at their facility and begin to plan for tours or modify existing programs, the following list can be helpful to identify some of the more critical areas of visitor services. Every location has its own specific criteria, however, and these are some of the more common considerations. In many cases, the final product can only be determined by the organization, taking into consideration its layout and specific needs. The following questions are provided to aid in problem solving for the site. These topics may not all apply to every circumstance, so focus on the ones appropriate to your own situation.

TOUR SIZE What constitutes a tour? One thing to consider is the minimum/maximum number of people required for a group tour. What is the minimum to be considered a tour? Ten is a common number required for a tour, but it can be whatever number makes sense to the organization to bring in someone to lead the tour. Some organizations like their tours for special-needs groups to be smaller than other tours. In order to set the maximum number, the organization will need to know:

- What is the maximum number of people the space can handle? It is important to have the fire code requirements for every space/room.
- How good are the acoustics and functional layout of the room/hall? How many people/tours can be accommodated comfortably and still hear their docent speaking? Also consider the physical movement of a number of tours and how they would all interface. The layout of the building and exhibits will dictate this organization. What about microphones? Would they work/help? How many docents will be needed for each tour?

Then the museum will need to determine maximum size of a tour for one docent. This will allow whoever is booking tours to ensure there are enough docents available. (For example, one docent will lead a tour of up to 20 people, two docents will split a group of 21 to 40 people, and three docents will divide a group equally of 41 to 60 people. Perhaps, no more than three tours can be running at any one time.) Sometimes organizations will have two docents, one to do the tour and the other to keep groups together and objects safe from probing hands. These parameters are to be determined by the site and what works best for it. Large facilities can often run more tours at a time.

Many museums limit school groups to no more than 60 at a time. This allows room for the visiting public along with tours. Availability of docents and types of activities included in the tour are also an important part of the decision of how big a tour can be. Sometimes groups are split and taken into different galleries, the research library, or even collections. The answers to these questions need to be determined by the size of the area, what is the purpose of the visit, how many docents can be provided, and the size of the

facility. It is also good to discuss this with local schools, finding out their average class size, and how many students can fit on one school bus.

TOUR DESIGN AND SPACE Design the tour to include the best use of space, which includes flow of visitors through the exhibit and allowing room for interactive areas and enough space to see and read the information. If there are 30 students, then possibilities include dividing them into five groups of six, three groups of ten, two groups of fifteen, or one group of thirty. In a small area, the tour should be kept to a smaller number, while in a big space the tour could be broken up into small groups to focus on specific areas or activities, or remain one big group. In the exhibit hall it is important for the visitors to be able to hear the docent, and also for the docent to be able to hear questions and respond to the visitors.

TIMING How long will your tour take, and how close together can you reserve tours? A tour length of one hour usually works well for visitors and school groups. Remember to think about where the tour will end and how the visitors will exit the area without becoming intertwined with another tour. The answers to these questions need to be determined by each site based on the layout, size of tours, and frequency of tours. What if one tour starts late? How do you get everyone back on schedule?

STUDENT–ADULT RATIO How many adults are required relative to students? Many museums require one adult for every ten students. However, for the younger children, preschool through second grade, one adult for every five children is sometimes required. Again, this is based on the needs of the site and activities. Always be prepared for fewer adults than required and determine in advance how the shortage of chaperones will be handled.

ROLE OF CHAPERONES It is important to indicate to the school before the visit that the role of the chaperones is important, and that they will be expected to control the group they are monitoring. This can be included in written information with the confirmation. Docents are not disciplinarians, but museum "experts" who are sharing special information with the students. However, docents can somewhat control discipline problems by involving students with questions and changing the pace of their tour to pull curious and fidgety students back into the topic.

BUS PARKING Any institution that wishes schools to visit needs to define a place for the buses to park and safely drop off and pick up the children. This is also true for tour buses.

JOINT TOURS   Is there another site such as library, city hall, park, or museum that the organization can coordinate with and switch tours or groups? Coordinating with another facility can allow bigger groups. One half of the group will be at one facility while the other half is at another, and then they will switch. It is important that both organizations coordinate the length of tours and time at both locations so groups can switch at the same time, and remember to build in time for the switch itself. For example, the tour is 30 minutes, 15 minutes to switch from one site to the other, and then the second tour is 30 minutes. The group in this example can expect to be away from school for at least 75 minutes excluding travel time and disembarking.

WHEN TOURS WILL BE OFFERED   Will the museum be closed on certain days of the week? Will tours be offered during regular open hours and/or extended hours? Does the organization need one day a week or more to maintain the area and, thus, not offer tours? Are there other programs that the tours could conflict with such as lectures, staff meetings, society or friends meetings, etc.?

LUNCH   Identify a place for groups to eat lunch. Many school field trips seem to include lunch. Lunch is served earlier at schools than one would think. Remember their day is usually over by around 3 p.m. Often groups can eat on a grass lawn, but if there is bad weather, then they will need a covered or indoor place. The backup position in milder climates is for them to eat on the school bus. However, the bus is not always available and waiting at the site for the students. Sometimes the bus drops off students, goes somewhere else, and then returns to pick them up.

- What if the group brings lunches? Where can they leave them? What about backpacks, notebooks, pencils, pens, etc.? Is there a place they can get drinks, or should they bring some? Do they need money to purchase drinks?
- Adult groups often like to have a business meeting with lunch and then tour the facility. Is there a place in the museum for groups to eat lunch? Will this space need to be reserved separately?

RESTROOMS, DRINKING FOUNTAINS, FLASH PHOTOGRAPHY, BABY STROLLERS, AND COATS   Identify the locations of the restrooms and drinking fountain(s). Everyone is more comfortable in the museum if they know where the restrooms are located. School groups traveling long distances need to allow time to visit the restrooms prior to the start of their tour. It is good to include this in the material going out before the visit.

Will the visitors carry their coats or is there a place to check them or leave them? Baby strollers should also be considered. Can they be rented? Some exhibitions do not permit baby strollers; is there a place to check them? Some museums do not permit flash photography. Some do not permit cameras or any other recording devices (even pencils and drawing paper). Now cell phones are so popular, and pictures can be taken with them without using a flash. What are the specific requirements of each exhibition within the museum? Also, are there special requests to turn off cell phones in the facility?

MUSEUM STORE   If you have a gift shop, can students visit it, and how will you keep the store informed about scheduled tours? How many people are allowed in the shop at one time? Are there safety concerns such as glass items? Can prearranged gift packets be made and purchased for school groups?

HANDICAPPED ACCESS   Are there wheelchairs, translators, signers, and visual information available? How do visitors access these services? If there are multiple floors, are there elevators? In historic buildings there may not be an elevator. How do you make the building accessible to the handicapped? (*Idea*: Make a video of the exhibits on other floors, or have pictures available.)

GREETER   Who greets the tour, checks them in, and organizes groups, and where will they do this?

EMERGENCY PROCEDURES   What if the fire alarm goes off, a weather advisory is sounded, a student gets sick or faints, or a visitor trips and falls? It is advisable and sometimes required that museum education staff receive basic first aid training, and that they become familiar with using a fire extinguisher, pressing the fire alarm, and dialing 911 in order to respond appropriately to medical emergencies. Docents need to be trained in moving groups efficiently whether inside the building as in the case of inclement weather, or outside for fire or bomb threats.

NAME TAGS   Can you provide name tags, perhaps with your logo on them—one for each student? Can you do this prior to their visit, so they come wearing their name tags? The use of name tags will help involve the students and personalize the visit for them because the docents will be able to call the students by name. Also provide name tags for your docents.

Docents and Their Tour Needs

Now, let's look at the tours from the perspective of the docent, and what the museum can do to help the docent do a better job and enjoy his or her experience as a docent.

TOUR SETUP What are the logistics of the visit? Will it be a tour, special activities, storytellers, or ask me cart? Who coordinates the activities and creates the handouts? Will there be a need for any tables, chairs, carts, copied information? Who will gather everything and set it up and when—just before the tour, the night before? What are the docents' responsibilities? Are they to get anything out, put anything away, and if so, does it involve signing out keys or going into restricted areas? If there is more than one tour in process at the same time, how do they move their group so the tours will not "bump" into each other and become entangled? With school students this is particularly important to consider, as the students can extend the "time of chaos" while the tours separate from each other. Docents also need to know if hands-on exhibit areas are out of service or if supplies are low.

DOCENT PARTICULARS What is appropriate dress for the docents? Where should the docents put their purse and/or jackets when they come in to lead a tour? Is there a safe place for them to store valuables, such as in a locker? What is the procedure for recording their time? Do they sign in when they come in, and out when they leave, and where will the book be located? Where do they start their tours, and where does the tour end? Where are their name tags stored?

STAFFING TIME PERIODS Can you run your program every day and keep it staffed? How many docents do you currently have? How long a time period should you schedule docents to be there? Two, three, or four hours is a common length of time for docents. Remember, it needs to be long enough to make it worth their while to travel to your site. They could be there for a whole day, but then be sure to include breaks.

TRAINING How do the docents learn the material? When and where will your training be? Who will coordinate and teach this? Will there be packets of information available? (See Chapter 3 on docent training.)

SCHOOL PACKET It is a good idea to send a packet to the school to prepare students for their visit. Who will be contacting the school, developing the packet, and seeing that it gets to each class? Make sure to include instructions, name tags, and evaluation forms in this packet for the teacher, chaperones, and students. Other items to include are a brochure on the museum, specific information about their upcoming visit with a special activity, and bus parking information, as well as a map of the museum including locations of bathrooms and drinking fountains and specific areas related to the tour experience. Share this information with the docents. (See Sample Form 4.1 for an example of an information sheet sent prior to the visit.)

TOUR NO-SHOW How long do the docents wait? At what point in time should the incoming tour group be called to see if they are on their way, and who should do the calling? Set a time limit for docents to wait, i.e., 30 minutes. If there is a problem making the group late, but it is still coming, then poll the docents to see who can stay for the tour. The incoming group will be told that all of the docents may not be able to stay or that their tour may be shortened due to time constraints.

DOCENT SCHEDULES Who schedules the docents, and how do they do this? Some organizations create a calendar of tours and send it out to all the docents every two, three, or more months. Then the docents call in to sign up for the tours they are interested in doing. Or, another approach is to create a calendar of tours, call the docents giving them the list of tours, and asking them to sign up for when they are available. Other organizations ask the docents to sign up for their next tours when they come in to lead a tour. Perhaps there is a special monthly meeting for docents, and scheduling could be accomplished then. Scheduling can also be done online; however, some docents may still prefer paper schedules. Alternatively, some docents sign up for a particular day of the week and give whatever tour is scheduled in that time slot. In some cases, docents must be trained to give all tours because any tour might be booked on their day; in other situations docents sign up for a particular day of the week and specify the tour or activity they will present that day.

DOCENT NO-SHOW What if docents do not show? When should you start calling the docents? Always call docents immediately to check to see if they are okay, and to make sure they know they were scheduled. However, never be upset with them about not being at the museum. Leave a message if they do not answer the phone. By contacting them, you let them know they have missed a tour and that it is important. This is also true when docents call to cancel for something they had signed up to do. Always thank them for calling, accept and understand their reason for canceling, and tell them it is not a problem, you will take care of it. The docents need to know they can cancel and still be appreciated. Believe it or not, if this is handled in a positive way, they will work harder and try to do more. The opposite is also true; if docents miss a tour or call in to cancel, and the person they talk to gets upset with them, docents will be less likely to sign up again because if they have to cancel, they might get yelled at. Remember, docents are volunteers and not paid staff. Wait five minutes after official start time before starting shorthanded. In the meantime, the other docents should have developed their contingency plan for the tour.

NO RESERVATION What if a group drops in without a reservation? Be gracious and offer them what you can. If there are tours in progress and everything is full, show the leaders of the group so they can see for themselves and then offer to schedule them for a tour. Perhaps, if you are not too busy, a quick tour can be arranged led by the educator or staff. Training all staff to lead basic tours can be very helpful at moments like this. Use this opportunity to pass out your brochures with information about programs and making reservations and contact numbers.

EARLY FOR A TOUR What if the tour group is early and all the docents have not arrived? Front-desk people often want to start a tour the minute the group arrives, but as long as they are there before the reservation time, it is not necessary to push to start when all the docents are not yet there. Some museums have a special place or classroom for visiting groups to go to wait for the start of the tour, whereas others do not.

DOCENT PHYSICAL ENVIRONMENT When docents are leading cart activities or special programs in the exhibit halls, consider:

- Can the docents sit during or between the presentations? Docents get tired when doing multiple presentations, and it is helpful to have a chair for them to sit on between presentations; or sometimes they can even sit as they do their special program, depending on what they are doing.
- In case of a quiet day, may they read? Is the lighting good?
- Are there breaks, and what happens if they need to go to the restroom?
- Clarifying all the logistics up front helps set the expectations for the presentation and clear away potential obstacles.

It is also good for the educator to personally conduct some of these presentations to experience firsthand what the docents are encountering and to determine how well everything is working.

VISITOR PREPARATION Are the visitors adequately informed about the activities being offered? How will the visitors find out about the special programs or activities of the day? If they know there are special presentations going on that day on a topic and located at a certain location in the building, the visitors will be more comfortable and more likely to participate. One solution is for the person in admissions to either tell them, or hand them written information, or both. A sign board at the entrance announcing special programs and activities of the day can be useful in keeping everyone informed. What is most important is to prepare the visitors for what will be happening in the exhibit halls.

GENERAL EXHIBIT HALL QUESTIONS How to answer the general questions about the exhibit halls can be frustrating for a specialty docent and also make the museum look unprepared. For example, if docents in the exhibit hall have been trained only to do special presentations, they may not be able to handle specific questions on other topics in the exhibit halls. It is helpful to always have a senior docent in the exhibit hall, so visitors may be directed to them as a knowledgeable docent who could answer these inquiries. When questioned, a docent may respond, "I have been trained to do this presentation. The docent you see over there is more knowledgeable about the exhibit hall. I'm sure he or she could answer your question." This allows the museum to be able to handle visitors' questions, and not have a docent be uncomfortable because of what he or she does not know. The front desk can also be a backup, answering general questions about the exhibit halls.

SCHOOL ISSUES Can the students sit anywhere at anytime? It is difficult for students, especially young ones, to stand still for long periods of time. Giving them opportunities to sit down helps keep the group together and also offers them a chance to rest. They will be better listeners if they are comfortable. Benches and chairs can be set up before tours, or if the floor is clean, students can often sit on the floor at a longer stop on the tour, or a small area rug used only for school tours is another seating option. Sitting for too long in one place can also be detrimental to the tour. Ideally having opportunities to sit, stand, and walk is an effective management technique.

VISITOR ACTIVITY NEEDS If an activity is part of the visit, do you have the tools required for the visitors/students? Examples of this might be a clipboard to write on, paper, pencil, and printed directions/activity. Pencils, and not pens, should be used in the gallery, since ink makes a permanent mark that is very hard to remove.

DOCENT EVALUATION/CONVERSATION Consider docent evaluations for them to fill out at the completion of each tour. Include questions about the group reactions to exhibit, what questions the group asked, and the docent's reaction to the group's interest in the exhibit and presentation as well as the group's behavior.

Feedback from docents about their experiences can be invaluable. They often have good advice for ways to improve the presentation/exhibit and can share the comments of visitors.

A variety of educational offerings is not only interesting and exciting to the public, but it also offers new and interesting opportunities to the docents besides the traditional tour. For example, some of the different programs that can be offered include tours, seasonal programs (such as at the holidays), curriculum-based school programs, family-based activities, and special events.

CONCLUSION

Logistics often get overlooked in program development, but taking care of these details will ensure a happier docent, safer environment for all, and a better experience for the visitor. Once your organization has set in place a well-organized tour program and developed a framework or format for its tour, then docents will be more accurate and more engaging, and the tour programs will run more smoothly. Public programs will be enjoyable for the docents, the staff, and the public!

NOTES

1. Kathy Matheson, "Heard the One about Betsy Ross? Not True," *Arizona Republic*, June 3, 2007.
2. *Merriam-Webster's Collegiate Dictionary*, 11th edition (Springfield, Mass.: Merriam-Webster, Inc., 2003), 368.
3. Anna Johnson, "Using Transitions to Teach Touring,"

PROGRAMS AND OUTREACH

Illustration by Larry R. Warner

CHAPTER 5

Professional Development for Teachers

MELISSA BINGMANN

> I know I should say something about learning theories, pedagogic strategies, educational technologies, and instructional models that are unique to museums, but I keep coming back to one thing: It is how we share our collections and stories with our visitors and communities. When it comes right down to it, for me, museum education was recently given voice when one of the second graders who toured my museum walked up to me and said, "Thank you. I really like your museum. And I'm sure happy we don't use a chamber pot in my house."
>
> —*Keni Sturgeon, curator, Mission Mill Museum*

Professional development for teachers serves many functions that benefit participants and the museum. It can enhance teachers' mastery of a subject, increase their level of comfort using museums as informal learning environments, enhance their ability to integrate field trips into classroom curriculum, introduce them to visual thinking skills, and develop proficiency in artifact analysis while earning required credit toward their professional license.[1] Museums benefit by better prepared students who participate in field trips and the opportunity to collaborate with teachers. Professional development can be an efficient means of educating large groups of visitors by reaching only a few. Many museum educators have found that teacher training can be an important complement to and sometimes replacement for school outreach. By training teachers to use museum resources and prepare students for field trips, museum educators are relieved of this essential, yet often time-consuming responsibility. Once skilled in artifact and visual analysis skills and comfortable with the content of your museum, K-12 teachers will be better able to incorporate museum resources and experiences into existing classroom curriculum than any outside provider. This chapter will explore reasons why museums offer professional development for teachers, useful approaches for creating a meaningful experience, background on national educational models, and tips for building an audience by incorporating workshops into existing state and district professional development requirements.

Adding professional development to a museum's existing cadre of educational opportunities is based on the idea that by empowering teachers to use museums, they will be able to bring these resources to hundreds of children over the course of their careers. In theory, teachers' mastery of exhibit content combined with their pedagogical expertise will enable them to tie the content of the museum to lessons taught in the classroom. With the addition of interpretive skill training, teachers will also be able to lead tours of the museum and engage students in exhibits and artifacts. Taken a step further, some museum teacher training programs embed a curriculum development component with the intent that teacher-created projects will be shared and disseminated by the museum. Museum educators, especially those who do not come from a K-12 educational background, need access to teachers for advisement, teacher-developed lesson plans, and a gateway into the professional world of this significant museum audience. Many teachers are introduced to museums through field trips and, increasingly, through professional development, and expand their involvement by joining the museum, serving as docents, and becoming involved in professional development planning.

Once you decide that providing professional development can achieve several institutional goals, the next step is to assess what your institution has to offer K-12 educators. This must be balanced by what teachers need. Museum educators should easily be able to create a list of topic ideas for lectures by content experts on staff, exhibits that need interpretation beyond what can be offered in a 60-minute tour, and overlooked artifacts that when time is allotted for expanded context, will dazzle and amaze educators. If you are just getting started, review your docent training schedule and think about which topics and activities have the most impact on docents and which content experts work well with public audiences. If you adhere to the philosophy that an important goal of professional development is to make teachers more proficient at preparing students for field trips and postvisit activities, elements of your docent training program will be easily adapted to teachers. Think about how ideal it would be if all teachers who brought students to your institution could lead their own tours and then create their own pre- and postvisit discussion because they are versed in the content of your museum.

MUSEUM EDUCATION SKILLS THAT BENEFIT TEACHERS

An often less-thought-of expertise that all museums can offer is instruction in artifact analysis, visual thinking skills, and the interpretive training that is embedded in everything that museum educators do. These skills are lacking from most undergraduate and graduate education programs but can be essential tools in cultivating lifelong learners who can gather and interpret visual as well as textual data. Museum professionals specialize in these skills but often forget that most visitors think of the content presented in displays and programs as fact, rather than an interpretation of artifacts within a context of available scholarship. David Thelen and Roy Rosenzweig's study illustrates that the public, although extremely enthusiastic about museums, lacks understanding of their interpretive role. In their analysis of data collected via phone interviews, respondents stated that museums were the most trusted source for learning about the past. Touted at almost every American Association of Museums (AAM) conference since the study was published, what is not revealed is the reason why the public trusts museums more than personal accounts from grandparents, college history professors, nonfiction books, movies, and television. People believe that artifacts are "pure" and unbiased sources of information.[2] This perception is highly inaccurate, as even if an artifact is displayed with no text or other interpretation, the mere selection of that artifact is, in essence, someone's construction of meaning. By discussing interpretive techniques, choices embedded in the messages conveyed by displays, and other museum trade secrets, teachers will witness a more significant educational value in museums that goes well beyond the subject content of your institution's displays. Museums are excellent places for teachers and students to explore historical thinking skills and the scientific method if the experience is framed specifically to meet these educational objectives.

To convey this idea in a way that is familiar to most educators (and may be useful to you when developing learning objectives for any program), consider incorporating Bloom's Taxonomy into your educational outcomes. The traditional use of Bloom's Taxonomy implies that students need to master the prior skill or ability before moving on to the next level of the hierarchy. Some educators have found that one lesson plan can include all cognitive steps and that some steps may occur simultaneously. The latter is less time-consuming and could be employed on museum tours. There is also the potential for working with teachers to break out which skills should be developed prior to the museum visit, those that could occur on-site, and those that would be best completed after the tour. As you study Textbox 5.1, think about where your museum's typical school visit falls and the potential all museums have to engage students in the three higher order thinking skills: analysis, synthesis, and evaluation (see Textbox 5.1). By emphasizing activities, concepts, and discussion in professional development workshops with the purpose of building up to higher order thinking, you will begin to instill a greater sense of the educational value of museums.[3]

The study of dinosaurs is an excellent example of how educators can use children's natural interest in topics conveyed in museums to cultivate higher order thinking skills. Anyone who has worked in a natural history museum has at one time or another been dazzled by a preschooler's knowledge of dinosaurs. Young dinosaur enthusiasts can tell you the name of almost every skeletal mount and a few details about that particular species. Some of you (myself included) have even experienced the humiliation of being corrected by a seven-year-old when you accidentally confused an

Textbox 5.1. Bloom's Taxonomy

Categories in the Cognitive Domain:

1. Knowledge: Remembering or recalling appropriate, previously learned information to draw out factual (usually right or wrong) answers. Verbs describing cognitive tasks: defines; describes; enumerates; identifies; labels; lists; matches; names; reads; records; reproduces; selects; states; views.
2. Comprehension: Grasping (understanding) the meaning of informational materials. Verbs describing cognitive tasks: classifies; cites; converts; describes; discusses; estimates; explains; generalizes; gives examples; makes sense out of; paraphrases; restates (in own words); summarizes; traces; understands.
3. Application: The use of previously learned information in new and concrete situations to solve problems that have single or best answers. Verbs describing cognitive tasks: acts; administers; articulates; assesses; charts; collects; computes; constructs; contributes; controls; determines; develops; discovers; establishes; extends; implements; includes; informs; instructs; participates; predicts; prepares; preserves; produces; projects; provides; relates; reports; shows; solves; teaches; transfers; uses; utilizes.
4. Analysis: The breaking down of informational materials into their component parts, examining (and trying to understand the organizational structure of) such information to develop divergent conclusions by identifying motives or causes, making inferences, and/or finding evidence to support generalizations. Verbs describing cognitive tasks: breaks down; correlates; diagrams; differentiates; discriminates; distinguishes; focuses; illustrates; infers; limits; outlines; points out; prioritizes; recognizes; separates; subdivides.
5. Synthesis: Creatively or divergently applying prior knowledge and skills to produce a new or original whole. Verbs describing cognitive tasks: adapts; anticipates; categorizes; collaborates; combines; communicates; compares; compiles; composes; contrasts; creates; designs; devises; expresses; facilitates; formulates; generates; incorporates; indi-

vidualizes; initiates; integrates; intervenes; models; modifies; negotiates; plans; progresses; rearranges; reconstructs; reinforces; reorganizes; revises; structures; substitutes; validates.
6. Evaluation: Judging the value of material based on personal values/opinions, resulting in an end product, with a given purpose, without real right or wrong answers. Verbs describing cognitive tasks: appraises; compares and contrasts; concludes; criticizes; critiques; decides; defends; interprets; judges; justifies; reframes; supports.

In the 1990s, a former student of Bloom's, Lorin Anderson, led a new assembly, which met for the purpose of updating the taxonomy for the purpose of making it usable for broader purposes.

- Remembering: Retrieving, recognizing, and recalling relevant knowledge from long-term memory.
- Understanding: Constructing meaning from oral, written, and graphic messages through interpreting, exemplifying, classifying, summarizing, inferring, comparing, and explaining.
- Applying: Carrying out or using a procedure through executing, or implementing.
- Analyzing: Breaking material into constituent parts, determining how the parts relate to one another and to an overall structure or purpose through differentiating, organizing, and attributing.
- Evaluating: Making judgments based on criteria and standards through checking and critiquing.
- Creating: Putting elements together to form a coherent or functional whole; reorganizing elements into a new pattern or structure through generating, planning, or producing.

Adapted from Benjamin S. Bloom, *Taxonomy of Educational Objectives: Cognitive Domain*, 1956; Mary Forehand, projects.coe.uga.edu/epltt/index.php?title=Bloom%27s_Taxonomy; and www.ntlf.com/html/lib/suppmat/84taxonomy.htm.

For more information on the new phrases and terminology, see Anderson, L. W., and Krathwohl, D. R. (Eds.), *A Taxonomy for Learning, Teaching and Assessing: A Revision of Bloom's Taxonomy of Educational Objectives*, complete edition, New York: Longman, 2001.

Apatosaurus with some other long-necked prehistoric skeleton. Identification, the lowest of the taxonomy, is an important skill because it is part of "Knowledge," which is the foundation of the higher order skills. However, if this is the only skill we are asking children to hone from their museum experience, we are missing an important opportunity. At the lower grades, children may be asked to develop identification skills, but they are usually very specific and are not always applicable to the artifacts in your museum. However, state and national standards emphasize classification and mastery of the scientific method. Dinosaurs, geological collections, and living collections have the power to challenge students to develop their ability to classify, form, and test a hypothesis, and engage in other aspects of the scientific method.[4]

APPROACHES TO DESIGNING A PROFESSIONAL DEVELOPMENT CURRICULUM

Assessing Teachers' Needs

As an academically trained public historian, I was extremely sensitive to the fact that in order to cater to various public audiences, I had to understand their needs. I must admit that at first, I found it difficult to break into the realm of K-12 education. I attended national and regional social studies conferences, completed a couple of graduate courses offered through the local university, participated in professional development workshops before I attempted to coordinate one myself, read the latest books, and have recently substituted for an eighth-grade history teacher. Familiarity with approaches, theories, and terminology is empowering and enables better communication with teachers. Listening to teachers' professional discussion at conferences and at workshops hosted by other agencies is extremely useful (I highly recommend registering for and participating in a professional development program before organizing one). However, there is another efficient and insightful means to assess what teachers want and need from professional development—ask them!

Educators' Advisory Committee or Task Force

An educators' advisory committee or task force is an extremely important resource that can help guide the development of effective programs, publications, and curriculum materials for students and teachers. Technically, an advisory committee is a permanent group whereas a task force is temporary and is dissolved once the task is completed. Either would be useful in launching a professional development program or series. A standing advisory committee needs to be carefully structured with a balance of current users and nonusers, administrators and teachers, representatives from different school districts, and a mix of elementary, middle, and high school teachers (see Sample Form 5.1). Representatives from educational organizations, for example, the local chapter of the National Council on Social Studies, Geography Educators' Network, National History Day, or Council on Economic Education, should also be invited. Most of these organizations have experience designing and implementing professional development for educators and can provide programmatic expertise. A rep-

resentative from the state, district, or city department of education who oversees professional development credit should also be included. In some states, professional development is overseen by the school of education at one of the universities, while in others the district is the ultimate authority on professional development guidelines and regulations. If you have a docent or board member who is a retired teacher, you might consider adding one person who is already intricately knowledgeable of your museum. However, because this is your opportunity to gather outside expertise and new ideas, you need to be certain to limit the number of staff, board members, or volunteers who are already embedded in the current operations of your department. Sample Form 5.1 provides a sample matrix for recruiting members who meet several criteria, allowing for overlap so that your committees and task force groups are not too large.

Discussion questions for your advisory committee or task force could include:

- Tell me about a professional development opportunity that you really enjoyed and valued. (Probe to find out what exactly they liked about it.)
- When faced with a variety of choices, what factors weigh into your decision?
- What time of year do you and your colleagues prefer to participate in professional development? If during the school year, do you prefer Saturdays or after school?
- What major initiatives is your school or district currently engaged in?
- What aspect of the museum would you like to know more about? Which exhibits or experiences do you think would most interest your students?
- How do you and your colleagues find out about professional development opportunities? How do you suggest we reach teachers?

Grade-Specific Programs

Another question you may want to ask is how to make the program grade-specific, but only if you are prepared to do this. If you ask, "Do you want or need professional development to be grade-specific?" the guaranteed answer is, "Yes." This can be difficult because it will entail either offering multiple programs or choosing which group of teachers to cater to. There are several ways to address this. If you approach teachers as adult learners, rather than purveyors of information to specific grades, gear your program toward them and not students. This is a good option if you are not skilled in K-12 education and is also a preferred philosophical approach advocated by many professional development providers. While teachers are trained in pedagogy, many may lack the content knowledge necessary to expand beyond the limits of the students' textbook. The assumption of this approach is that teachers, who are experts in the art of educating specific age groups, will be able to adapt material to their classes. Another reason for this approach is to cultivate a collegial relationship between museum staff, presenters, and teachers. Rarely do teachers have the opportunity to participate in programs for themselves and become part of a scholarly, intellectual community. Many go into the profession because they are intrinsic learners, and all too often this is taken for granted. Furthermore, few teachers remain in the same grade level their entire careers. Therefore, professional development that is too grade-specific may limit teachers' ability to adapt materials to other grade levels, if they are not trained in the content that should make up the foundation of the lesson. This approach places responsibility for translating newly gained knowledge on the participants, not the museum.

Some programs consist of content delivered to adult learners, others showcase activities and curriculum offered by the museum that can be implemented in the classroom on completion of the workshop, and many others are a combination of both. For example, if you choose to gear your program to teachers of all ages rather than a specific grade level, you could consider having all teachers participate in lectures and adult discussion, but offer break-out sessions based on grade level. If you do provide activities created by the museum or generic material that can be used to enhance the content of your exhibits, be certain to allot time to model the activities. In any approach you choose, make sure at least half the time is spent in active participation. This does not mean that you need to have activities geared to age groups. Science experiments, analyzing primary sources, and reading discussion all serve to engage teachers in the content of your program. Teachers expect you to model best-practices in education and know that people learn best through active participation rather than passive listening.

WORKING WITH MULTIPLE DISTRICTS OR ONE DISTRICT: CASES FOR COLLABORATION AND VERTICAL TEAMING

Networking with museum professionals and contact with other teachers needs to be an important aspects of professional development. It was surprising to me

that most teachers are rather isolated in their professional lives. Some school districts promote team teaching and others have a "block" system where two class periods are combined for English and history, for example. Aside from these arrangements and lunchroom conversations, most are unable to take time away from their classrooms for regional or national conferences and rarely have other opportunities for meaningful collaboration. Teachers value the opportunity to meet and work with teachers in their own school district, and from other school districts. Knowing this, you need to factor in time for networking and socializing beyond breaks. Group discussion, modeling activities, and intensive exploration in the museum should be structured to facilitate teacher interaction.

It is important to note that if you are going for a major federal grant, some agencies advocate that you work with only one school district. The reason behind this is that major grants want you to demonstrate that a result of your program will be systematic, sustainable district-wide reform. This only comes from an extended time period (major federal projects range from one to three years) and intensive interaction among teachers in one district. I used to think this was an undemocratic approach and believed that it would be better to reach one teacher from many different schools who would then bring back material to their individual institutions. While the latter is possible, it does not have the same impact as participation on a school or district-wide basis. Think about your own museum staff. Suppose you attended a workshop on ethics or some other topic about which you would really like to engage in dialogue with your colleagues and possibly implement some of the ideas presented in the program. You might make copies of material, send out an e-mail with highlights of what you gained from the program, or outline a plan describing how the ideas might be implemented at your site in a staff meeting. Suppose no one read the material, most staff only glanced at the e-mail before "filing it," or most people focused on their own report during the staff meeting rather than listen to your necessarily brief report. Could you really hope to implement the ideas in a meaningful way? Reverse the scenario to one where everyone on your staff participated in the same workshop. Throughout the program you had time to discuss ideas and how they could be implemented at your site and left with a plan for implementation. Interacting with colleagues from different institutions has its benefits, including exposure to new ideas; however, sustained institution-wide change requires participation by many from one district over a longer period of time.

"Vertical Teaming" is an educational approach that is achieved by working with one school district. A vertical team is a group of educators (teachers, counselors, administrators) from different grade levels who work together to develop a curriculum that provides a seamless transition from grade to grade. In a vertical team approach, elementary curriculum is linked with middle level curriculum and middle level curriculum with high school curriculum to build students' skills and knowledge incrementally by grade level. It is purported that "through vertical teaming, school districts can strengthen the opportunities for all students to have access to—and be successful in—rigorous coursework" that builds on previous knowledge.[5] For example, a district may require that American history be taught in fourth grade, eighth grade, and at some point in high school. It might also be part of geography, economics, and other subjects at different points in a student's academic career. If a district adopts vertical teaming, then the eighth grade teachers will understand and build on what is taught in the fourth grade, and the high school teacher will do the same. The fourth grade teacher will have a better understanding of eighth grade standards and attempt to prepare students for what they will learn as they advance. Instead of repeating the same content on the Civil War in high school that was taught in eighth grade, teachers from different grade levels would work together to structure an integrated approach to the topic that builds on knowledge and skills designated for each stage of intellectual growth.

I like the idea of vertical teaming for another reason. It creates greater understanding and sensitivity among educators for each other. Before engaging university faculty in Teaching American History grants I randomly heard complaints about how freshman were ill-prepared in high school for college work. Working with teachers, I often heard elementary teachers say that junior high teachers blamed them for students' poor performance and for the fact that many were unwilling to do homework. Since participation in the grant, many university faculty stated in focus groups that they better understood the work of K-12 teachers. In addition, teachers expressed their appreciation for working with teachers from other schools within their district to have a better understanding of the challenges each other faced. In other words, there has been a lot less blaming of teachers and more focus on student needs as a result of bringing K-16 educators together.

STANDARDS

The ability of your program to address state and national standards will greatly enhance the value of the professional development opportunity. Teachers must adhere to state standards and are evaluated based on student performance on exams. Keep in mind that there may not be standards in every subject in every state, and even if there are standards for every subject, students may not be assessed on these standards. It is important to be familiar with state requirements for the subjects related to your collections for several reasons. By linking the content of field trips and professional development programs to the standards, not only will teachers see greater value in your museum, they will more easily be able to sell the program to administrators who allocate funding. Knowledge of the standards may also affect the structure of your program. For example, in Indiana, elementary and middle school teachers cover the Colonial period through the Civil War, and in high school, teachers must cover the twentieth century. In this scenario, you could introduce grade-specific lesson plans based on the topic of the workshop. Most state standards are broad, so you should easily be able to relate the content of your museum to standards.

Federal initiatives require every teacher to address math and literacy standards. Because these two subjects trump all others, educators have had to find creative ways to infuse history and other subjects into their curriculum. An easy way to provide teachers with a valuable classroom resource to meet literacy requirements is to develop bibliographies. Work with a local librarian to identify fiction and nonfiction books that pertain to topics explored in your museum. The titles can be listed by grade level. Requiring students to read a book about some of the subjects in your museum prior to their visit will help contextualize the experience in addition to working toward goals for literacy. As part of your professional development program for teachers, consider providing participants with one or two copies of a book from your bibliography, or have several copies available for teachers to peruse throughout the program and raffle off items toward the end of the series. You could also provide lists of terms to be used in spelling and vocabulary lessons. Developing the word lists could be part of your professional development program. Ask teachers to come up with these lists after they become more familiar with your museum during the professional development program.

PROFESSIONAL DEVELOPMENT CREDIT

In order to keep their licenses current, teachers must participate in some form of professional development throughout their careers. The requirements vary by state, and the rules seem to change frequently. The result is that there could be two, three, or more different sets of criteria for different teacher populations in any school, district, or state. In some states, teachers need to earn their master's degree within a certain period of time from the date they were hired, while others must earn a specific number of Continuing Education Units (CEUs) and/or Professional Development Points (PDPs) during a defined period of time (in most cases, it is a five-year cycle).[6] There could be salary incentives for earning a certain number of graduate credits above the minimum requirements for licensing. It is important to contact the State Department of Education to determine whether professional development is administered by the state, district, or both; to learn about teachers' requirements; and to understand how to register your program so that teachers can earn the credit they need for licensing. For example, if five contact hours count as .5 CEU and this is the state's standard of measurement, you would not want to offer a program that is only four hours in length. In most states, one contact hour of instruction is equivalent to one PDP (see Textbox 5.2). In Massachusetts, within a five-year cycle, teachers need to earn 150 PDPs, and ten PDPs are equivalent to one CEU.

Registering with or applying to the State Department of Education is usually not too taxing for the value it generates. If you register or inform the State Department of Education, your program can usually be included in a statewide listing of professional development options. In addition to ensuring that teachers will earn the credit required of the state, this free publicity for your program and museum is well worth the time it takes to complete any required paperwork. Keep in mind that listings may only be created two or four times a year, so you will need to be mindful of deadlines. Registered professional development providers in Massachusetts are expected to:

- Know the content of the relevant state curriculum frameworks.
- Plan professional development with clear objectives, relevant learning activities, and conclusions.
- Incorporate technology tools and appropriate media.
- Build on educators' prior knowledge and experience.
- Use principles of adult learning theory to engage educators in professional growth.
- Employ a variety of teaching techniques such as direct instruction, practice, discussion, problem solving, Socratic dialogue, and research projects.
- Provide many and varied opportunities for educators to incorporate new knowledge and skills into classroom practice or school and district management.
- Assess proficiency through an appropriate end-of-course assessment.[7]

In order to streamline an otherwise cumbersome process in Pennsylvania, professional development providers like the Fort Necessity National Battlefield Friendship Hill National Historic Site, work through an intermediate unit of the Pennsylvania State Board of Education that covers three counties rather than register with the state. The intermediate unit charges a minimal administrative fee (around $5) and handles advertising and registration. Although this approach limits program visibility to the immediate region, the primary goal of the professional development program at Fort Necessity is to bring in school tours. By focusing on the region rather than advertising statewide, this goal is more likely to be met.

The Kansas 2007 guidelines reflect a recent nationwide trend in professional development to deemphasize goals in terms of numbers of hours and focus on institutional planning. In this case, teachers develop their own plans in conjunction with school-wide goals. In a recent change in Indiana, professional development providers outside of districts and the State Department of Education no longer have to apply to offer professional development credit. As long as the program fits in with a teacher's professional development plan, the program can be counted toward licensing. Although this relieves museums of having to register

---

Textbox 5.2.

In order for Kansas teachers to renew their licenses every five years, they must have either earned 120 PDPs under an approved professional development plan; earned 160 PDPs including at least 80 points for college credit (one semester hour of college credit counts as 20 PDPs), if the applicant does not hold an advanced degree; completed a minimum of eight credit hours in an approved program, or completed an approved program.

Kansas Professional Development Guidelines, 2006–2007, www.ksde.org (July 18, 2007).

or get approval from the Indiana State Department of Education, there is now more burden on teachers, who may be more limited in their options.

Oftentimes, teachers can earn additional PDPs for developing and delivering professional development. You may want to recruit/hire teachers to demonstrate exemplary curriculum materials related to the topic of your program or museum, especially if you are uncertain of your own capacity to develop activities that can be readily implemented in the classroom or are planning to do break-out sessions geared toward specific grades. Educators in Massachusetts who develop and present a minimum of three separate sessions in a professional development series are eligible to receive twice the number of PDPs given to participants, with the presenter receiving a minimum of ten PDPs and a maximum of 24 PDPs.[8] It is best to work with teachers who are intimately knowledgeable of the content of your museum, use your museum's resources beyond school tours, and have developed exemplary curriculum units that have been tested in a classroom setting.

Working closely with your State Department of Education has other rewards as well. You should keep abreast of new initiatives as your institution might be in a strategic position to help educators meet new requirements or fill a mandate that may be lacking in textbooks. For example, when I worked in Chicago for the Prairie Avenue House Museums (now separately the Glessner House and Clarke House), I developed a program to demonstrate the impact of the Industrial Revolution on women. I discovered a state mandate to teach women's history, but few resources to introduce this topic in classrooms. The State Department of Education had funding for curricula that could be used to meet the mandate and awarded the Prairie Avenue House Museums a couple of thousand dollars to develop the school tours and accompanying material. In Indiana, there is a new requirement to teach an interdisciplinary class in world history and world geography. Teachers, who for the most part are trained in only one subject or the other, are quite concerned, especially since there is no textbook that integrates these two disciplines. An institution that can fulfill this need would have a successful program and guaranteed attendance.

A good way to keep on top of these initiatives and statewide changes in curriculum is to become involved in the state affiliates of the National Council for Social Studies, National Council on History Education (34 states currently have state affiliates), National Geographic Education Network (48 state affiliates and the District of Columbia), and the National Council on Economic Education (affiliated network of state councils and 275 university centers). These are also excellent avenues for informing teachers about professional development programs offered by your museum. Several state affiliates host annual or biannual statewide conferences and are always looking for quality session proposals and presenters. In addition, because many state affiliates have experience offering professional development workshops, staff and board members will have tips for registering your workshop for professional development credit, advice on appropriate registration fees, and guidance on workshop logistics.

PARTNERING WITH UNIVERSITIES

In some cases, museums work with universities to offer graduate credit in addition to continuing education credit. This may or may not increase enrollment. Several U.S. Department of Education Teaching American History grant projects offer graduate credit as part of the three-year program, but many program directors have found that this is not truly an incentive to participation, even though the credit is paid for through the grant. In states where a master's degree is a requirement, the opportunity to earn graduate credit may be more worthwhile. There are several types of "credit" offered by universities. There is continuing education credit that is specifically for teachers that does not count as graduate credit, graduate credit that does not count toward a master's degree, and graduate credit that will count toward a graduate degree. If a local university offers the first two options, usually the course is not graded, but will be included on a transcript. The university will approve the syllabus and, in some cases, the credentials of the lead instructor. Benefits include listing in the university's course schedule; registration is taken care of by the university; and in some people's minds, the fact that the course will show up on a university transcript and that the syllabus is vetted by the university carries additional weight. For example, the Historic Landmarks Foundation of Indiana (HLFI) works with the Indiana University–Purdue University, Indianapolis (IUPUI) School of Education Summer in the City program to offer its two-week program on Teaching with Historic Places. Participants register through the School of Education and earn three graduate or undergraduate credits. The course is not graded, rather participants either pass or fail. HLFI does not have to market its program or manage registration (which always fills at maximum capacity of 25 teachers), and receives a portion of each participant's fee paid to the university.

If you want to offer graduate credit that will apply toward a master's degree, you need to partner with university faculty in a specific department that has a degree-granted graduate program. Keep in mind that someone on your staff may already have adjunct status in a department or have the credential to be considered adjunct faculty. Depending on the individual university, faculty may be able to simply approve your syllabus and set up a line number for registration. In this scenario, museum staff would be responsible for developing the course syllabus, instruction, and assessment, and the university would collect tuition fees. On the other end of the spectrum, faculty will need to assume responsibility for these tasks and will need to be compensated. There are many alternatives for the latter, for example, museum staff develops a syllabus that includes a variety of instructors, and one faculty member from the university is designated as the instructor on record who is responsible for assessment. In this case, your institution would pay honoraria to speakers (if that is your policy) and to the instructor on record. In order to assess whether or not graduate credit is appropriate and should be awarded based on performance, the instructor on record will need to be involved with developing assignments to be assessed. Professional development programs that offer graduate credit usually charge one fee for the program (which goes to the museum), and a separate fee for graduate credit (which goes to the university). You may be able to negotiate that the instructor on record can count the course as part of their teaching load, but more than likely, you will need to pay an honorarium. If it is optional and you anticipate only a few teachers taking advantage of this opportunity, the amount does not need to be extravagant. As a faculty member at IUPUI, I make arrangements for teachers participating in our Teaching American History grants to earn graduate credit by requiring participation in a certain number of workshops with the addition of six précis for the assigned monographs. Most departments have generic line numbers that can be used to offer credit for professional development programs (for example, "Independent Readings" and "Special Topics"), but university rules and regulations regarding course development truly run the gamut. In some instances, if you have a master's degree or above, the department might be willing to give you adjunct status solely for this purpose. If you do not have a relationship with a specific university faculty member, contact the chair to discuss your ideas.

NATIONAL MODELS AND POTENTIAL PARTNERSHIPS

Partnering with national professional development programs relieves some of the burden of having to create programs from scratch, assists with participant recruitment, and adds an interdisciplinary aspect to your curriculum. Earlier in the chapter I advocated several reasons for consulting with state affiliates of the National Council for Social Studies (NCSS), National Council for History Education (NCHE), National Geographic Education Network (NGEN), and the National Council on Economic Education (NCEE). The latter two, especially, offer interdisciplinary lesson plans and have excellent name recognition among teachers in providing quality professional development and creating published material. Most institutions can find a connection to these subjects and build on these organizations' established practices and materials. By expanding into different subject areas through these national organizations, your museum will also reach new audiences, develop a more interdisciplinary approach to interpretation, and enhance your museum's ability to meet state standards. For example, in 2007, the Virginia Geographic Alliance sponsored an eight-day institute for K-12 teachers to commemorate the 400th anniversary of the Jamestown Settlement. Participating teachers focused on two themes relative to the lower Chesapeake Bay: historical geography of early settlement and environmental geography of the estuary as a natural resource. Daily schedules included lectures, discussions, field trips, laboratories, and teaching workshops. The institute included three graduate credits in geography and cost $1,450 per participant. Field excursions included Historic Jamestown and Jamestown Settlement, historic Williamsburg, a day on the Chesapeake Bay, Westover Plantation, First Landing Site, Virginia's Eastern Shore, and the Mariners' Museum in Newport News.

In addition to excelling in professional development for teachers, NCEE has published several books that contain curricula and activities that may be applicable to a variety of museums. *Economics in U.S. History* contains 39 activity-based lesson plans that range from "European Contact" to "The No-Good Seventies." An online lesson, "Marketplace: To Show or Not to Show," explores the effects of the rising cost of insurance for high-profile art exhibits since September 11th. Students examine the "economic decision making of both art owners and the museums that want to display borrowed works." In addition, because NCEE has affiliates in every state, with 275 university centers, it is likely that your museum will have access to an expert who would be willing to implement activities for teachers as part of your professional development program. In many instances, the director of the state and university center is a full-time employee with the primary responsibility of professional development for teachers. Museum professionals will most likely have to take the initiative for incorporating artifacts and exhibit content into the unit, but this effort will be worth the time by building on this existing program and national expertise.[9]

Another national program that some museums can readily incorporate into their menu of offerings is the U.S. Department of the Interior, Bureau of Land Management's (BLM) Cultural Heritage Education Program called Project Archaeology. This program started in Utah in 1990 in an effort to educate the public on cultural resources and vandalism and is now based at Montana State University in Bozeman. Project Archaeology has since expanded to twenty-one states and is currently developing in twenty more. Project Archaeology uses archaeological inquiry to foster understanding of past and present cultures; improve social studies and science education; and enhance citizenship education to help preserve our archaeological legacy. This archaeology-education program for teachers and its companion textbook, *Intrigue of the Past: A Teacher's Activity Guide for Fourth through Seventh Grades*, offers a series of extensively tested and teacher-friendly lessons designed to draw on students' interest in archaeology to enhance their skills in science, math, higher-order thinking, and communication. Lessons also foster a sense of responsibility for stewardship of archaeological sites. The BLM encouraged states to write state specific supplements to *Intrigue of the Past*, and currently Alabama, Alaska, Arizona, Colorado, New Mexico, Pennsylvania, and Wyoming have state handbooks. See Sample Form 5.2 for a sample lesson from *Intrigue of the Past*.[10]

In order to lead a Project Archaeology workshop, facilitators must complete training offered at various locations throughout the country. However, it is not necessary for museum staff to be facilitator trained to take advantage of this nationally recognized program. Staff can contact the state coordinator (or nearby state) for a list of facilitators and archaeologists. The role of the museum educator would be to link the artifacts and objects in the museum to Project Archaeology in order to tailor the experience to meet institutional goals.

PBS may be another resource for your museum as you begin to develop professional development opportunities. There is a website for teachers with a host of curricula tied to programming (www.pbs.org/teachers), which may be applicable to the content of your museum and workshop. As you peruse the site, think about topics or documentaries that would assist in preparing students for field trips. Consider introducing a clip and reference the curriculum activity in the workshop if your goal is to aid teachers in preparing students for an educational experience at your museum. There may also be funding available for teacher workshops in conjunction with new releases. For example, in conjunction with the PBS documentary *The War That Made America*, launched in January 2006, the Corporation for Public Broadcasting awarded grants to PBS stations to offer educational programming throughout the nation. French and Indian War 250, Inc., a consortium of sites in southwestern Pennsylvania, received a grant to host workshops for educators across Pennsylvania and in New Hampshire, North Carolina, and South Carolina during 2007.

Federal Funding Opportunities

Other national partners include federal funding agencies. The National Endowment for the Humanities (NEH) has a long track record of funding professional development for teachers. The first program it sponsored was called "Schools for a New Millennium." Currently, the NEH provides funding through its "Landmarks of American History and Culture: Workshops for School Teachers." The one-week, residence-based workshops for K-12 educators incorporate historic sites to "address central themes and issues in American history, government, literature, art history, or other related subjects in the humanities." The goals of the project are to:

- provide teachers with training and experience in the use and interpretation of historical sites and the material resources and archival evidence of American history and culture;
- increase knowledge and appreciation of places significant to American history and culture; and
- encourage historical sites to develop greater capacity and scale for professional development programs.

As with all NEH projects, applicants must demonstrate how the site or museum can be used to engage audiences in the rigorous study of a humanities topic; involve humanities scholars in the planning and development of the program; include a description of how participants will engage in the scholarly research, discussion, and interaction; and a plan for how the program will be evaluated.[11]

Another example of a large, federally funded professional development program is the U.S. DOE Teaching American History (TAH) program that started in 2001. The purpose of TAH is to raise "student achievement by improving teachers' knowledge and understanding of and appreciation for traditional U.S. history." Its guidelines state that a Local Education Authority (LEA) must partner with a museum, library, institute of higher learning, or other entity with content expertise. These are intensive, three-year programs that often offer graduate credit. Your museum may not be ready to be the main partner on such a project, but it can be a good way to begin working with teachers. For example, on two TAH grants in Indiana, Indiana University–Purdue University at Indianapolis (IU-PUI) and the Indiana Historical Society (IHS) are the two lead partners with the LEA. IUPUI subcontracted several museums to deliver specific workshops as part of the three-year syllabus. Some had experience with professional development, while others had none. The benefit to those willing to participate with no experience is that they did not have to worry about advertising or recruiting teachers to participate; TAH project staff could provide guidance as to how to structure the five-hour workshop; the museums reached a group of teachers who, for the most part, had never been to the site; and funds were available to hire a scholar of their choosing who could also extend their stay for an additional public program or to meet with staff. Because each museum and historic site was selected based on the historical content, the site also had the benefit of knowing how much content background teachers participating in the program brought to the workshop. The idea was that after participating in TAH, museums would be able to replicate the workshop for other groups. Over the five years TAH has been in existence, there have emerged certain leaders and centers of grant activity in most states. If your museum would like to be involved in TAH but is not ready to initiate a program, peruse the DOE website to find active TAH participants and contact the project director to see if your institution could be involved in an existing or future project.[12]

In addition to the NEH and U.S. DOE, there are other government agencies that offer funding for professional development for teachers. The National Science Foundation's (NSF) Informal Science Education (ISE) program funds "projects that develop and implement informal learning experiences designed to increase interest, engagement, and understanding of science, technology, engineering, and mathematics (STEM) by individuals of all ages and backgrounds, as well as projects that advance knowledge and practice of informal science education." The primary audiences are the general public and professionals in informal STEM education. Secondary audiences can be formal educators and students. As long as it is not the primary deliverable, teacher professional development can be included in the proposal.[13]

LOGISTICS

When working with teachers, there are several nuances of this audience to keep in mind as you develop your syllabus and workshop schedule. Whether you are working with one school or one district, or decide to have open enrollment, you need to keep in mind that professional development for teachers is also their time for networking. In addition to vertical teaming, you also need to be aware of horizontal teaming (a group of teachers from the same school or grade level). If you have open enrollment, you may have a group of teachers from the same school participating who will want to work together. The workshop agenda should reflect your understanding of the significance of teaming and networking by including group work, discussion groups, and extended breaks.

A standard model for professional development consists of 50 percent lecture or guided discussion and 50 percent active learning or modeling. If you suggest an activity, make sure you allow teachers to try it out (model it) during the workshop. Modeling gives participants the opportunity to review directions, determine potential pitfalls, take home a completed example to show students, work with peers, and develop a level of comfort with the activity, which will increase the likelihood that they will use it with students. After the activity is completed, be certain to leave time for reflection and discussion. Lead with "Would you be able to use this in your classroom? How? Does it need to be modified?" Oftentimes teachers will immediately come up with ways to adapt it to the grade level of their students and will share this with the other participants if you allow time for this reflective activity. If modeling the activity involves using materials or a photocopy, be certain to provide each participant with two—one to use in the workshop, and one to take back to the classroom (see Textbox 5.3).

In addition to handouts and materials, consider providing participants with books or other resources.

Fort Necessity offers two curriculum-based programs. The 4th through 6th grade curriculum focuses on the French and Indian War and the 3rd grade program studies the National Road. The professional development workshop outlined below is an example of one that is primarily designed to increase 4th through 6th grade class visitation by showcasing its curriculum-based programs. Notice the emphasis on modeling the hands-on activities that students will engage in if they visit the site as part of a class field trip.

French and Indian War at Fort Necessity National Battlefield
4th–6th Grade Field Trips and Materials Workshop
Oct. 22 or Oct. 29, 2005

9:15–9:30 Registration

9:30–9:45 Introduction

9:45–10:45 Classroom element, *The French and Indian War 1754–1763* Teacher's education kit

10:45–11:00 Break

11:00–12:00 On-site *Three Cultures in Conflict at Fort Necessity* workshop section—hands-on activities to teach about the three cultures and how they interacted through trade. Students

- Learn about emigration to New France and Pennsylvania
- Learn American Indian skills needed to help them be successful and get furs for trade. These include

  o Planting a garden
  o Grinding corn
  o Identifying furs
  o Identifying tracks
  o Determining how to fire a musket

- Make decisions about trading with the French or British
- Trade the furs they have "earned"

12:00–12:30 Lunch

12:30–1:30 On-site *Three Cultures in Conflict at Fort Necessity* tour of Fort Necessity section—hands-on activities during the tour highlight the different positions and situations of the three cultures. Students

- Learn about the event leading up to the battle at Fort Necessity
- Identify why the meadow was a good location for a fort
- Measure the distance to the historic tree line, which was influential in the battle
- Learn about George Washington's situation through a hands-on activity
- Find out about the French situation
- Tie it all together with a time line leading to the American Revolution

1:30–2:00 Discussion of bookstore/theater/exhibits

2:00–2:45 Tour exhibits—tour the exhibits in the new $12 million interpretive center, especially concentrating on the exhibits featuring the French and Indian War.

Submitted by Jane Clark, Fort Necessity National Battlefield

At a minimum, include a bibliography of resources to consult. In addition to reference books and children's literature, it should also include documentaries, websites, outreach kits or programs, and a list of speakers from your museum who are willing to visit classrooms. If you cannot afford to provide copies of books or curriculum material, create a sample display of the resources for teachers to peruse during breaks and plan to raffle off individual items at the end of the program. I have observed programs where participants earn raffle tickets for arriving on time in the morning and after lunch. It is a good idea to guide teachers through the websites included on your resource list. As part of their professional development offerings, the National Archives and Records Administration (NARA) spends half of a day showcasing its website, explaining how to access primary documents, and demonstrating online exhibits and other classroom resources. Many teachers use media and value expert-approved online resources. If you are emphasizing teaching with artifacts, it would be highly useful to provide each participant with a replica artifact in addition to a list of suppliers vetted by museum staff.

The registration fee will depend on what the market will bear, the resources you would like to include, honoraria for outside speakers, hospitality, promotional costs, and whether or not you will pay teachers a stipend. Assuming that you will not have to pay a rental fee for space, there should be little overhead expense involved. Factor in the value of museum admission when figuring out a registration fee and be certain to include free museum admission as a selling point. If you are only focusing on part of the museum, consider giving each teacher additional passes to return. Your goal should be to break even or earn modest revenue. Oftentimes teachers pay out of pocket for workshops. The other option is to secure funding through granting agencies or sponsorship.

If you are seeking outside funding, you need to include teacher stipend or substitute pay in the budget.

In many states, union contracts set the amount, but the rate can vary by district. If the professional development is to occur during regular school hours, the budget needs to include money to hire substitutes. When the activity occurs after working hours, plan to pay teachers a stipend (usually around $20 an hour, but this will vary by state). It is difficult to find a time that will be convenient for all teachers. Some teachers do not like to meet on weekends, while others prefer it. Coaching and other after-school activities make it difficult for many to attend workshops at this time of day. Summers work for some teachers while others reserve this time for vacations or seasonal employment. This adds another benefit to working with one school district because you can survey teachers before creating your schedule and get a handle on other school-wide initiatives that might affect participation. In an ideal scenario, a museum would repeat programs on weekends during the school year, after school, and during the summer to maximize the potential of convenience for all.

There is also the potential to offer professional development through in-service. Most districts have four to six days of professional development each year during school hours. Students are released early in order for teachers to attend workshops either sponsored by the district or offered by outside service providers. If a district is involved in a major initiative, a Teaching American History grant, it may focus on this training during in-service. Oftentimes a district will recruit a variety of outside educational agencies to sponsor sessions that will be of interest to a select audience. In-service sessions are relatively short—one to three hours in length. Given the brevity of the time, most museums develop presentations that showcase the variety of offerings for schoolchildren and teachers, while some focus on a specific topic, providing a content overview or introduction to working with artifacts. In-service is ideal for introducing and providing content training for traveling exhibitions and is an excellent way to reach out to teachers who may have little or no experience with your institution. Staff typically meets with teachers at their school or district, making it extremely convenient for teachers to participate and learn more about your museum.

Evaluation is another significant aspect of any teacher professional development program. If you seek federal funding, you will need to include money to pay an outside evaluator to assess the program beyond logistics. For example, TAH grants require that evaluators assess the ability of the program to improve teachers' understanding of American history as well as student learning. Sample Form 5.3 is an example evaluation form developed by the Kansas Department of Education. It is geared to teachers but will be useful to museum educators as it articulates its criteria for a quality professional development experience.

CONCLUSION

A professional development program can meet several institutional goals because it can be an efficient means of reaching K-12 educators. Once empowered with content and museum learning skills, teachers who bring students on field trips to your site will be better prepared to introduce the museum experience prior to arrival, reinforce learning in the classroom, and integrate the field trip into classroom teaching. Even if participating teachers do not plan to take a field trip to your museum, you are still enhancing the educational mission of the museum if you treat teachers as adult learners in their own right. By giving a cursory overview of how professional development works, including sample schedules, and providing several national models and ideas for partnerships with organizations that currently do professional development for teachers and do it well, my intent was to take away some of the mystique of reaching this important museum audience.

NOTES

1. For more information on Visual Thinking Strategies (VTS), developed by Abigail Housen and Philip Yenawine, see www.vue.org. VTS is a learner-centered approach to visual thinking that uses open-ended questions to guide learners to think about and interpret visual clues.

2. Roy Rosenzweig and David Thelen, *The Presence of the Past: Popular Uses of History in American Life* (New York: Columbia University Press, 1998), 21–22. Chapter 4 further explains people's desire for an unmediated experience.

3. Benjamin S. Bloom, *Taxonomy of Educational Objectives: Cognitive Domain* (New York: Longman, 1956).

4. Craig A. Munsart, *Investigating Science with Dinosaurs* (Englewood, Colo.: Teachers Idea Press, 1993); Craig A. Munsart and Karen Alonzi VanGundy, *Primary Dinosaur Investigations: How We Know What We Know* (Englewood, Colo.: Teachers Idea Press, 1995). Both sources contain multiple activities with this approach that can be easily adapted to museums. If you do choose to adopt activities from either source, be certain to gain permission from the publisher and credit the source. If you purchase these books for teachers (*Investigating Science with Dinosaurs* is currently in print, but *Primary*

Dinosaur Investigations is not), you can model the activities, adapting them to your museum's content.

5. Penny H. Kowal, "Vertical Teaming: Making Connections across Levels," *Middle Ground* 6, no. 1, August 2002, www.nmsa.org/portals/0/pdf/publications/On_Target/transitioning_hs/ (July 15, 2007).

6. The Continuing Education Unit (CEU) was created by the International Association for Continuing Education and Training (IACET) as a measurement of continuing education in 1968. One IACET CEU is equal to ten contact hours of participation in an organized continuing education experience. The website includes "Criteria and Guidelines for Quality Continuing Education and Training Programs," which may be of use when designing professional development for museums. For more information visit the website at www.iacet.org.

7. Massachusetts Department of Education, "Recertification Guidelines for Massachusetts Educators," 2000, 11, www.doe.mass.edu/recert/2000guidelines/ (July 16, 2007).

8. Massachusetts Department of Education, "Recertification Guidelines," 9.

9. Go to www.ncee.net/ for information on the National Council on Economic Education. Mark C. Schug, Jean Caldwell, and Tawni Hunt Ferrani, *Economics in U.S. History* (National Council on Economic Education, 2008). Online Lesson, "Marketplace: To Show or Not to Show," available through EconEdLink, www.econedlink.org/lessons/index.cfm?lesson=EM354&page=teacher.

10. Project Archaeology operates under a partnership between BLM and Montana State University in Bozeman; www.projectarchaeology.org/ (July 17, 2007). Shelley Smith, Jeanne Moe, Kelly Letts, and Danielle Paterson, *Intrigue of the Past: A Teacher's Activity Guide for Fourth through Seventh Grades*, 1993, reprinted 1996. See www.learnnc.org/lp/editions/intrigue and www.blm.gov/wy/st/en/programs/Cultural_Resources/edtools for an overview of the program and examples of how states have adapted this program.

11. www.neh.gov/grants/guidelines/landmarks.html.

12. www.ed.gov/programs/teachinghistory/index.html.

13. www.nsf.gov/funding/pgm_summ.jsp?pims_id=5361&org=EHR&sel_org=EHR&from=fund.

CHAPTER 6

Families and More

Intergenerational Learning

MELISSA BINGMANN, TIM GROVE, AND ANNA JOHNSON

> **Museum educators are matchmakers. They research the background and interests of visitors in order to pair them with ideas, experiences, objects, and people that will inspire a lifelong commitment to learning.**
>
> —*Sandra Harris, deputy director, Hearst Museum of Anthropology, UC Berkeley*

Family audiences have long been a staple of museum visitation and currently comprise the largest percentage of visitors.[1] Contemporary research shows that Generation X parents, the generation that followed the Baby Boomers born between 1965 and 1980, are particularly interested in finding unique ways to interact with their children. Generation X children visited museums with their families and understand the value of museum experiences to lifelong learning.[2] Educational programming, exhibitions, and institutional resources, however, rarely address the needs of this group in a holistic fashion or emphasize interaction among varied age groups. Rather, educators tend to develop a diverse range of programming based on age groups, for example, school tours (further divided by grade levels), adult lecture series, summer and weekend workshops (again, segregated by age), or Elderhostel programs, to name a few. If you were to create side-by-side lists of programs that are developed for specific age groups and those geared toward intergenerational audiences, our guess is that the former would overwhelm the latter. Festivals and other events that offer several different activities are one means of attempting to provide programming for diverse age groups, but again, certain activities target children, some adults, and others seniors. Oftentimes museum professionals write labels for an assumed median level of education rather than initiate inter-generational conversation. This chapter will explore successful methods of facilitating interaction among intergenerational groups and will include a discussion of theoretical approaches to family learning, including exhibitions, hands-on rooms, family gallery guides, homeschool programs, and teen programs.

RECENT RESEARCH

To better understand the theory and practical implementation of programs that serve intergenerational audiences, it is useful to examine family learning initiatives that include a research component as part of a family learning initiative. Funded by a National Leadership Grant through the Institute of Museum and Library Services, the Family Learning Forum conducted research to develop models for family learning at the USS Constitution Museum in Boston. Through its website (www.familylearningforum.org), roundtable reports from the "Family Learning Roundtable" can be accessed in addition to reading lists, frequently asked questions about family learning, model labels from the new family-friendly exhibits at the USS Constitution, and research data on families in museums. One of the main goals of the project was to create an exhibit that fosters family-learning conversations in the gallery.[3]

In a paper developed for the Family Learning Forum in 2005, Beverly Sheppard, executive director of the Institute for Learning Innovation, suggested the following characteristics for family learning opportunities:

- Empowerment for both parent and child—where each can feel competent and contributing. To accomplish this, museums should offer activities that respect the abilities and insights of all ages.
- Instruction for both parent and child—where each can learn something through multiple levels of learning.
- Creative and purposeful play—that affords making, creating, experimenting, demonstrating, or proving something. Activities should strive toward being open-ended, offering multiple interpretations or discoveries.
- Positive learning behaviors—where visitors can take risks, ask questions, experiment a bit, try something out, without the risk of embarrassment.
- A degree of necessary collaboration—the success of the experience is linked to the engagement of all. Cooperative learning leads to shared success and something you can talk about or simulate later.
- Opportunities to reflect or celebrate—reward collaborative learning to reinforce it as a truly meaningful accomplishment.
- A component to take home—consider ways to provide reminders of the shared experience, reinforcing the positive aspects of learning and doing together. Be creative about follow-up—whether a photo, an e-mail, a packet of ideas, a reference to other similar experiences, etc.
- Transferable—a skill that can be repeated—try to suggest a link with what activities families may engage in at home with similar skills.
- Direct links to other resources—guide families to the library, other museums or sites, the community, the school curriculum, or even television programs. Show them how learning opportunities are accessible everyday in our lives.[4]

The Philadelphia-Camden Informal Science Education Collaborative, PISEC, was one inspiration for the Family Learning Forum. PISEC, composed of the Academy of Natural Sciences, the Franklin Institute Science Museum, the New Jersey State Aquarium, and the Philadelphia Zoo, began the Family Learning Project in 1994 to study learning in family groups in these museums and then created exhibits that would facilitate and enhance social learning. The project had three phases:

Phase 1—What is family learning and how can it be measured?
Phase 2—Do specific exhibit characteristics facilitate family learning?
Phase 3—Do exhibits that have the seven characteristics of family-friendly exhibits produce measurable increases in family learning?[5]

Family was defined as a multigenerational visiting unit of no more than six members, with at least one child between five and ten years of age and one adult, age nineteen or older. The PISEC study identified seven characteristics of family friendly exhibits:[6]

1. Multi-sided: Family can cluster around exhibit
2. Multi-user: Interaction allows for several sets of hands or bodies
3. Accessible: Comfortably used by children and adults
4. Multi-modal: Appeals to different learning styles and levels of knowledge
5. Multi-outcome: Observation and interactions are sufficiently complex to foster group discussion
6. Readable: Text is arranged in easily understood segments
7. Relevant: Provides cognitive links to visitors' existing knowledge and experience[7]

Broader scholarship on learning in museums reinforces several of these findings and conclusions. John Falk and Lynn D. Dierking in *Lessons without Limit: How Free-Choice Learning Is Transforming Education* affirm that humans are social and "live in societies, among other humans, and the other humans we interact with to a greater or lesser extent play a role in shaping our ideas, our beliefs, and our behaviors."[8] As one looks at the seven characteristics of family-friendly exhibits, it becomes obvious that creating an environment that supports social interaction is integral to the experience. Free-choice learning, learning how, when, and where one chooses, also considers social interaction a key element in the experience. Conversations help to build the shared meanings and bonds that are fundamental to relationships.

CHILDREN'S MUSEUMS AS MODELS

Children's and youth museums, with their inherent mission to serve children and families, have excelled in intergenerational programming for years, especially in the development of hands-on interactive exhibits.[9] The Providence Children's Museum,

Every Friday morning preschoolers and their parents, grandparents, or other caregivers gather at Providence Children's Museum for 30-minute intergenerational classes. Preschool Friday gives children, ages three to five, a structured, safe, and short class period with an experienced educator. Each class is carefully planned to ensure the following:

- Children are active participants, whether they are making their own puppets or stirring melting ice in a simple science experiment.
- The variety of modalities in a program might include listening to a story, engaging in a discussion, making something, or even tasting something.
- Children make choices from among a variety of materials and ways to use them—no two children come away with identical products.
- Children are independent; they are encouraged to do what they can do themselves, to find their own ways of succeeding.

- Programs are creative experiences; they encourage children to think with flexibility, fluency, and originality.
- Developmentally appropriate activities take into consideration the shorter attention span of the preschooler.
- Programs use interesting, inexpensive materials, including common reusables like cardboard tubes, manufacturing leftovers, or natural objects.
- Parents are facilitators; accompanying adults have an important role as supporters of their children but not "doers-for." Written resource material is often available for parents to extend the activity at home.

Parents and caregivers are encouraged to:

- Have fun and learn along with their children.
- Use activity ideas at home.
- Ask questions about why a particular activity or material is used.
- Share thoughts about Preschool Friday to help ensure responsive programs.

—Janice O'Donnell, Providence Children's Museum

for example, uses the power of interactive play to help strengthen parent-child bonds and build parenting skills (see Textbox 6.1). The museum has taken this approach a step further. In 1991 the Providence Children's Museum worked in partnership with the Rhode Island Department of Children, Youth, and Families (DCYF) to provide comprehensive services to families affected by child neglect or abuse. Based on the belief that families in the child welfare system could benefit from the positive shared experiences offered by the museum, the museum's Families Together program employs family therapists who guide and supervise court-separated families' visits at the Providence Children's Museum. While children are in foster care, regular supervised parent-child visits are part of the family rehabilitation process. The purposeful nature of parent-child interaction at the Providence Children's Museum makes it an ideal environment for fostering this aspect of family rehabilitation.[10] The success of this program and its ability to bring together severely distressed families greatly attests to the unique position of museums to facilitate highly meaningful intergenerational experiences. The museum was honored with a Promising Practices Replication Award by the Association of Children's Museums (ACM) and MetLife Foundation for this program. More information can be found on the ACM website (www.childrensmuseums.org).

HANDS-ON LEARNING

Reaching multigenerational audiences requires recognizing various learning capabilities common to specific age groups. While an adult can be satisfied with a lecture-format tour, an eight-year-old learns more from concrete examples like artifacts and demonstrations than from verbal descriptions. It means understanding that a five-year-old doesn't have the sense of history that a teenager does. Teenagers are preoccupied with themselves, and to reach them you need to show how something relates to them and their world. Whatever format, whether tours or family programs or exhibitions, museum programming should be accessible to all ages (see Textbox 6.2).

The best way to reach multigenerational groups is through activities that a family can do together. Whether in an exhibition, a separate learning gallery, or a portable interpretive cart, such activities present a challenge for a group to work on together—something to build, create, solve. One commonly held misconception is that hands-on learning is just for children. The many natural history museum and science centers that feature discovery rooms and the hands-on nature of children's museum exhibitions testify that children learn through touching. Yet, many adults are hands-on learners. Most learning theorists acknowledge that a person's learning style doesn't change with maturity. We all know people who do not like museums where

Textbox 6.2. Age Chart

Ages 3–5	Egocentric Discovering themselves as individuals Short attention spans Limited number of choices Literal minded No sense of history
Ages 6–7	Generally uninhibited Active imaginations Curious and eager to please Limited number of choices No sense of history
Ages 8–11	Interests extend to the wider world Longer attention spans Just beginning to feel effects of peer pressure Consider differing viewpoints Have a sense of the past
Ages 12–14	Egocentric again Interested in themselves and their peers Huge swings in energy levels and emotions Intensely curious Heavily influenced by peer pressure Want to be adults Good understanding of chronological time
Ages 14–18	Preoccupied with themselves, their peers Want to be "cool" Can think like adults Can think abstractly Must appeal to their interests and concerns
Ages 18–30	Limited leisure time Want to be cool Must appeal to their interests and concerns

visitors are not permitted to touch anything. Exhibitions and programs need to support the learning styles of all the family members. If an exhibition fails to do that, and is no longer enjoyable, the family will leave.

In 1985 the Smithsonian's National Museum of American History experimented with hands-on learning by creating an activity-based gallery within the Life after the Revolution exhibition. Visitor response was overwhelmingly positive, and as a result, in 1992 the museum opened an expanded space called the Hands On History Room (HOHR), a self-directed, activity-based learning center devoted to 35 hands-on activity stations. Visitors could ride a highwheel bicycle, harness a life-sized model of a mule, assemble a Chippendale chair, gin cotton, make rope, send a message by telegraph, and many other activities. The goal of the HOHR was to provide museum visitors with the opportunity to gain a deeper understanding of American history by making a personal connection to history and creating meaning for themselves. The goal was achieved in three ways: direct access to reproductions of primary sources, focus on the stories of real people from history, and information presented in a variety of ways. Visitors enjoyed an opportunity to manipulate reproduction artifacts, and to examine documents and other primary sources. This direct access to primary sources allowed them to do their own rudimentary detective work and to gain an understanding of the historical process. Each activity related directly to exhibitions in the museum. This clearly defined link encouraged visitors to apply what they had just learned and to seek out the related original artifacts on display.

The recognition that people learn in diverse ways is vital to understanding hands-on learning. In developing the HOHR, educators at the museum studied the educational theories of Jean Piaget and John Dewey, who advocated the idea that learning is an active process based on personal experience. Learners must actively manipulate material mentally and/or physically to create meaning for themselves. Museum staff also used the theories of Kieran Egan about the importance of using stories to teach history, especially for children. The HOHR was also based on Howard Gardner's theory of multiple intelligences.[11]

The various remarks visitors recorded in the comment book and the fact that families did not want to leave when their designated time was up testified to the room's success in meeting its goals. The cotton gin activity, for example, encouraged many visitors to share personal stories of their experience with cotton culture. Grandparents told their grandchildren about picking cotton in their youth. Many adults remarked that they learned about the cotton gin in school but never really understood the process until they had the opportunity to gin cotton in the HOHR.[12]

SEPARATE LABELS

Within an exhibition context, educators also face the challenge of engaging many ages and learning styles. There is no easy solution to this challenge, and educators have tried various creative ways to make exhibitions intellectually accessible. Depending on the subject material, sometimes it makes sense to target the exhibition script to older students and adults. But there are ways to engage children. One way is to create a separate series of labels targeted to a younger age group. The National

Hands-on Activities—Wild Wednesdays

During the summer I instituted a program called Wild Wednesdays. Every Wednesday in June and July the museum presented special activities and invited the public in to have fun with history. These activities, which were targeted to family groups, were generally related to exhibitions in the museum and community history, the museum's focus. Over the years, there were storytellers, puzzles that had to be assembled by the visitors using clues, artifacts to match from different time periods such as a rug beater with a vacuum, special activity carts, scavenger hunts, a specially programmed cash register tracing the history of sales tax from 1890 to 1998, and much more.

For example, one of the games was called Discover Estelle! Estelle, now deceased, had lived in the community a long time, and her house was a historic home in the downtown now turned into a gift shop. Many people visited the shop, but didn't really know about the building's namesake. There were four types of question cards: action (good for young children to join in the fun), information, document, and photograph (also good for young children). The game board was a big outdoor tic tac toe board. So there were 9 squares, and each turned independently. We chose a good picture of Estelle and blew it up, so it was the same size as the game board. Then the pieces were cut and glued on each of the squares. As the participants played the game and answered the questions, they turned over the squares until they had a complete picture of Estelle. The questions were answered by looking at objects located in a purse, a set of photographs in a manila envelope, a set of documents, and an exhibit in the hall. This was a successful family activity, as the adults learned with the children, and they were using the tools of history as they proceeded through the game. The instructions explained that action and photograph cards were best for young children. When visitors had completed the game and discovered Estelle, then they received a prize.

Through the years, creating games for these special programs became a fun and interesting challenge. There are three elements that were always needed:

- Topic—often the smallest little detail can become an interesting and challenging game, but choose the topic with care.
- Research—the key is uncovering enough information to make an interesting activity and exhibit. If you can't find much information, it may be time to move to another topic.
- Game format—sometimes a common game format may work, such as "Who Wants to be a Millionaire Historian?" or adapting the tic tac toe bean bag game, and other times this will be something created fresh for your topic.

When developing activities, it is good to look at the list of seven characteristics of family friendly exhibits as an aid to a better end product.

—Anna Johnson

Air and Space Museum's newest permanent exhibition, America by Air, features a series of labels targeted to a younger audience. The educators on the team struggled with a name for these labels. They ultimately became known as the "family labels" to staff, but visitors identify them by their distinct design, which sets them apart from the main text labels. In the years before the exhibition opened, the education staff had experimented with printed guides for families to use in the museum's exhibitions. Testing of these guides revealed that many visitors would prefer the information on panels within the exhibition instead of in publication form. So, the family labels were an experiment in an effort to increase intellectual access to the exhibition.

The goals for the family labels were:

- Illuminate the main themes presented in the script.
- Expand on topics of interest to younger ages that are only slightly covered in the script.
- Promote directed looking at primary source materials—artifacts, photographs, and documents.
- Promote discussion within a visitor group through questioning strategies.
- Help the visitor make personal connections to the exhibition.

- Include short "fun facts" of interest to a variety of visitors.
- Offer comparison/contrast opportunities to expand on visitor understanding of themes.

FAMILY GALLERY GUIDES

Gallery guides or activity sheets can be an important means of meeting the characteristics for family learning. Although the National Air and Space Museum found that visitors preferred information on panels to printed guides, there may be circumstances that make printed or web-based family guides a better or an additional option. Guides empower and instruct adults and children and foster collaboration by encouraging families to work together to complete suggested tasks. The National Park Service Junior Ranger program provides both a reward and take-home materials. Packets include simple activities that require children to look for artifacts or natural features, answer questions, and also include postvisit activities. On completing the activities, children receive Junior Ranger badges and certificates. By working through the activities with children, adults gain a better idea of the significant aspects of the tour. The Park Service recently developed a WebRanger program, where children can become

Educators often look for a "hook" that will attract children and draw them into the exhibition content. Animals can serve this purpose since children have a natural affinity for animals. The Smithsonian National American Museum of American History incorporated a graphic of Bud, a bull terrier, into a series of labels in the transportation exhibition "America on the Move." Bud was a real dog who went along with his owner on part of the first transcontinental automobile journey. The car is featured in the exhibition. The labels encourage visitors, especially younger visitors, to look for specific items in various settings in the exhibition.

Highlighting pets or using them as text panel guides who "speak" to visitors may also help make your exhibition, website, or printed material appear more family friendly. An exhibition at the Little White House in Warm Springs, Georgia, mentions Fala, F. D. Roosevelt's dog, and the national attention he received as the president's amiable companion. Including images of Fala at various points in the exhibit and at a height accessible to children could be a creative way to engage younger visitors.

—Melissa Bingmann, Tim Grove

Junior Rangers online. Many of the activities included on the website help prepare families for visits to various Park Service sites across the country.

While NPS Junior Ranger worksheets require little advance preparation and are designed to be picked up at the ticket counter and easily perused while on the tour, other museum family guides are designed to provide an abridged overview of the content of the museum in addition to activities and objects to look for while visiting the museum. *Inside the Museum: A Children's Guide to the Metropolitan Museum of Art* is an example of an in-depth gallery guide that incorporates several common strategies for engaging family audiences. Published in 1993 the introduction promises that it will introduce readers to a sample of the museum's treasures and includes "stories to surprise you, facts to amuse you, questions to puzzle you, and activities to entertain you."[13] Artifacts include a wooden Egyptian coffin with a detailed explanation of how the Temple of Dendur was transported to the Metropolitan Museum in 1968. Historic photographs aptly demonstrate the intensity of the process, adding a story to the exhibit that children or adults could share with the group on visiting the exhibition. The guide also includes several "Eye Spy" activities, asking readers to look carefully at artifacts contained in the guide to identify specific details explained in the text. "Your Turn" shaded boxes suggest activities to complete at home. Readers are challenged to try making models out of simple household materials, replicating an ancient Chinese seal using a potato, and creating "stained glass" like the window from the 1440 Carmelite church in Germany that is featured in the guide. Notice how many of the features of this guide fulfill several of Beverly Sheppard's suggested characteristics for family-learning opportunities, including empowerment, instruction, creative and purposeful play, take-home activities, and transferable skills.

Some adults may be overly concerned about answering children's questions and may avoid museums out of discomfort. Gallery guides and websites can greatly reduce any anxiety over their perceived lack of knowledge. *Museums & Learning: A Guide for Family Visits*, created by the U.S. Department of Education's Office of Educational Research and Improvement in partnership with the Smithsonian Institution's central education office, suggests to parents that they encourage children to bring a notebook for reflections and unanswered questions. After the tour, together, children and adults can review their unanswered questions to conduct further research or contact the museum. Since many families may not know whom to contact at the museum, it is a good idea to guide them in this direction.[14] For example, in the last page of *Inside the Museum: A Children's Guide to the Metropolitan Museum of Art*, readers are directed to "Ask William," the Egyptian hippopotamus featured earlier in the guide as the museum's unofficial mascot. Inquiries are to be addressed to "Ask William" and mailed to the museum.[15]

The goal of *Museums & Learning: A Guide for Family Visits* is to help parents facilitate meaningful museum experiences with their children by providing suggestions that are intended to be applicable to all museums. The guide explains what a museum is and defines the various kinds of museums (i.e., art, history, natural history, science and technology, children's and youth, zoos, aquariums, cultural heritage, historic homes, botanical gardens); includes activities for children and families to do before, during, and after the museum visit; and ways to inspire children to hone thinking skills. The publication could be a useful addition to any museum's gift shop, but could also serve as a template for developing web-based or printed activities tailored specifically to your museum.

A common aspect of many gallery guides, including both the Junior Ranger activities and *Museums & Learning: A Guide for Family Visits*, is a focus on directed-looking at specific artifacts or details. This solid educational approach is also a simple form of play that can promote visual literacy skills. By providing directed questions to help adults lead discussion about specific

The Desert Detective©

In the 1980s the Desert Botanical Garden developed a discovery game for children, to be used on the Garden's trails. The game is engaging and inspires learning rather than boredom while looking at plants. Originally developed by the Garden's educators, Kathleen Socolofsky and Diane del Gaudio, with updated versions still highly popular today, the *Desert Detective*© game incorporates line drawings, each in its own "clue box," and each focusing on an aspect of desert plants. Each box has a line or two of information about the concept represented by the plant, and a detective clue. The small box in the lower right corner is for tallying finds. An example of a clue box follows.

The 11-by-17-inch page is folded in half to create four pages. The front page explains how to play the

Small plants often grow under the shade and protection of larger plants. These larger plants are often called "nurse" plants.

CLUE: Find a nurse plant with at least 3 plants growing under it.

Figure 6.1. Sample clue box for *Desert Detective*©
Courtesy of the Desert Botanical Garden

game and the back page is for scoring to find out "What Kind of Detective Are You?" It includes a *Desert Detective*© Certificate, certifying the participant's name, the date, and the type of detective status earned based on the number of points earned for finding the clues and completing the clue boxes. For example completing 4 to 8 clue boxes earns the title of Desert Detective, 9 to 11 clue boxes wins the title of Agave Ace, and completing all 16 clue boxes makes a Super Saguaro Sleuth, which anyone who is engaged with the game will easily attain. The game is a take-home memento of the visit and a reminder of simple concepts about plants that thrive in deserts.

This game sheet has been found to be an effective tool for engaging families as well as school groups and homeschool groups. Not only does it focus attention and empower young visitors to explore and discover interesting desert plants and animals, it also makes learning a social experience, encouraging parents, older siblings, and others to work together in making discoveries. If children cannot read, the companions who can are empowered to explain concepts and help younger children find and discover. Children who can read are empowered to tell adults or others what they are learning about desert plants while still working together to make discoveries. The *Desert Detective*© game is flexible enough to work throughout the Garden, since examples are abundant and do not require a set route. It also works well with other interpretive formats such as tours or discovery stations.

—Nancy Cutler

aspects of artifacts or exhibit context, the activity empowers adults and helps both children and adults learn how to interpret artifacts based on visual cues. A museum can develop simple printed handouts or a website with images of artifacts, architectural features, or other items to look for in order to guide visitors' experience to those museum elements that best stimulate dialogue and convey important learning objectives. Online gallery guides can be an excellent way to introduce intergenerational audiences to specific information about visiting the museum in addition to highlighting selected exhibitions or artifacts. *Museums & Learning: A Guide for Family Visits* suggests an additional way to focus family visits and visual thinking skills. If the museum does not have the resources to provide games, adults (or museum staff) can make a "postcard game" by purchasing postcards at the museum gift shop and turning children into detectives who must find the pictured items. "Later at home," the guide suggests "the cards can be arranged for a home exhibition."[16]

Most successful printed or online gallery guides contain a postvisit element. If carefully structured, postvisit activities can further intergenerational learning by serving as a reminder of the shared experience, reinforcing the positive aspects of learning and doing together. *Museums & Learning: A Guide for Family Visits* also suggests several postvisit activities and states that "many museums maintain websites that feature information about their exhibits and interactive activities for children." The Web is an excellent means of providing pre- and postvisit activities. If your museum develops web-based activities, be certain that family visitors are aware of this resource either by printing it on activity sheets to be used in the museum or other resources that adults can take with them.

HOMESCHOOLERS

Homeschool groups have certain similarities with multigenerational audiences. Educators can often repurpose programs developed for one of these audiences for use with the other. As informal learning environments that emphasize free-choice, object-based education and authentic experiences, museums are ideally suited for homeschool curriculum.[17] Leading homeschool advocate and educational philosopher John Holt used museums as an example of the type of stimulating environments that are rich in resources, focused in their scope, and have the potential to allow children the freedom to explore and learn naturally.

Homeschoolers are neither exclusively a family group, nor are they a traditional school group. They are an amalgam of both audiences, according to researcher Melinda Adams.[18] She further states that there is frustration expressed by the homeschool community regarding the tendency of museums to approach homeschoolers much like traditional school groups by focusing on state standards or expecting that homeschooled children will have familiarity with standard school rituals (i.e., standing in a straight line or raising their hand to ask questions).[19] For the practical purpose of facilitating homeschool learning experiences, museum educators should focus on homeschoolers as a family audience rather than treat them as traditional school groups. Homeschoolers can spend more time than is generally allotted for standard school tours, so they are often looking for greater depth of content. Slightly altering or replicating school tours does not usually facilitate the type of visit homeschoolers are seeking, so it is often better to create a new and different experience for them. On the other hand, when developing homeschool programs based on the philosophical approaches described below, think about how these could be translated to family programs or exhibit elements intended for intergenerational audiences.

A tour may be part of the homeschoolers' museum experience, but they will also want the opportunity for in-depth exploration of subjects through primary research, volunteerism, and mentoring by professionals, especially when a child-centered educational philosophy is employed. "These direct experiences," according to Adams, "deepen and personalize the meaning for the learner." In addition to child-centered learning, homeschool methodologies include the child-parent collaborative. In this approach, both the child and the adult make decisions about the subjects studied and together choose the course of study. Parents provide a variety of environments and experiences, offering assistance and guidance when needed. Children's interests, developmental level, and learning style are taken into consideration when developing experiences that meet the educational goals of the parents and children. Homeschooling is interdisciplinary, and many parents approach topics thematically rather than adhere to traditional delineations in subjects like math, history, science, social science, and language.[20]

Child-centered philosophy and child-parent collaborative are just two approaches to homeschooling but are probably the most applicable to general family visitors and translated most easily into museum education theories. For example, if your museum or your educational philosophy tends toward constructivism, you are more in line with a child-centered approach. "Constructivist learning situations require learners to use both their hands and minds to interact with the world: to manipulate, to experiment, to reach conclusions, to increase their understanding about the phenomena with which they are engaged."[21] If you espouse the discovery approach, homeschool parents who embrace the child-parent style may relate more to these elements of the museum. Most museums are an amalgam of many learning theories and have a mixture of those elements embedded in programs and exhibits. To appeal to homeschool groups, start with those aspects of your museum that best incorporate constructivism or a discovery approach, as these will naturally coincide with the pedagogy of most homeschool philosophies.

When developing programs specifically targeted to homeschoolers, consider the value of behind-the-scenes tours and time with museum experts. Homeschool advocate John Taylor Gatto emphasizes education based on self-directed study, apprenticeships, and community involvement, among other attributes.[22] In this vein, homeschoolers may benefit from existing or specially created volunteer opportunities for youth. Access to curators, historians, paleontologists, archivists, and other museum staff can provide the type of in-depth skills training needed for homeschoolers to learn by participating in firsthand authentic experiences that are self-directed and intrinsically motivated. For example, a thematic program on World War II might include a bibliography of reference material, training in oral history methods in order to enable children to conduct interviews themselves, a behind-the-scenes tour of the collections area to see how World War II artifacts are preserved, a guided activity in the archives that could include volunteer work organizing a collection, periodic meetings for children to express their own research interests, and time to collaborate with museum staff on continued research or the development of a culminating project that could be used by the museum. Because homeschoolers will make time for in-depth, meaningful experiences and have demonstrated willingness for extended stays (up to five hours) and repeat visits, this type of program is entirely feasible. By collaborating with homeschool networks, museum staff will get a feel for the types of thematic programs desired by this audience and, in some cases, guidance on how to facilitate an interactive intergenerational experience that may have the potential to be replicated for general family audiences (see Textbox 6.3).

Some museums cater to homeschool audiences by hosting "homeschool days" that include a multitude of in-depth, hands-on activities for a variety of age groups; speakers; behind-the-scenes tours; and demonstrations. (See Textbox 6.4 for more ideas about working with the homeschool community.) Stations with different activities that appeal to varied learning styles and developmental stages allow visitors an element of free-choice learning (and are an excellent method for engaging nonhomeschooled families as well). This type of event has the added bonus of providing a social setting for learning, advocated in most homeschool philosophies. While one-quarter of the respondents to Adams's research questionnaire felt that days designed specifically for the homeschool community served them well, others expressed that homeschool days were "chaotic, crowded, and do not allow for the in-depth experience that they seek." The Monterey Bay Aquarium in California attracted over 750 participants for its homeschool day in April of 2005. Staggered entry times helped avoid chaos and allowed each group to assemble for an orientation on arriving.[23]

TEEN VOLUNTEERS

Teen volunteer programs often attract homeschoolers and can be an extremely rewarding intergenerational experience if structured in a way that integrates teens into existing volunteer programs. At the Arizona Museum of Natural History (formerly known as the Mesa Southwest Museum), staff developed a teen volunteer program that rapidly grew to over 100 participants over the course of three years. The underlying premise was that teens work directly with museum staff, in the same capacity as adult volunteers, but also have the opportunity to participate in activities and social events specifically geared to middle- and high-school students. The format worked because it empowered students to structure their volunteer experience to meet their interests and allowed them to meet peers with similar interests.

Prior to the development of a structured program for teens, several students were already engaged in volunteer work in the paleontology lab, on excavations, and in special events through one of the museum's associated volunteer organizations. Some sought out the museum because of their interest in paleontology and archaeology; others were encouraged to volunteer through parents or grandparents who also volunteered at the museum. Word of mouth and city-sponsored newspaper inserts introduced others. There are two intergenerational aspects of this teen volunteer program. Students who discovered the museum on their own worked primarily alongside adult volunteers and participated in the same docent training, orientation, and recognition events as their senior counterparts. In addition, many became the channel for the involvement of their entire family. Teens encouraged their parents and grandparents to register younger siblings for summer camp, and parents, who often provided transportation for students, often became intrigued by museum programs and volunteer opportunities. Teens were the initiators of family participation while retaining a degree of independence through the social events and volunteer activities reserved for their

Textbox 6.4. Tips for Working with Homeschoolers

General

- Be willing to share authority. Homeschool parents, conscious of their child's learning style, take an active role as educator even when a museum educator is present.
- Learn about the philosophy and methods of homeschooling and gain a better understanding of the homeschool community. Join listservs, talk to homeschool parents who already use your museum, and meet with homeschool support organizations at a minimum. See below for a list of recommended resources.
- Do not make assumptions about the religious beliefs of homeschoolers.

Programmatic considerations

- Do not expect that your existing school tour program will work for homeschool groups.
- Actively cultivate homeschool audiences with programs geared to their needs. These include multimodal (kinetic, auditory, visual, and tactile) activities for multiple age levels that achieve the same learning objectives.
- Make sure that staff and volunteers understand that homeschoolers learn by asking lots of questions that may require extra patience. View their inquisitiveness and enthusiasm for learning in a positive light.
- Develop programs that are multidisciplinary.
- Form collaborative relationships with local businesses to create homeschool day events. The Space Center in Houston and the St. Augustine Lighthouse and Museum in Florida found that homeschoolers are willing to travel up to four hours to participate in homeschool events. Museums should approach local restaurants, hotels, bed and breakfast businesses, and other educational institutions to offer complete travel packages.
- Develop pre- and postvisit materials that include recommendations for books, articles, documentaries, and websites for in-depth exploration of the museum content.
- Carefully consider the staff-to-learner ratio. Homeschoolers are seeking individualized attention, and whether your event is an afternoon program or a homeschool day event, parents will want to know this information in advance.
- Offer behind-the-scenes experiences and tours.
- Overnight events work well with many homeschoolers.
- Provide depth of engagement with collections and subject experts.
- Offer professional development workshops and benefits for homeschool educators.

Logistics

- Make sure the museum store is well stocked and staffed. Homeschoolers rely on teaching materials, books, and other resources often available in your museum shop to further children's interest in the subject areas of your museum.
- Schedule homeschool programs during nonpeak visitation hours that may include weekday afternoons or during state-mandated testing periods. Homeschoolers have flexible schedules and desire more in-depth programming.
- Communicate and clearly define program content and expectations. In addition to standard logistical information, homeschoolers may need additional instruction about behavioral expectations that may not be part of their regular schooling experience (i.e., raising hands to answer questions, standing in line). Addressing the role of the homeschool educator—that is, observer, participant, or collaborator—will also prevent potential misunderstanding and frustration.
- Because homeschoolers often need to document their learning experience for personal portfolios or to fulfill requirements of local school boards, communicate your institutional photography policies in advance. If your museum does not permit photography, brainstorm other ways to help homeschoolers document the experience.
- Make programs fee-based or require a returnable deposit as homeschoolers may not always show up for programs.
- Make accommodations for infants and toddlers who accompany most homeschool group visits.

Selected Reading

Gatto, John Taylor. *Dumbing Us Down: The Hidden Curriculum in Compulsory Schooling*. 2nd ed. Gabriola Island: New Society Publishers, 2002.

Holt, John, and Pat Farenga. *Teach Your Own: The John Holt Book of Homeschooling*. Cambridge: Persus Publishing, 2003.

Richter, Katrina. "Homeschoolers Are Always Late: What Every Museum Needs to Know about Alternative Learners." *Museum News*, March/April 2007: 47–51.

Websites

Homefires: The Journal of Homeschooling. www.homefires.com.

National Home Education Research Institute (NHERI). www.nheri.org/.

Adapted from Melinda Adams, "Optimizing Homeschoolers' Experiences in Museums," master's thesis, John F. Kennedy University, 2005.

age group (i.e., summer camp counselors, specific exhibition fabrication tasks, designing and building parade floats), which gave them a sense of importance and leadership in their households. Parents and grandparents greatly appreciated programs that encouraged teens to participate in the museum activities. It was much easier for older relatives to "sell" a family program when they could highlight special teen events like the once-a-year overnight program reserved solely for teen volunteers in addition to volunteering in the museum store or serving Dutch-oven biscuits at special events. An intergenerational program of this sort requires a recognition of the special needs of each family member in addition to those that can be a shared experience.

In cities and states that have a traditional school calendar, teens are often limited to summer volunteer work, which could hinder their ability to be readily incorporated into an existing program. On the other hand, by focusing on teens during the summer, there is a clear beginning and end to the season, which also has benefits. For example, at the Tempe Historical Museum, teens filled out applications and interviewed with staff in order to assist with summer programs. Students completed training for their summer positions leading hands-on activities in the exhibit halls, and met every Friday morning for behind-the-scenes tours and other skill-building activities. Each summer, teens developed a family night. This culmination of their summer experience gave them the chance to research a topic of their choice, create an activity

for intergenerational audiences, work in teams with other students and curators, and present their project to the public. The most successful teen programs give students authority for creating something that will be used by the museum, training in order to have the skills and knowledge to complete a project, and clearly outlined expectations. (See Sample Form 6.1.)

CONCLUSION

Museums will always be places that families can go on a social outing. But programs developed by skillful educators who plan for intergenerational visits by families and friends can turn a wonderful social outing into a meaningful experience laced with many opportunities to learn and create memories. As cultural institutions continue to compete with other leisure-time activities, it is important that museum educators find creative ways to engage all ages and types of learners. Teens who enjoy working at your institution will invite their families to visit. An intergenerational group that has fun together will remember the experience and be more likely to return. Designing fresh and more effective intergenerational experiences presents new and exciting opportunities for the future of museums.

NOTES

1. Lynn Dierking, "Families and Free-Choice Learning," (unpublished paper delivered at "Family Learning Roundtable: Successful Strategies for Engaging Families," June 14, 2005). Notes available online at www.familylearningforum.org/current/roundtable.html.

Communicating with Parents of Homeschooled Teen Volunteers

Homeschooled teens are often drawn to museum volunteer work because it provides access to experts in the field, the type of in-depth experience that homeschoolers value, and the chance to socialize with people who have similar interests. As a museum educator in Mesa, Arizona, I appreciated the flexibility of their schedules, their ability to work well with a diversity of age groups, and the perspective of students who have learned to excel in a free-choice learning environment.

In my experience, I found homeschooled teens extremely adept at conversing with adults on sophisticated topics. Concerned over how some homeschooled students would perceive our paleontology wing and its clear demonstration of evolution, I asked a teen I knew was homeschooled for religious reasons, "How do you feel about the interpretation of the paleontology wing. It clearly discusses evolution. How do you feel about this?" The teen responded that although she believed in creationism, she understood that many people believed in evolution, and that she respected their differing views.

Avoiding potentially controversial issues with homeschooled teens who may come from a religious background may be unnecessary, but communication with parents is essential. I found that parents who homeschooled their children for religious reasons wanted a higher level of detail, which in actuality was beneficial for all parents of teen volunteers. For example, once a year the museum hosted an overnight retreat for teen volunteers. Most parents asked about the adult to student ratio, while parents who homeschooled for religious reasons also wanted to know the content of videos students would view, the evening's agenda, and details about the activities. This served parents who might want to pick up their teen at a certain point in the evening, but mostly parents wanted to help students address what they learned from the experience. Prompted by these inquiries, we started providing all parents with additional information that helped them better engage teens in discussion about the museum and its programs.

—Melissa Bingmann

2. Comments delivered by Anne Grimes Rand and Beverly Sheppard, "Family Visitors Are the Bottom Line," (American Association for State and Local History Annual Meeting, Atlanta, Ga., September 7, 2007).

3. www.familylearningforum.org/whatis/overview.html (September 16, 2007).

4. Beverly Sheppard, "The Learning Bond," (unpublished manuscript delivered at the "Family Learning Roundtable: Successful Strategies for Engaging Families," Boston, Mass., June 14, 2005), available online at www.familylearningforum.org/current/roundtable.html. In her remarks she cites Sir Christopher Ball's five C's for the successful learner: "Choice, Confidence, Challenge, Clarity, Comfort"; and Mihály Csíkszentmihályi, *Flow: The Psychology of Optimal Experience*. Sheppard stated that Csíkszentmihályi writes about the influence of the family context in promoting a child's ability to have an optimal experience and lists five characteristics that are quite similar: clarity, centering, choice, commitment, and challenge.

5. Minda Borun, Jennifer Dritas, Julie I. Johnson, Nancy E. Peter, Kathleen F. Wagner, Kathleen Fadigan, Arlene Jangaard, Estelle Stroup, and Angela Wenger, *Family Learning in Museums: The PISEC Perspective* (Philadelphia: Philadelphia/Camden Informal Science Education Collaborative, The Franklin Institute, 1998), 3.

6. Borun et al., *Family Learning in Museums*, 10.

7. Borun et al., *Family Learning in Museums*, 30.

8. John Falk and Lynn D. Dierking, *Lessons without Limit: How Free-Choice Learning Is Transforming Education* (Walnut Creek, Calif.: AltaMira Press, 2002), 48.

9. According to the Association of Children's Museum website, "a children's museum is defined as an institution committed to serving the needs and interests of children by providing exhibits and programs that stimulate curiosity and motivate learning. Children's museums vary greatly in style, size and content. Because of this creativity and diversity, the field is on a continuum of exciting change." The mission of the Association of Children's Museums is to build "the capacity of children's museums to serve as town squares for children and families where play inspires creativity and lifelong learning." www.childrensmuseums.org/programs/start.htm#CM (September 12, 2007).

10. www.childrensmuseums.org/programs/providence toolkit.htm (July 18, 2007). In 2005, Providence Children's Museum published *Play with Your Kids!—A How-to, Why-to Guide for Parents*, based on Families Together philosophy and practice. The booklet is available to social service agencies as a resource for parents and family welfare professionals as well as museum professionals seeking to replicate this model.

11. Kieran Egan and Howard Gardner have written numerous publications of use to museum educators.

The educators who developed the Hands On History Room drew from Howard Gardner, *Frames of the Mind: The Theory of Multiple Intelligences* (New York: Basic Books, Inc., 1983); and Kieran Egan, "Accumulating History," *History and Theory* 22, no. 4 (December 1983).

12. Tim Grove, "I Never Knew History Could Be so Fun," *History News* (Autumn 1999): 18–20.

13. Joy Richardson, *Inside the Museum: A Children's Guide to the Metropolitan Museum of Art* (New York: The Metropolitan Museum of Art, Harry N. Abrams, Inc., Publishers, 1993), 3.

14. Wilma Prudhum Greene, *Museums & Learning: A Guide for Family Visits* (U.S. Department of Education, Office of Educational Research and Improvement and Smithsonian Office of Education, 1998), 14.

15. Richardson, *Inside the Museum*, 3.

16. Greene, *Museums & Learning*, 16.

17. The majority of this section is summarized from Melinda Adams, "Optimizing Homeschoolers' Experiences in Museums" (master's thesis, John F. Kennedy University, 2005). She defines "homeschoolers as parents and children who do not utilize structured education within an institutional setting" and restricted the range of her research to homeschoolers who prescribe to the movement for philosophical and educational reasons. The study does not "address the needs of people who choose to homeschool for purely religious ideologies" (p. 24). Research conducted by Melinda Adams for her master's thesis, which included a survey of 155 homeschool parents in California, concluded that 99 percent of the families surveyed visit museums. Forty-four percent visit museums six to twelve times a year and twenty-three percent visit three to six times a year.

18. Adams, "Optimizing Homeschoolers' Experiences in Museums," 86. Adams asserts that John Falk and Lynn Dierking "examine and advocate the type of learning environments that homeschool parents seek for their children" in *Learning from Museum Visitor Experiences and the Making of Meaning* and *Lessons without Limit: How Free-Choice Learning Is Transforming Education*.

19. Adams, "Optimizing Homeschoolers' Experiences in Museums," 8, 10.

20. Adams, "Optimizing Homeschoolers' Experiences in Museums," 47–48.

21. George Hein and Mary Alexander, *Museums: Places of Learning* (Washington, D.C.: American Association of Museums, 1998), 37.

22. Adams, "Optimizing Homeschoolers' Experiences in Museums," 65–66. Adams draws from John Taylor Gatto, *The Underground History of American Education* (New York: Oxford Village Press, 2000).

23. Adams, "Optimizing Homeschoolers' Experiences in Museums," 108–110.

CHAPTER 7

Reaching Out into the Community

NANCY CUTLER

> A museum educator is the bridge between the objects and the visitor. Their job is to take "So what?" and turn it into "A-ha!"
>
> —*Sarah Gamble, The George Washington University Museum Education Program class of 2008*

WHY OUTREACH?

Museums have a limited impact when their audience is confined to the people who visit within their walls. Extending beyond the museum walls into the community to demonstrate why your museum matters can benefit both the museum and the community in innumerable ways. Outreach is any type of museum-related program that extends beyond the museum walls, bringing a part of its mission and collection into a classroom or other off-site location, including into your home via the Internet. An off-site visit can include materials and/or activities related to the collection that will enhance or can even replace a museum visit. Like any exhibit, an outreach program should be enticing and engaging, as well as informative and related to the mission of the museum.

What Are Some Benefits of Doing Outreach Programs?

Off-site programs are often used as a teaser to introduce the museum to an audience that might not otherwise visit, with the hope that participants will then visit for a more in-depth experience. Off-site programs can either stand on their own, or they can be used to enhance a museum visit, such as a preview—setting the stage for a visit—or a postvisit wrap-up to reinforce concepts learned. Outreach programs to schools are especially valuable for remote areas or for "underprivileged" schools, where students cannot go on a field trip to a museum. Many programs can be used at events or fairs, either on- or off-site, as well. Or, in uncommon circumstances, perhaps due to lack of space or staff, or due to a renovation, activities cannot be presented at the museum, and outreach provides venues for presenting educational activities related to the museum's mission. The puppet shows described below serve as one example that developed due to lack of both space and personnel. I also know of a history museum that used living history characters as outreach while waiting for the museum to open. Those living-history interpreters also serve as a teaser to visit the museum.

What Are Some Challenges of Creating Outreach Programs?

Outreach projects require significant resources dedicated to developing and maintaining the programs, as is indicated in the list that follows. Sometimes museums, especially small museums, do not have the manpower or resources to manage some types of outreach programs. Developing the program is only the first step. The project then needs a dedicated champion to oversee and maintain the program, perhaps do scheduling, replace consumables or repair items, keep an electronic site up-to-date and functioning properly, or even to secure funding. Without that dedicated champion the program will not survive.

SOME EXAMPLES OF OUTREACH PROGRAMS

Successful outreach programs can provide many of the benefits described above if they are planned carefully and creatively. This chapter suggests several possibilities to consider and describes in-depth three projects that have proven successful as potential models. A sampling of several forms of museum outreach follows.

Programs for Schoolchildren and Homeschoolers

TRAVELING TRUNKS/KITS Boxes or trunks with themed activities for learning about the museum's exhibits, collections, or themes. School-directed kits usually contain activities that are grade-appropriate and interactive and are presented to students by museum volunteers or the classroom teacher. They often have some type of visual component such as a video, a slide show, or a power point presentation. The most successful kits have some hands-on, experiential, problem-solving elements that are more than just show-and-tell. Ideally the programs correspond to national and/or state education standards. (Detailed discussion appears on page 90.)

DISTANCE LEARNING OR VIDEOCONFERENCE OR VIRTUAL CLASSROOM Brings the excitement of the museum into the classroom in real time. Through electronic productions the museum offers programs, presented by museum staff and/or docents, so that students can interact with the museum without leaving their classroom. This type of program can reach classes that may be unable to physically attend the museum for a variety of reasons. These interactive learning opportunities can be exciting when they feature the museum's collection along with kid-friendly activities and allow students to ask questions of the museum presenters that can be answered on the spot. Programs are relevant when the lesson plan augments teacher lesson plans, and corresponds to national education standards. These programs are broadcast over the Internet or via satellite and require the use of videoconference equipment at the school, which can be costly. (See Chapter 9, "Education Online," for additional information.)

MOBILE MUSEUM Some type of van, bus, or vehicle outfitted to bring portable exhibits from the museum to the school or classroom. For example:

- The Phoenix Zoo has a *Zoo-mobile* that will bring a menagerie of portable desert animals to schools all over the state of Arizona. This is often targeted to remote areas or schools where students cannot go on a field trip to a museum. Curriculum can focus on Arizona state social studies or science using the animals.
- *The Van of Enchantment* is a converted RV that tours New Mexico carrying exhibitions and educational material from the collections of the state museums and monuments.[1]

SCIENCE EXPO The New England Air Museum participates with exhibits in several regularly scheduled community events, including the CPTV Science Expo, where it reaches out to the public.[2]

ART CONTESTS The New England Air Museum participates in the International Aviation Art Contest.[3] Other museums also participate in or hold art contests to get students involved.

LIVING-HISTORY CHARACTERS/INTERPRETERS Volunteer or paid staff are actors who take on the role of a historical person related to the museum's collection and mission. They are outfitted with the type of clothing that historical characters may have worn in his or her time (perhaps gathered from pictures) and also some appropriate props. The character could be a specific historical person or a composite of people using period clothing, dialect, articles, and social customs to depict a sense of the period. Research is required to learn the customs of the times, or for a particular person, who the person was and what they represent to history. A script is often developed of things the character might say in a presentation or in a conversation with students. In the museum this becomes a mini-immersion experience. As outreach this becomes a taste of the world the character comes from and is most effective when it relates to a classroom lesson. It can be used in schools, fairs, or as entertainment for any outreach project. A system of booking, scheduling, and confirming, and some type of funding for the characters and travel are required.

PUPPET SHOWS The Desert Botanical Garden partnered with the Great Arizona Puppet Theater in the 1980s and 1990s and cocreated three educational puppet shows about the desert environment using puppets of desert plants and animals that went out to classrooms. Shows are musical, fun, and interactive and relate to students in grades K-6. Curriculum foci included social studies (Arizona), science (how desert plants and animals survive), and art (the art of puppetry—how puppets are made and function). A system of booking, scheduling, and confirmations, and some type of funding are required. This is a good example of a successful collaboration between two nonprofit organizations with different missions working together to enhance both missions. (Detailed discussion appears on page 89. Also see Chapter 13, "Collaboration," for additional information.)

WEBSITES Museum websites may have online exhibits and/or educational activities along with general information about the museum, its amenities, and its collection. (See Chapter 9, "Education Online.")

MASTERPIECE ART PROGRAM An art museum outreach program that trains parents to take prints of art masterworks into classrooms once a month to discuss the artist, his or her times, and the techniques used in the art piece, and then lead a hands-on activity related to the art. The art print is then left in the classroom for one month for the children to become familiar with the piece until the next session, where a new piece of art will be introduced. Check with art museums in your area for a similar program. (Detailed discussion appears on page 92.)

Several of the programs listed are also appropriate for community groups or students of all ages.

Programs for More Mature Groups

SPEAKERS BUREAU Lectures covering a variety of topics related to the museum's collections and mission. Trained volunteers or museum staff offer formal or informal lectures to schools and community groups. Presentations often include a video, slide show, or power point presentation that lasts between 30 and 60 minutes. Speakers can bring hands-on items for people to handle. An organization may charge a fee for presentations to adult groups to cover costs and perhaps a little more.

ONLINE EXHIBITS Many museums offer online exhibits. As technology advances, museums are growing into using the new technology to keep their collection information current as well as available to the public. (See Chapter 9, "Education Online.")

LIFELONG LEARNING CLASSES For example, a collaboration between Arizona State University and Del Webb's Sun City Grand offers a huge variety of classes at the Sun City Grand Community Center in Arizona, making learning accessible for senior citizens. The Desert Botanical Garden was one of the institutions that presented classes, focused on the ecology of the Sonoran Desert and landscaping with desert plants which were of interest to new homeowners.

This is just a sampling of how a museum can reach out into the community. The possibilities are bounded only by imagination. Funding is sometimes an issue because programs have costs associated with the outreach, but funding is often available from arts, science, or humanities agencies; school PTAs; or other foundations or entities that see education as a valuable priority. (See Chapter 11, "Financing Museum Education Programs.")

THREE SUCCESSFUL PROJECTS

This chapter highlights, as examples, three outreach projects; the goals of each; the process of development; and some benefits, outcomes, and comments:

1. A collaboration with the Great Arizona Puppet Theater and the Desert Botanical Garden, developing three outreach puppet shows.
2. Traveling trunks for the Gilbert Historical Museum.
3. A volunteer experience with the Phoenix Art Museum's Master Arts Program.

Puppet Shows

The Great Arizona Puppet Theater (GAPT), established in 1983, presents workshops, residencies, and classes for children and teachers throughout Arizona and performs educational shows for outreach that have been codeveloped with the Desert Botanical Garden, the Craniofacial Society of Arizona, and the Water Conservation offices in Arizona. GAPT has a repertoire of over 50 shows that include classic fairy tales, original stories, and educational programs. In 2007 it served over 400 schools, preschools, and child care centers with shows and workshops; it has been the recipient of several local awards including the Mayor's Environmental Award for Education.[4]

In 1986 one of the goals of the Desert Botanical Garden was the development of educational programs

---

National Portrait Gallery Outreach Program

In the 1990s I was part of a team of educators at the National Portrait Gallery that presented programs to secondary students in the metropolitan Washington, D.C., area. The first part of the program took place in the classroom and the second part at the gallery. The programs used role-play as the central teaching format. Students might be settlers to a new town in colonial Connecticut and decide whether to build roads or a church or school first, or they might be participants in a Harlem town meeting gathered to discuss the condition of the black race in 1919 America and ways to improve

the situation. Once students became comfortable with playing a role, they were ready to explore the topic and then looked forward to their visit to the gallery. The gallery visit focused on portraits of personalities of the time period and introduced them to the historic building. The two-part program served to introduce education staff to students in their setting, present a program that engaged the students and prepared them for their site visit, and then expose them to a wonderful museum in hopes that they would return on their own time with family.

—Tim Grove

that teach about the importance of the desert environment. In keeping with that goal, the education department created an innovative outreach program partnering with the Great Arizona Puppet Theater and featuring two puppet presentations, "Hotel Saguaro" and "Seasons of the Desert." Through the drama of animated puppets, the goal of both presentations is to introduce students to basic ecological concepts and to the interrelationships of desert plants, animals, and people. The dramatic presentations include musical ditties, which enable children to learn the concepts by holding their attention and help them remember the information. In addition, these professional puppet shows introduce children to the art of different types of puppetry. After the show the puppeteer shows students how the puppets work, building on familiar puppetry forms seen in children's shows on television. Coproduced by the Garden and the Great Arizona Puppet Theater, and presented by professional puppeteers, the presentations traveled to elementary schools throughout the Phoenix metropolitan area.[5] In 1998 a third show was funded and added to the repertoire. "Desert—Day and Night" focused on the different niches of certain desert plants and animals in the heat of the Arizona summer.

Local teachers at the elementary school level are required to teach about Arizona and often want to teach about the desert environment as well, but most were not well versed in desert ecology. These shows give teachers a jumping-off point for teaching about the Sonoran Desert. Shows can be used as the introduction to a desert or an Arizona unit, an orientation to a field trip to the Garden, or as a culmination activity for extended learning and reinforcement after a field trip. Sometimes these shows are the only information the children receive about desert plants and animals. Along with the shows, teachers were given an activity packet of ideas to use for follow-up lessons about the desert. Children (as well as adults) who watch the performances leave with a better understanding and appreciation of the fragile balance of living things in the desert and how their actions can affect what the desert will be in the future, for better or worse.

The Garden's innovative program grew dramatically in the first four years with audiences increasing by over 275 percent. During the same period, school group visitation to the Garden grew by over 235 percent. Responses from teachers, school administrators, and students were overwhelming, and funders, impressed with the responses from the education community, committed over $27,000 to the Garden's outreach program. Ten years later, over 11,000 children annually were treated to one of these puppet shows in their schools. The program was so popular that the funded shows were fully scheduled within four weeks. When the Garden's annual funding for the program was exhausted, an estimated 10,000 additional children whose teachers requested presentations were unable to see the shows unless they acquired funding from other sources such as PTA or PTO organizations.[6]

The shows have also been presented at the Garden. They were advertised to entice families to visit the Garden, and all ages enjoy the stories.

THE PROCESS To create a similar outreach program note these six basic steps:

1. Team up with a professional, nonprofit theater company that has experience designing programs for school audiences and a mission similar to yours.
2. Write a contract stating the responsibilities of both parties. The contract should include a budget that defines costs and what to charge per performance as well as financing and scheduling agreements.
3. Work together with the theater company to identify the target audience and develop accurate educational presentations, materials, and follow-up lessons.
4. Solicit funding—the theater could solicit from cultural arts organizations for development of the program, and the museum would be responsible for securing funds for sponsoring school presentations.
5. Jointly publicize the outreach program.
6. Develop a system for scheduling and confirming performances.

There are many advantages to such collaborative ventures. Museum educators work with the theater director and ensure that all information is accurate, while the theater director develops entertaining professional presentations featuring experienced actors. The partnership between two nonprofit organizations presents more opportunities for funding, because each institution provides a different focus for fund-raising efforts. The combined marketing efforts of both institutions also provide increased opportunities for advertising, and both receive added publicity.[7] It is a win-win opportunity for all!

Traveling Trunks or Kits

In the township of Gilbert, Arizona, the Gilbert Historical Museum received a $15,000 grant to develop traveling trunks targeted to local third- and fourth-grade classes to teach the history of this Arizona community. Although several teachers use the museum for tours, the goals for this small museum were to provide a more hands-on experience for the students as a supplement to the visit, and to encourage more teachers to use the museum as a resource for teaching about the history of their town. The museum staff, volunteers, and consultants worked first to define the messages to be communicated using the museum's exhibits. They next formed an advisory panel of interested, local third-grade teachers to help design activities based on those messages and related to their current curriculum, and a Teacher Resource Guide to go along with the traveling trunks. The activities chosen were to teach Gilbert history and to supplement the Arizona history curriculum in accordance with the state standards. The activities were designed to be used in the classroom for a variety of purposes. They could stand alone as lessons on the history of the town of Gilbert or supplement curriculum as pre- or post–museum field trip activities.

THE PROCESS Once the messages were defined, the teacher advisory panel selected, and a teacher survey of the exhibits developed, there were two meetings of the teacher advisory panel. The first meeting included:

- Goals for the grant
- A tour of the museum exhibits using a survey designed for the teachers with preselected topics based on the themes and messages for each exhibit, which asked them to prioritize the selections according to what they considered most to least important to teach. The teachers were then asked for any other suggestions they might have. (See Sample Form 7.1, "Teacher Survey, Gilbert Historical Museum" in the appendix.)
- The teacher panel then brainstormed ideas based on the survey to suggest as many ideas as possible that might be used to create hands-on activities for the traveling trunks and resources for the Teacher Resource Guide.

An extensive list was compiled from the teachers' suggestions. The ideas were grouped into categories of suggestions that worked together, or were eliminated. After examining the exhibits in light of the suggestions, some ideas emerged on how to create engaging activities to help students learn about some of the major historical events and people in the formation of the township, and to understand a sense of place by locating "Where in the World is Gilbert?"

Three trunks based on different themes of Gilbert history were developed. Each includes a Teacher Resource Guide with background information on historical events and people in Gilbert, and some primary resource information in the form of copies of newspaper articles covering certain events. Each trunk also has its own spiral-bound Teacher's Guide with tabbed sections informing the teachers how to use the activities in the trunk; how each correlates with the state education standards; an overview of the exhibits in the museum; how to sign up for a field trip; and teacher and student evaluation forms to fill out and return with the trunk. (See Sample Form 7.2, "Teacher's Trunk Activities Evaluation," and Sample Form 7.3, "Student Evaluation," in the appendix.)

At the second teacher advisory panel meeting, two months later, teachers were asked to respond to the following:

- Review and evaluate the information assembled for the Teacher Resource Guide and the proposed format for ease of use.
- Review and evaluate the modular classroom activities that were developed in prototype or in the process of being created. Did they compliment or enhance the curriculum already being taught? What else should be included? Are the activities meeting the state standards as you understand them? Any suggestions on logistical usage of the trunks and recommendations on how to check them out for use? How many sets of each trunk should be created? Are there any other suggestions you may have at this point?

THE TRUNK THEMES The first trunk is "From Alfalfa to Butter." In 1918 Gilbert was called the "Alfalfa Shipping Capital of America" because of the tremendous amount of alfalfa grown in this little farm area and shipped by rail from Gilbert. This was also an important dairy producing area, due to the abundance of alfalfa feed for dairy cattle. Students participate in activities that help them understand the importance of alfalfa as a farm crop and to make the connection from planting and growing alfalfa hay to seeing how the hay is food for cows that enables cows to produce milk that can be made into butter. Hands-on activities for students include examining dried, pressed, and laminated alfalfa plants, sprouting and growing their own alfalfa from seeds, and making their own butter to eat from cream (supplied by the teacher).

The second trunk theme is "Early Gilbert in Time and Space." Using materials provided in this trunk, students create and use a variety of maps and aerial photos, create a time line that includes historic photos, and put together chronologically a "Fascinating and Fun Facts Fan," to recognize some of the significant events in the town's history and Gilbert's location on the earth.

The third trunk theme is "Gilbert at Work and Play." This trunk contains items that were used in the home and on the farm at the turn of the twentieth century, when the town was just beginning. Students have to identify the items and match them with a modern-day counterpart. Discussion focuses on comparing the items from then and now and on how lifestyles are different, giving them a sense of how life was at the turn of the twentieth century and how it was different from today.

When the trunks are returned to the museum, volunteers check each trunk (against a checkoff sheet—which is also supplied to teachers with the trunk) to make sure all supplies are in order, clean, and ready for the next teacher to use. There are two complete trunks available for each theme.

These trunks have been popular with Gilbert teachers, serving over 2,000 students in the first year, according to the museum; "From Alfalfa to Butter" was the most-requested traveling trunk. As word of these trunks spreads through the schools the museum anticipates an increase in their use.

A Master Arts Program: Training for Parents

The Phoenix Art Museum has, for many years, offered Master Arts Program training to parents who volunteer to introduce masterpieces of art into school classrooms. One goal of the program is to introduce art to young students so they can begin to develop an appreciation of masterpieces and will one day visit and support art museums.

THE PROCESS Training was offered once a year in the fall, once a week for 7 weeks, to parent volunteers interested in taking an outreach art project into their child's class based on an art masterpiece. Developed and taught by the Phoenix Art Museum docents, the training introduces parents to "The Basics of Art" including design, space, movement, lines, shapes, color, perspective, and composition. Docents model for parents the techniques to use with students, using the prints of masterpieces that could be taken into a classroom. They demonstrate how artists use lines to give feeling and direction, repetition of shapes and designs to create movement of the eye and hold the picture together to tell a story. A selection of significant art pieces were chosen to be used in the classrooms; the pieces represented a variety of well-known artists from a variety of time periods and schools of technique. In the two-hour training sessions each week, a little information about the artists, their lives, and their techniques was shared, as well as ideas for related art projects to use with the students.

The goals of art in the classroom are to:

- make art alive for students
- explore and validate the emotional response to art by understanding how the artist is creating that response
- develop an awareness and appreciation of art
- peek at history through art—art reflects the artist's life and times
- create support for the arts

Discussing the art pieces with children also builds their visual, verbal, and writing skills along with problem-solving skills and their attitudes toward art. The training taught parents how to construct good questions to encourage the children to discover elements about the art pieces and also let them know that while we are learning things about the pictures we are also enjoying them as pieces of art.

The parent training was fun, informative, and inspiring. Taking the art into the classroom inspired creativity for engaging the students and the pleasure of sharing important lessons of culture that are otherwise not available through the school.

The experience was so inspiring and straight forward that I believe the model could be modified to be used by any museum to take outreach programs into classrooms. The benefits of using volunteer parents are as follows:

- Provides outreach that does not mean a big increase in staff—only teaching of parents once a year, and maintaining the kits
- Engages parents in learning science, history, art, or whatever the focus of your museum is as well as methods of teaching
- Empowers parents to be involved in their child's classroom
- Puts relevant, local, hands-on science, art, or history projects into classrooms, enhancing their curriculum
- Introduces your museum to parents and to schools
- Program can grow—limited only by resources and imagination
- Sensitizes participants to your museum's topics and themes

- Connects museum with schools and parents from the community
- Promotes school tours to your museum as well as teacher trainings
- Is possibly grant worthy for funding

Your proposed model should include:

- Goals of the program
- The objective of the outreach. For example: to have trained parents take [art, history, or science] kits to their child's classroom and present a 45- to 60-minute hands-on lesson about [topic of the kit]
- How the training and the program will work
- An example of a kit and the objective of the lesson

- The process necessary for implementation. For example:

  o Begin by promoting to members to participate.
  o Design the training sessions, the dates, and who will teach.

- Plan for and pursue funding
- Put together concepts and kits with the help of whoever is doing the teaching (such as a teacher advisory panel)
- Additional outreach kit ideas

(See Textbox 7.1 and Sample Form 7.4 in the appendix.)

Textbox 7.1. Model for Desert Discovery Program Proposal: An Innovative Outreach Program

Objective—Have trained parents take desert ecology "kits" to their child's class and present one 45–60 minute hands-on lesson about the desert—based on Desert Botanical Garden (DBG) themes.

Goals—Students will recognize elements of the Sonoran Desert as their home.
Develop skills of observation, compare and contrast, and problem solving.
Whet the appetite to want to know more.

How— Based on the "Masterpiece Art Program" at the Phoenix Art Museum. DBG would develop and offer, once a year, in the fall, a once-a-week training course for 6–8 weeks, to parent volunteers interested in taking an outreach project into their child's class.
Training would cover how to use each "kit," background content on desert ecology, and methods for presenting the information to students at various grade levels.

Example—Sample kit

Why Do Cactus Live in Deserts? (or What's So Great about a Cactus?)
Kit includes hands-on items and activities used on the cactus stop of the *Secrets of Desert Plants* tour and a few other items to illustrate concepts.
CONCEPT to learn —Cactus is a living plant.
—How and where does cactus survive in deserts?
—Some varieties of cactus and their features.
Do a project that stays in the class room—like planting cactus seeds or a prickly pear pad, create a paper saguaro with pleats, create a diorama or class mural, create a "feeling" poem, or . . . (other ideas).

Benefits—
- Engages parents in learning science, desert plant adaptations, and methods of teaching.
- Puts short, age-appropriate, hands-on science projects into classrooms.
- Introduces DBG and its teaching methods to parents and schools.
- Program can grow—limited only by resources and imagination.
- Sensitizes participants to desert topics and scientific process.
- Connects museum with schools and parents from the community (collaboration).
- Promotes teacher trainings and museum classes.
- Promotes school tours.
- Provides outreach that doesn't take much staff—only in the teaching of parents and someone to maintain kits.
- Is probably GRANT worthy for funding.

Process—
- Develop the proposal enough to get funding to develop the project.
- Begin advertising by promoting to members—especially through preschool and camp sessions.
- Spend the summer putting together kits for fall.
- Design training to be offered in the fall—see if volunteers want to help with training of parents.

Conclusion—
It is a traveling trunk kicked up a notch!

Other Outreach Kit ideas—using concepts we teach, but in a different distribution method.
- **Secrets of Desert Leaves—Large and Small :** aloe, agave, mesquite, palo verde, creosote, jojoba.
- **Flowers—Sex in Your Garden**
- **What's So Hot about Botanical Art?** Includes Herbarium pressing of a plant and classification.

CONCLUSION

Should your institution have some type of outreach program? Before committing resources to such a project you must decide how the program would benefit the museum and the intended audience. The decision requires looking at the goals and objectives of your proposed outreach, your target audiences, resources available or attainable (including manpower), possible collaborations, venues, funding, and some form of cost/benefit analysis.

Planned carefully and creatively and using members of the target community to help assess the need, the impact, and the resources available, outreach programs can touch people in the community and provide value to both. Creating successful programs is fun, and the possibilities are bounded only by imagination and the resources available. So, investigate, collaborate, create!!

NOTES

1. New Mexico's Van of Enchantment is on the Web under Educational Programs at www.museumeducation.org/ (October 16, 2007).
2. The website for the Science Expo is www.cpbi.org/local/special/scienceexpo/ScienceExpo_features.asp (October 16, 2007).
3. The Virginia Department of Aviation International Aviation Art contest. www.doav.virginia.gov/art_contest.htm (July 5, 2007).
4. Great Arizona Puppet Theater, www.azpuppets.org/ (July 5, 2007).
5. Kathleen Socolofsky, "A Collaborative School Outreach Program in Phoenix," *The Public Garden* 5, no. 2 (April 1990): 17.
6. Socolofsky, "A Collaborative School Outreach," 17.
7. Socolofsky, "A Collaborative School Outreach," 17.

CHAPTER 8

Planning and Managing Museum Programs and Special Events

KIMBERLY A. HUBER AND ANNA JOHNSON

> **A museum educator piques the interest of the public about a subject that they may have never known they had any interest in.**
>
> —*Emily Pope, student, The George Washington University Museum Education Program, class of 2008*

Museum educators at some point will need to expand their activity repertoire to include programs and special events, which attract a wider audience and keep their members satisfied over the long run. That means that the educator can be responsible for developing, coordinating, and managing all types of visitor activities. This chapter will take a look at programs and special events—what they are, why museums have them, and how to plan and manage them. In the appendix you will find a sample time line/checklist for planning programs and special events and an event budget information sheet. These sample forms will help you plan almost any program, but you may need to modify them to accommodate your specific needs. For large-scale special events such as fairs, grand openings, markets, or regional celebrations you may need to add subcategories to some items on the time line/checklist and budget to ensure you have included every detail. For smaller programs, the planning time line may be compressed from one year to as short as three to six months, but no less than three. Depending on the scale of your program you will need at least three months to successfully promote it. Develop a calendar of educational programs and museum events for the year. Include anything that might impact the education department.

PROGRAMS VERSUS SPECIAL EVENTS

A program can be broadly defined as an activity or series of related activities that present information and entertainment to an audience at a specific time and place.[1] Examples of programs may include lectures, forums, seminars, films, puppet shows, presentations, storytelling, or workshops. Programs can be targeted to any age group or any size audience. We define a special event as a large, multifaceted program. An event would typically involve several hundreds or thousands of visitors and might last all day or several days. How do you determine when a program is a function of the education department of a museum, or are all programs managed by the education department and/or educator? Educators need to clarify these questions in order to understand their job and its parameters.

Let's think about programs from a managerial perspective. What distinguishes educational programs from those of other museum departments is that in order to justify the immense commitment of resources, there must be a strong educational component. Increasing public awareness of the museum and fund-raising events, in most cases, do not make for an educational program. In midsize and large museums, exhibit openings, donor events, and facility rental are best handled by development, facility, or public relations staff. Although other museum departments may sponsor some events, sometimes all museum personnel may be called on to assist with some museum activities. However, each museum has to determine who will manage events relative to its own situation. This chapter emphasizes programs the museum educator or education department is responsible for.

The following diagram shows a couple of approaches to structuring programs. The diagram illustrates that education generally runs through all programs put on at a museum. However the frequency with which a program is presented and the external resources required to organize and manage the program can all be indicators of how big a factor education will play in the final product. The more external resources needed to develop and manage an event, the more likely it is that the education factor will be less significant. The more frequently a program runs, the more likely it is that it is being done in-house by the education staff/educator.

Now let's look at the frequency of programming and how that also might impact the role of the educator. How frequently can you consistently run programs at your facility, and what types of programs would they be? It is important to lay out your programs in an orderly fashion. This will help with setting priorities, determining staffing and the workload in general. Your museum may choose to do one annual event and nothing else. Or your museum may prefer to focus on monthly programs and add weekly programs. This diagram is merely an organizational tool to help you look at the big picture of programming in your museum while focusing on the role of education within the institution. This pyramid can be completed in any way you think reflects your programming. The categories in the boxes serve as common sample programs to get you started thinking. For example, there may be a class one month, a series of lectures for the next few months, a workshop for teachers in another month, and docent training and then touch carts in the exhibit halls in other months. Newsletters are often done on a quarterly basis by museums, and in each quarter there may be different programs for students such as fourth graders, fifth graders, or high-school students along with special summer programs. If looking at your programs from a time line basis is not helpful, then fill in the boxes at the base of the pyramid with your core educational programs. As you work up the pyramid, you are creating a priority of importance for the programs developed by the education department. Complete or modify the blank pyramid form (Sample Form 8.1) in the appendix or create your own diagram template. Use whatever format works best to meet your needs.

No matter what size program you are planning, one

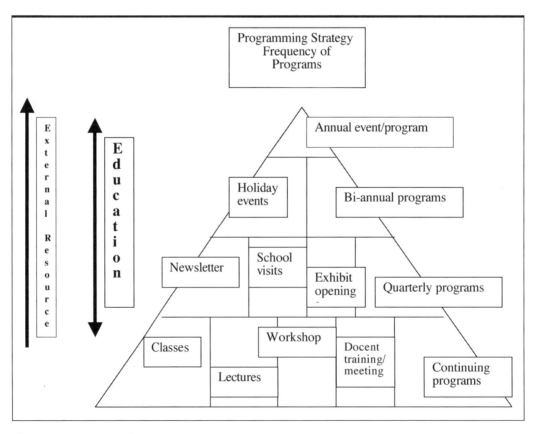

Figure 8.1. Programming Frequency
Courtesy of Anna Johnson

person should be designated as being in charge of the program. Often the person in charge is the educator or director of education. However, for large programs like events someone is often appointed as chair of the program committee. Even if many others help throughout the process, and especially if committees are formed, the person in charge or the program chair is the key person to whom everyone will report; the person who has the plan responsibility and who understands the details of the event. Fortunate program managers will also have an assistant who serves as second-in-command and can step in if the chair drops out for any reason. Event committees can also be used to aid in the planning. Each committee member can oversee a portion of the event, with all members meeting regularly and reporting directly to the event chair. Even if you don't have program experience, you can manage well if you thoroughly plan, work with a dedicated committee, stay organized, remain flexible, and keep calm, because even the best-planned programs will experience some unexpected situations.

Effective programs seem effortless, yet they take detailed planning and lots of work. Very early on, as much as one year out (or sometimes several years prior to a major event like a blockbuster exhibit), you should ask yourself the following questions:

- Does the program fit within the mission of both the museum and the education department?
- Does the program or event relate to the collections or site?
- Do the institution, director, and board support and approve of the program?
- Who will be the target audience?
- How do I know the target audience will be interested in the program?
- What will this program accomplish for the museum?
- How will the program be funded?

Once you have satisfactorily answered these questions it is time to start planning your special event. To help you begin we have identified the major categories you must address during the planning process. We refer to them as *The Event Eight*. *The Event Eight* are itemized later in this chapter. Although every category is important for any size program, details become more complex for large special events. Attending to the details is often what makes an event seem exceptional, but do not focus on any one detail at the expense of satisfying the big-picture objectives. Look

in the appendix for the many forms that will help you create and organize any program, large or small. Because events are the most complex and serve the largest number of people, the specifics of each area will be described from an event perspective with some references to other types of programming.

SPECIAL EVENTS

Educators must keep their core audiences and repeat visitors interested in museum activities while continuing to build and attract a broader public if they wish to operate as an integral part of their community. Much like traveling or changing exhibitions, special events help to emphasize that museums are dynamic, active places where there is always something new to experience. Special events have become a popular way to enhance museum visitation. Parades, powwows, cultural celebrations, festivals, fairs, and expos are all examples of special events. Large events take a lot of thought, planning, and time to put together. Again, each museum and site has to work out its own details; you may use our diagram and time line/checklist as initial templates. Many of the large institutions may have event-planning staff; however, in smaller ones museum educators often have this responsibility and will work with the rest of the staff to coordinate events. This section includes general lists of common concerns when putting together a large event. (See Sample Form 8.2, "Event Planning Time Line/Checklist," in the appendix.) Use what is appropriate to your situation, and remember your list may include other items in addition to what is stated here.

It takes approximately one year to put together a multifaceted event for over 1,000 people, not only to allow time for proper planning, but also to secure presenters or performers and for adequate promotion. One of the first concerns is selecting the date. If your city, town, or Chamber of Commerce creates a community calendar, look that over as you choose your date and avoid a day when another major activity is going on. You may also choose to avoid holidays, unless your event is directly tied to it, such as a Fourth of July celebration. It may be especially difficult to recruit volunteers during holiday seasons and summer vacations. Consider when locals are in town, when the peak tourist season is; then choose a date that will appeal to your target audience. As soon as the date is chosen, get your event on the local and state calendars as well as the museum's calendar. Often very large events become annual affairs; therefore document the process and reserve the same date, month, or season to help your audience remember your event from year to year.

As you consider hosting a large event, you must choose between outsourcing the program and doing it in-house. Some organizations choose to hire an event planning company and turn the running of the event over to them. The company will work with your organization to develop an event that reflects your museum. There is a cost for this service, but the company will handle the event scheduling, performance contracts, details, and problems. Another option is to ask an affiliate group of the museum, such as a historical society, a guild, or an auxiliary group, to run the event. Organizing and managing the event at the museum is a third option. There will be costs regardless of what decision you make, but running the event in-house is generally the least expensive way to go. However, the enormous amount of work involved is a different cost to consider, but you will have more control. If the museum is part of a larger organization such as a city, county, university, or state, then the resources of the larger organization can be very helpful in developing, staffing, promoting, and managing the event. It is useful to create a committee comprised of only staff or with staff, volunteers, board members, and others working together to create the event. Regardless of your approach, there always needs to be staff involvement and a staff liaison to keep the information flowing between the groups and to the program chair. Museum staff is ultimately responsible for the outcome of the event and the content presented through performances and other activities. Although this chapter prepares you to plan and manage an event in-house, the information can be useful even if you work with an event company. It will help you monitor the company to see that it stays on task, on schedule, and within the budget.

THE EVENT EIGHT

Once you know you will be planning a program or special event, how do you begin? We have broken down the event-planning process into manageable parts that we call *The Event Eight*. *The Event Eight* represents broad categories of activities and responsibilities that the educator must address while planning a program, large or small. We have further divided *The Event Eight* into subcategories to provide you with more specific areas of concern. Choose the details that are appropriate to your situation and modify our checklist to make sure everything you need is included. Additionally we offer suggestions, examples, and a time line that we

---

The Event Eight

1. Safety, Security, and Liability
2. Goal(s), Objectives, and Target Audience
3. Publicity and Publicity Materials
4. Budget and Sponsors
5. Site, Supplies, and Materials
6. Staff and Volunteers
7. Performers, Celebrities, and Dignitaries
8. Evaluation

Figure 8.2. The Event Eight
Courtesy of Kimberly A. Huber and Anna Johnson

have found useful when planning educational programs. A good organizational tool is to keep all the paperwork in a notebook with section dividers for each of *The Event Eight* categories or committees. The notebook is especially helpful if the event becomes an annual program. It can be referred to while planning in subsequent years.

1. Safety, Security, and Liability

Events have many component parts that must be carefully planned and administered; however, safety can truly make or break a successful program. Safety is a primary concern not only for your visitors, but for the volunteers, staff, performers, and everyone involved with the event. Safety issues involve everything: site, transportation, people, food, beverages, activities, sanitation, emergencies, and weather. The local fire station may be willing to work with you to make sure your site is safe and that you abide by fire safety standards. If your event is to be held indoors, you should know the maximum number of people your facility can safely hold based on local fire regulations.[2] Also, exits must be clearly marked and staff and volunteers should pratice evacuation procedures prior to the event. All fire extinguishers should be working and accessible and their locations clearly marked. A first aid kit should include bandages for minor wounds, but it is best not to dispense any medicine. Some fire personnel can also serve in an emergency medical capacity.

As you ponder your security needs, consider hiring off-duty police or guards to patrol the event. Security personnel should protect equipment and offer safe transport and storage of cash. They can also deal with crowd control, fights, emergency situations, and unlawful conduct. Do not let a few problem visitors spoil your event.

Liability and insurance issues always need to be examined and dealt with from the beginning and no later than nine months out. Permits and licenses will be necessary for some vendors, street closures, alcohol, and possibly the site. As you review your insurance policy, consider these questions:

- What happens if a person is injured at the event?
- Who covers the cost of the accident?
- Will the event-planning company have its own insurance or will it be under the umbrella of the museum's policy?
- Does the support organization's insurance cover accidents at the event if it is held at the museum?

Some museums that are affiliated with a local government or university system may have a risk management department that can help with these concerns. The participating groups should discuss and put in writing how to handle insurance needs prior to the event.

You must provide a safe and secure environment for any activity or suffer the possibility of a lawsuit if someone is accidentally injured or killed, or if something is damaged. Every program has potential risks that must be weighed in proportion to the benefits. Check your insurance policy for liability coverage, and always be sure that you and your institution are protected.

I helped to coordinate a large statewide Archaeology Expo for Arizona in 1995. I was the assistant director at the Deer Valley Rock Art Center, a museum and archaeological site that was affiliated with Arizona State University. For this three-day event we needed off-site parking and lots of portable signs. The weather that weekend was extremely rainy and windy. A wind gust blew one of the metal event signs onto a visitor's parked car, causing some minor damage. I filed a university incident report to deal with the visitor's complaint. Fortunately, I had checked with the risk management office prior to the event and knew our small museum was protected through the university's policy. Talking to the visitor, collecting his information, and filing the incident report was all I needed to do to handle the problem. The university took care of it from that point on.

—Kimberly A. Huber

2. Goal(s), Objectives, and Target Audience

We cannot overstate that the planning and execution of large special events is time-consuming, costly, and labor intensive. However, some organizations become so focused on the "to-do" list for the event they forget to consider the "why." What do you hope to accomplish with your event? Perhaps just as important: What does the museum director, board, sponsor, or committee want to accomplish? Determine the goals and

The target audience of the *Tardeada,* a community event at the Tempe Historical Museum, was the local population of Mexican descent. With an annual attendance of approximately 5,000 people, the goals were to engage the local residents through identifying and organizing the historical roots of Tempe and to educate the whole community about the Hispanic culture through this celebration.

—Anna Johnson

establish objectives in consultation with them during the first month of planning.

Every successful event must accomplish at least one significant institutional goal. Although other people have defined and redefined the differences between goals and objectives, for our purposes we keep the definitions simple to make the event-planning process run smoothly and efficiently. A goal is a statement of the overall purpose of a program or event. The objectives identify the steps needed to reach each goal. The objectives should be measurable and concise. Some events may have multiple goals, but limit your goals to no more than three, which you clearly define. Do not try to attract a new audience, educate everyone, bring in income, entertain, and promote your facility all at once. Although many of these things may be desirable results, trying to satisfy a multitude of goals at any one event can often lead to doing many things poorly instead of one or two well. Measure each objective during the evaluation process (see Sample Form 8.3) to know if your event succeeded.

Identifying your event's target audience should be done in conjunction with the development of goals and objectives in the first month of planning. Educators are acutely aware that knowing the needs and wants of your audience is essential to successful programming. Each event should identify a specific audience or audiences you are hoping to reach. If you are targeting families you have to consider the needs of parents and their children, which are different from a program designed just for adults, children, or some other specific group type. For example, families will need room to navigate strollers, restrooms should include changing stations, entertainment should be appropriate for children and adults, and food and drinks should take into account sensitive and youthful palates. Events for adults may include louder music, liquor, and a need for extra security to monitor alcohol purchases and consumption and potentially disruptive behavior. If your event targets a specific cultural community, bilingual signage and ethnic foods are recommended.

Event planners need to use whatever resources they have: past event evaluations, demographics, statistical information, and learning theory to collect useful data to meet the needs of the intended audience. Following the event you must verify that you have reached your target audience. This will be discussed later in the evaluation section of this chapter.

3. Publicity and Publicity Materials

Publicity, *promotion*, *marketing*, and *advertising* are terms that are often used interchangeably, but they actually have specific meanings depending on the user. We use "publicity" in a broad sense to include promotion, marketing, and advertising in order to provide information to the public about your event. Publicity is a key program concern because it does not matter how great your event is if no one shows up. Promote your event to the target audience in a timely manner (as early as nine months out but no later than three months prior to your event). Depending on your budget, you may choose paid or public service advertisements in the press, on the radio, or on television; however, it is necessary to reach your target audience in ways that are meaningful and accessible to them. For example, if you are hosting a Cinco de Mayo festival and want to reach the Hispanic community you will need Spanish-language materials sent to local churches, media outlets, community centers, and places where Hispanics gather or shop. No matter whether you choose print or other media, you must saturate your target audience with program information on a regular basis. Good and frequent publicity attracts the target audience to your event.

Publicity materials can include a number of different components: logo, printed materials, advertising, and signage. If you are planning to use a logo for your event it needs to be chosen carefully and developed as early as nine months before the event in order to appear on all promotional materials, banners, programs, and mailers. A logo gives the promotional materials a unified look, and it will become a symbol for the event. The logo must be ready by the time you send out your first press release. The logo design should be unique and reflect the nature of the event. Your logo and event name should not violate another organization's registered trademark or copyright.[3] It may help to hire a graphic designer to aid in logo design. Once the logo is developed, then work can begin on other advertising designs. If the event is expected to be an annual occurrence, the logo becomes even more recognizable as a symbol for it. If you have

sponsors, their logos may also need to be displayed. For example, Arizona's annual museum association conference often receives free printed programs from a local utility company. The sponsor's logo is included as an acknowledgment of its support; however, the event logo is primary and should be separate from and larger than sponsor logos.

Almost any type of program you develop will have likely been tried by some other institution. Because every program had some kind of printed materials, you can benefit from other museums' experiences if you are developing promotional materials for the first time. Start by collecting publicity materials from other museums to use as examples for preparing your fliers, brochures, site maps, or other printed items. Do not copy their materials; rather, review their style and format to aid you in determining attractive and effective design. If you do not have design experience you may want to look online for graphics and figures, recruit volunteers with design experience, or hire a designer to help you with the process. Just remember that publicity must include the essential five "W's" and one "H": who, what, where, when, why, and how. The rest is up to you.

Printed materials include brochures, banners, fliers, billboards, inserts in newsletters (yours and the sponsor's), event schedule, and a map. If you mail fliers directly to your members, sponsor staff, and target audience, include a map to the event. Take the time to collect and cull your mailing list to avoid duplicates and return mail. Work with a printer and a design company or a design student who is willing to offer free printing or design services as community service or a class project. In the Phoenix metropolitan area many of the city utility bills include local-event advertising for city-run museums. There are a number of opportunities for "freebies" if you are willing to take the time to ask for them; however, acquiring free services often takes longer than purchasing materials or services, so factor in extra planning time and start early.

Set a budget for advertising, no later than nine months prior to your event, and then start making contacts with the appropriate media outlets. As you prepare your budget, find out if the museum will allocate money for paid advertising. Consider print, radio, and television media if your budget allows. Perhaps a local newspaper would be willing to be an event sponsor. Its support could include free advertising, with its art department designing the ads. Do not be afraid to contact the press to ask what kinds of ways they will publicize your event. A paid advertisement is different from a community calendar item, which is different from a news item, so you will likely need more than one press release to promote your event. After talking with the various media outlets, develop time lines for when material has to be ready for each medium and a mailing list for whom to include. Although paid ads are very useful, if you do not have an advertising budget, you can still promote your event by sending press releases. Most newspapers have a local calendar of events, especially for nonprofits, where you can list the details of your event. Television and radio stations also have a limited amount of free air time for public service announcements (PSA). Although these media outlets will not charge you to broadcast your PSA, you will still have to produce it. PSAs sometimes air very late at night or at times that will not reach your intended audience, so choose stations wisely and be strategic about spending your advertising dollars.

In some cases you may have a built-in audience. For example, if a holiday event includes a performance from a youth bell choir, family and friends will undoubtedly want to attend. Though you may not use all advertising mediums, you must let the performers and visitors know the basics about your event. Information can be sent via mail or e-mail, listed on your museum's website, and posted at the museum. You will get the best results when you promote your programs early and often.

SIGNAGE On-site signs and arrows help direct visitors and staff through the event, and prohibit entry and parking where not allowed. They should also identify separate locales such as the food court, stage, restrooms, seating, vendor entry, entertainers' access, first aid, water, and other important guest services. The signs need to be large, sturdy, weatherproof, and visible. Place banners high in order for people to see them. Each booth should identify what it is offering, such as an art activity, information, lemonade, and so on. Banners and some signs should also include the event and sponsor logos. Universally recognized symbols for male, female, handicapped restrooms, and handicapped parking can be used with or without lettering. To save on expenses, many signs can be printed in-house by using computer graphics. They can be glued, spray mounted, laminated, or otherwise attached to cardboard, foam board, or another firm backing. Make extra signs because you will not have time to make them during the event. Remember that visitor perception is important, so make everything neat, accurate, and grammatically correct.

4. Budget and Sponsors

Establish a budget within the first month of planning your event. Although many museum education programs or special events are not intended to be profitable, you do not want to overinvest time and resources if you only attract a few people. Review attendance numbers from your past programs and other similar events to set realistic expectations for attendance. If you have a maximum number you can accommodate, consider selling or giving away a limited number of tickets. When planning an event for the first time you may want to establish a formula to determine if your event will be cost-effective based on how much you are willing to pay per person: Number of people x cost per person = budget. If you have past event data to rely on, your formula might be: Cost per person = event costs divided by # of people attending. It is a very common but potentially disastrous mistake to base your budget on unrealistic figures and wind up with a much larger deficit than you had hoped.

Overall budget categories should include money the museum has set aside for the event, the costs of services and supplies necessary to run the program, projected support from sponsors, and the estimated income to be earned through admissions, fees, and a percentage of vendor sales.

Allow approximately 10 percent of the total budget for miscellaneous cost overruns.[4] During the event it is a good idea to have access to petty cash for small purchases. When preparing the budget, in-house copies, clerical support, mail, phone calls, and other administrative expenses may or may not be included. For large programs you will want to break down expense categories even further to include subcategories such as rentals, printing, performers, and so on, as well as subcategories for income. Be conservative with your income estimates and do not rely on sponsor funding without a written commitment. A computer spreadsheet is a good way to plan for and keep track of the actual event costs: Income Total – Expense Total = Total Event Profit/Loss. Many museum programs are not intended to make money, so the expenses may be greater than the income. That way educators can measure the real cost of hosting an event. See our sample budget information form 8.4 in the appendix to help you start your own event budget.

If sponsors are to be involved, it is important to start contacting and developing sponsorships during the first month of planning. A sponsor is a person, corporation, or business that helps to defray expenses or pays for a particular program, event, web project, or exhibit.[5] If the sponsors are actual event partners who share the costs, duties, and responsibilities, then it will be necessary to add them to the planning committee. Sponsors can offer a great deal to an event, but they generally want name recognition. They may ask to have their banners visible at the event, their logos included in all newspaper ads, a booth at the event, or perhaps to be listed on T-shirts or any other promotional materials. Some museums develop institutional guidelines that reflect the amount of sponsorship, exposure, how each party's name will be displayed, and what type of VIP treatment is available. If this is the case at your organization, a printed copy of the guidelines should be given to each sponsor. Other museums work with their sponsors to write a contract acknowledging the donation and what the benefits will be as a result. Remember to show all sponsors your appreciation after the event by presenting them with something meaningful such as a framed picture of their people at the event, a certificate, or a plaque, and always send a thank-you letter.

5. Site, Supplies, and Materials

Museum special events are typically held on-site, either indoors or outdoors. Because programs take place in a specific time and place, it is important to consider a multitude of location factors: space, temperature, audio/visual resources, seating, bathroom access, and the ability to provide parking and public access. Significant attention to logistical details is imperative because an uncomfortable and unsafe environment can often supersede the impact of the program and leave the participants with bad memories. If over 1,000 people are expected to attend the event, it may be necessary to get an event license or permit from local authorities. Look into this during the early planning stages (nine months out). Consider all these factors and more as you plan your program or event.

In order to determine an appropriate location for your event, consider the following logistical questions:

- How many people can the site safely accommodate?
- What type of event will it be?
- Will this be a two-hour, four-hour, all-day, or multiple-day event?
- Is there adequate parking?
- Can the streets be closed or the area secured?
- Is electrical service available at the site, or can it be brought in?

These questions are critical in determining whether to hold the event indoors or outdoors. Events for thousands of people are generally held outdoors, or in very large convention halls. Answering these questions will influence and aid your planning, including setting the date, times, and location of your event.

Once you select the site, begin to plan the event layout. For example, 5,000+ people in two hours may be very high volume, whereas 5,000+ people over two days is quite different. Use space planning software or graph paper to make it easy to calculate space dimension ratios. Measure and locate where every activity will take place along with their accompanying booths, tables, chairs, stage, and sound system. These measurements will help you determine how many and what size areas the site can hold. The site map should include:

- Entrance/exit points
- Vendors
- Food and drink booths
- Shaded areas and seating
- Information booth(s)
- Communication center
- First aid station
- Stage(s)
- Electrical outlets
- Restrooms
- Parking
- Bus access
- Activity areas
- Trash

Discussed below are some of the supplies and materials you will need for your event including booths, tables, chairs, electrical equipment, and anything else specific to your particular event.

BOOTHS Coordinating booths takes a great deal of organization. If the event is outside, it is important to consider the weather and how to keep exhibitors comfortable, shaded, and protected from the elements. Contact local rental companies for open or enclosed tents to create individual booths. Frequently booths are 10 feet by 10 feet, but check with the rental company to verify the tent/booth size. Determine what style and size booths you will need, and then consider what will fit in them such as a six-foot table and chairs or whatever else is appropriate. Using the computer or graph paper, determine how many booths you can safely accommodate, how each will be set up, and the electrical needs for each. Rental companies will set up large tents or booths and take them down. They may also be able to set up an outdoor stage and even a dance floor if necessary, all for a fee.

What will you need booths for? It is important to determine what types of activities will go on in the booths such as selling food, creating crafts, selling souvenirs, or information sharing. Will vendors be charged for them? Some museums charge vendors for the booths to recoup some of the cost of renting the tents, chairs, and tables. Other museums might require a percentage of the overall sales, whereas others do not charge vendors at all. If you are going to charge it may be easier to charge based on price per size of booth rather than trying to keep track of and calculate vendor sales.

Food booths will likely need tables and chairs and a separate area for visitors to sit and eat, plenty of trash containers, and someone to empty them periodically. Even if food vendors sell drinks, plan to have at least one booth for water and other drinks to prevent long waits in food lines. Some food and information booths have additional considerations. Food vendors often need to be close to electrical outlets. Do you group them all together or spread them out throughout the whole event? Be sure to set a limit for how many food booths you need at the event because all will want to make money. The food vendors will also need a special food handler's license or permit to prepare and sell food. Check your local health inspection and food service laws (city and state) to prevent problems. It is also a good idea to find out what equipment the vendors will be bringing and what their power needs will be. If cooking is part of food preparation, you may need to have fire extinguishers or some other type of fire suppression on hand. Check with your local fire department to see what it requires for fire safety and proper disposal of cooking oils.

INFORMATION BOOTH The information booth can be a central place to coordinate activities. If placed by the entrance to the event, the information booth can supply visitors with programs and maps, volunteers can sign in and out, staff can check in, newspaper reporters can find representatives to interview, and it might otherwise serve as command central. Depending on the size of the event, this booth may also serve as a lost and found area or any other number of functions. For very large events with multiple entrances, you may need more than one information center. For smaller events, the people in the booth might also collect admissions. If collecting money, have plenty of bill denominations to make change, and it is also helpful to be able to ac-

cept credit cards. Large amounts of money should be collected frequently and safeguarded throughout the event. Keep an event information notebook or two as a reference guide so booth staff can answer any questions, and have several people scheduled for each shift. Finally, if the information booth is used as a central communication point, walkie-talkies or some other form of instant communication will be necessary for all key staff. Fast and effective communication before, during, and after an event can be handled with walkie-talkies, two-way radios, phones, or some other means to talk to other staff members. Walkie-talkies have become fairly inexpensive to purchase or rent and are a necessary part of any event.

FIRST AID BOOTH Some large events may require on-duty medics. Ask your local fire department to send people on-site to provide minor medical services. Provide a place for them to set up and be available to help anyone in need. Check with the local city or county authority to see what first aid service is required.

STAGE AND SOUND SYSTEM Events with performers, speakers, or entertainment will need to have a stage, sound, and speaker system set up in advance and sometimes during the event as performers rotate. Although musicians usually want to bring their own sound system, an independent audio system can be very useful. Musicians can still bring their own equipment, but your microphone and audio system will then be available during the time between performers. It can also be used for backup if the performer's equipment fails. In fact, extra lights, bulbs, batteries, and similar items are a must. If there is only one performer for the event, it is much easier to coordinate the audio requirements than if the performers change several times, but it is often not as interesting for the visitors. If you have multiple performers, allow plenty of time between them for setup and takedown. A covered stage is necessary for daytime events. It may be too hot for the performers and equipment without one and will help to protect against inclement weather, day or night.

ELECTRICAL NEEDS The food booths will need power, as will the stage and sound system. Find out what other booths may need electricity. Will the site be able to handle all the power requests? You may need to consult an electrician to verify that you will have adequate power. There may also be a need for additional lighting, especially for an evening event. A good electrician should be able to resolve all of these concerns. Electrical expertise will need to be available for the entire event in case of problems, power outages, overloads, or simply to resolve connectivity issues.

TOILETS Survey the site to determine how many bathrooms there are and map their locations. If you need more, order portable toilets, including handicapped stalls. Rental companies can tell you how many stalls are needed based on the number of expected visitors. Consider more toilet facilities for women and include family restrooms if possible. Determine where they will be placed, but be mindful of privacy, odors, accessibility, and ease of cleaning and placement. Good signage is a must.

PARKING Parking is an important consideration for any program that attracts more than your normal amount of visitors. You must consider not only the number of available spaces but their location in proximity to the event. The public will need to walk safely to the activities, or you will need to arrange bus or shuttle service. How many handicapped spaces will you need, and where can they be located to make the event accessible to the mobility impaired? Entertainers, especially musicians, need a place close to the stage to unload and load their equipment. That will often be done in the middle of the event if there are a number of bands performing. Also, designate places for vendors to unload and load near their booths. Sponsor or VIP parking, if you have it, needs to be located close to the event. Remember staff and volunteers will also need reserved parking nearby. Parking signs, traffic cones, barriers, and tape to mark off special parking or loading areas are necessary supplies for all special events.

DIRECTING TRAFFIC It is a good idea to bring in trained people to direct traffic. Experienced volunteers or off-duty police can be used to help direct traffic. Perhaps there are high school students who work with the local police, such as the Explorer Scouts, who can assist. Concerns include crossing busy streets to get to the event, multiple parking lots, and moving people safely to and from the event. To accommodate lots of people you may have to use off-site parking. In that case, consider running shuttles from outlying parking lots to the event and back. If you have an orientation DVD or other museum-produced DVDs, consider showing them on the shuttle. Many participants will not have time to truly enjoy all that your museum has to offer during the event, so you might want to use the shuttle time as an opportunity to educate them. Well-produced information can entice first-time visitors to return for an extended visit. If you hire buses and drivers, they may come with their own liability insurance, but you will need to review their coverage along with your own. As you map the site, leave room for emergency equipment to get through.

PUBLIC BUS SYSTEM If a city bus system serves the area near your event, consider tying in with it to meet your transportation needs. Perhaps it would bring people to the event free for the day, especially if your institution is part of the local government. Public transportation can also be a great place to advertise. Promoting the use of local bus services can also help alleviate parking demands.

MAP Developing a good working map of the site will be invaluable. It can facilitate the placement and number of booths, stage, activities, parking, electrical outlets, bathrooms, water, and many other considerations. The map can be used to provide directions to participants, and it should be passed out to the attendees as they enter and be available at the information booth. Maps are very helpful to the people doing the booth setup, electrical placement, and to other support services. Vendors, staff, entertainers, and volunteers should receive a site map in advance of the event. Highlighting or marking the specific location where vendors and staff will be located will expedite their setup on the day of the event.

SETUP/TAKEDOWN When will the event be set up? Often for large events, the setup will need to start one or two days in advance. If tents are needed, streets are closed, and special parking areas are designated, overnight security may be necessary. Takedown is just as important as setup. Make sure you plan to have enough people and time to return the site to the same condition it was in before you started. You will be charged by the day for the booths, tables, and many other items, so be prepared to have them returned in a timely manner to prevent unnecessary costs. It is often easy to recruit enthusiastic volunteers to set up your event, but after working all day or over several days they may be reluctant to help with the teardown. If possible, include this service as part of your event booth, stage, or tent budget. If this is cost-prohibitive, consider asking some volunteers to only assist with cleanup, so at least some of your workers will be "fresh" for this duty.

TRASH For events, bring in extra large trash cans or bins and space them all around the site, especially in food and bathroom areas. This will help to keep the site pristine. Have someone responsible for checking and emptying trash cans several times during the event, especially the ones by food booths. You may also want to have volunteers pick up litter or have the area cleaned each night. Plastic gloves and/or trash pickers should be provided to the people responsible for cleanup. Visitors respond better to a clean and sanitary environment. A tidy site might encourage them to be neat too.

GOLF CART If your event covers a large area, you will quickly wear yourself out by repeatedly walking the entire site. Although it may sound like a luxury, renting a golf cart or two to provide quick and easy transportation for key staff is very helpful and well worth the cost. These carts can also help you deliver ice, small equipment, and supplies where needed. Add a golf cart or two to your budget or borrow one from a volunteer or sponsor. You will not regret it.

6. Staff and Volunteers

We use staffing here in the broadest sense: museum staff, event staff, volunteers, vendors, and anyone who will be working during the event. Staffing needs should be discussed throughout the planning process beginning as early as six months out. The project manager should limit himself or herself to hospitality and troubleshooting and should never be committed to a station or time slot. Part of the event-planning process should include the training for the staff and volunteers. Everyone must be clear about their roles and responsibilities and where to find the answers to their questions before, during, and after the event. Approximately one week prior to the event hold a walk-through, site maps in hand, for everyone who will be working. This will help people visualize the site layout. For large events an information packet should be prepared and distributed before the walk-through. Include a site map, rules, event description, important names and phone numbers, and copies of any printed materials that the event staff will need. Below we have listed some additional things to consider when staffing your event.

VOLUNTEERS Participating in special events is an excellent way to effectively employ those volunteers who do not want to go through the intensity of docent training but do want to contribute time to your museum. Volunteers are essential to the success of big events. They can be used to provide all manner of assistance. Volunteers might help vendors and exhibitors carry their things to their assigned booths, assist with setup or teardown, direct parking, staff the water and information stations, and so on. Consider students, business sponsors, or tour guides as possible volunteers. If volunteers are there for any length of time, have a place for them to rest, make phone calls, get supplies, and store their personal belongings. Their rest area should be private and away from the public if at all possible. Complimentary food, drinks, and snacks are always welcome. At the very minimum, you must provide water, lots of water, for all volunteers. There is no such thing as too much water!

RUNNER Designate one or two people whose sole responsibility is to be a runner for supplies, equipment, or whatever else may be needed.[6] This person must also have petty cash. No matter how well you have planned your event, unforeseen circumstances may arise where something extra is needed. Make sure the runner has access to communication, transportation, and supply keys so that he or she won't have to get assistance or permission to retrieve the needed items.

PHOTOGRAPHER Documenting your event can be useful for a variety of purposes. You may wish to hire a photographer, select a staff member, or assign a volunteer to take pictures throughout the event, but the pictures must be of good quality. These pictures can be used for public relations, media exposure, or newsletters. If a portrait view image of a minor is taken, release forms will need to be signed by a parent or caregiver to use the photograph. If you are expecting the media, especially to document celebrity performers or VIPs, send them a media information packet in advance. The packet should include the event schedule, parking information, site map, and contact person to assist them. Notify the media where to enter the event, and direct all staff to contact the project manager or media relations person once the media have arrived.

7. Performers, Celebrities, and Dignitaries

PERFORMERS AND CELEBRITIES Choosing and hiring performers can be challenging. Remember to use the goals of the event as a guide to selecting your performers. High-profile celebrities should be contacted as early as one year in advance. Contracts need to be signed, and then arrangements for payment must be made. Performers rarely come in costume, so a dressing room near the stage is important. If the performer/artist does not mention sale of their merchandise (e.g., books, recorded material, posters) you should approach the subject to (1) make sure you have an extra table available for this purpose and (2) make certain there is not an issue with your museum store if the performer sells his or her own merchandise independently. If the event is outdoors, consider which direction the stage faces, and try to keep both the performers and attendees from looking into the sun during performances. Shade and protection from the elements may be essential at some times of the year or in certain parts of the country.

DIGNITARIES You will want to give special recognition and treatment to local dignitaries, such as government officials, sponsors, the museum director, or anyone who is speaking at the event. Sponsors may want to present awards or provide an emcee. Write out the schedule for the day to give to the emcee, so he or she will know what is happening and when. Also, if there are announcements you want the emcee to make, provide them in writing. Choose your emcee carefully, as he or she will represent the "feeling" of the event. Certain speakers or celebrity performers may require additional security.

8. Evaluation

During the planning process it is important to define what success is in order to know if you attained it. In other words, did you meet your original goals and target audience? One way to measure your success is to create an evaluation form or comment card for the event attendees to fill out. Ask specific questions that will help you evaluate your goals. For example, if you want to know about specific performers, you may choose to ask your visitors to rate the quality of the entertainment on a scale of one to five. Always ask for suggestions or comments for future events/ activities. If you were targeting a new audience, ask them if they are visiting your event or museum for the first time, and collect the demographic information you need to discern this. You might consider giving away coded "two-for-one" passes that when collected will identify return visitors. The passes could also include a brief questionnaire. Do not discount personal observations, and be certain to create notes based on your reactions for your file a day or two after the event. These notes can be for your eyes only if you choose. As a novice event planner do not be too hard on yourself if you fall short on some goals. Instead make notes and discuss problems during the debriefing meeting. Use this valuable information to improve your event in future years. (For additional information about evaluation see Chapter 10 in this text.)

A debriefing meeting with your planning committee and staff is essential and should be held within one week following the event. Critique what went well and what needs to be done differently. The debriefing session is also a time to celebrate a successful event. The event manager should begin and end the meeting, thank the participants for their efforts, and recognize exemplary performance. A number of authors offer a series of postevent

questions to be asked. Bill J. Harrison, CFRE, a nationally recognized fund-raiser, has compiled 10 Questions to Ask *After* Your Special Event (Sample Form 8.3); Darcy Campion Devney's book *Organizing Special Events and Conferences: A Practical Guide for Busy Volunteers and Staff* offers her list of "Common Evaluation Questions";[8] and Carter McNamara recommends eight questions to ask when conducting a goal-based evaluation.[9] These lists can help you develop your own questions to determine if you met your event goals, managed the program well, identified problems, and stayed within your budget. At the meeting, compile a list of names and addresses of people to thank who helped along the way. Each committee member can write their own thank-you note, which includes a special note from the event manager or museum director. This meeting is also a time to discuss outstanding bills and review the budget so revisions can be made for the next large event. If digital photographs are available, the committee might review them to select images for use in-house, by the media, or to be sent to sponsors. Minutes of the debriefing meeting should be taken, distributed, and saved.

When I managed large events, I often found it useful to prepare a short summary report. I used the report for several purposes. It was included in my monthly or yearly report, sent to sponsors and interested participants, and used for postevent publicity for museum publications and the press. The report was included in the event notebook and reviewed when another similar event was planned. If the event was an annual one, the report was available to the planning committee to review along with the evaluations from the previous years to help them plan the next event.

—Kimberly A. Huber

You now have *The Event Eight* to help you begin your program planning, but know that your event may include other parts that do not neatly fit into these eight categories. Some events have a special party the night before the actual event to celebrate and to thank the sponsors, special performers, participants, donors, and those who helped create and organize the event. This minievent can require a caterer, renting tables, chairs, sound system, invitations, decorations, and whatever else might be needed. Another option is a postevent VIP party to celebrate the event's success and thank sponsors. Sometimes organizations develop an exhibit or a series of classes, programs, or activities to generate interest in the theme of the large-

At the Deer Valley Rock Art Center we hosted the Archaeology Expo as part of the State Historic Preservation Office's annual event. Museums, parks, and archaeological sites around the state sponsored their own activities throughout the month and all promoted the three-day statewide expo at our site.

—Kimberly A. Huber

scale event. This works especially well if connections with the community's library and recreation programs can be made, for example. Their related activities can supplement the primary event. Just make sure to have promotional flyers to pass out at each activity and organization.

For events with a theme, such as connecting to community history, a museum may also have a special exhibit related to the event. For example, the Tempe Historical Museum had an event related to Hispanic history. Members of the Hispanic community came to the museum and created family albums with support from the museum. Then these albums were exhibited at the *Tardeada* event.

So far in this chapter we have included tips and suggestions for planning your event. However, you will likely run into minor problems, changes, or surprises somewhere along the way. When you do, do not panic—some problems are to be expected. What you want to avoid are disasters or catastrophes. To prevent major problems you should consider the following: How soon before the event can it be canceled or postponed due to weather? How will you get this message to the public? What is the alternative to cancellation? Can the event be pulled indoors in case of inclement weather? What is the consequence or alternative for paid ticket holders?

If you accept a position as a museum educator, you will likely develop new programs, but you may also be responsible for preexisting educational activities as well. Many events or programs are done year after year because they have brought in people. Sometimes organizations repeat events without assessing the value of these activities. Institutions can find themselves in the position of being event-focused rather than goal- and outcome-focused. Educators should take an annual educational inventory to see if what you are doing is still needed, continues to fit the mission, is cost-effective, and accomplishes the educational goals. A good time to assess an event or program is after it has been completed. If the program has low attendance, costs more than it brings in, or does not meet institutional or educational goals, it is

appropriate to question whether or not it should be repeated. This information along with any recommendations for changes should be included in the evaluation final report.

In 1994 I worked at the Mesa Southwest Museum. This midsize, city-run museum sponsored the Indian Pow-Wow, a three-day event that drew over 20,000 people each year. After hosting the ever-growing event for more than 10 years, we realized that it had become too large to hold on-site and required so much time, staffing, and money that some of the museum employees dreaded it. At one debriefing meeting, I remember asking the question, "Do we still want to host the Pow-Wow?" My question was met by a stunned silence. I'm not sure anyone had ever asked that before. After the shock wore off, the staff agreed that the event had become bigger than what we could reasonably manage. It was really more appropriate to locate the event at a large park and include other city departments to help with the planning, promoting, and managing. Although it was difficult to let go of this project, ultimately the PowWow was made into a citywide event, drawing even larger crowds. However, significant citywide cutbacks in 2005 put an end to this special event. Even though the PowWow brought thousands of people to this unique cultural celebration, city management deemed it too costly to continue.

—Kimberly A. Huber

CONCLUSION

So, what can you learn from our experiences? All educators have limited resources to perform their job functions, no matter what the size of the institution. They must measure the cost of the activity—the staff and resources needed—against the number of visitors served and the ability to meet institutional goals. Tough choices need to be made to ensure that an institution maximizes its resources to serve the broadest public, meets the goals of its educational programs, and serves the museum's mission. We should all strive for excellence and quality over quantity in museum educational programming. The blank pyramid form, sample time line, and budget template in the appendix will help you with your planning. Review our Important Things to Consider (Textbox 8.1), add anything else specific to your event, and make sure you have included everything in your checklist. Revise each sample form to fit your event's needs. Work backward from the date of your event to see when you need to begin each phase of your planning and create your own time line. Use check boxes to indicate when each item has been completed. With good planning, good organizational skills, attention to detail, and a strong commitment from your staff and volunteers, your event can meet its educational goals while providing a safe and pleasant environment for your participants and visitors. That's when you know you have a successful program or event.

Textbox 8.1. Important Things to Consider

Maps, signs, banners
Directions
Tables, chairs, fencing
Booths, tents, canopies, decorations
Audio/visual/lighting equipment
Sufficient and safe power sources
Bathrooms
Food and beverages—necessary permits
Parking, barricades, closure permits
Media
Fire, police, security, setup, cleaning needs, inspections, and requirements
Communication equipment
Garbage/trash needs
First aid
Information
Lawn watering schedule
Special insurance
Proofread everything at least twice
Have extra light bulbs, batteries, extension cords, etc.
Needs of the disabled

NOTES

1. Adapted from National Park Service, "Glossary," U.S. Department of the Interior 2007, /home.nps.gov/applications/budget2/glossary.htm (June 12, 2007).
2. Darcy Campion Devney, *Organizing Special Events and Conferences: A Practical Guide for Busy Volunteers and Staff* (Sarasota, Fla.: Pineapple Press, Inc., 1990), 37.
3. Devney, *Organizing Special Events*, 11.
4. Devney, *Organizing Special Events*, 26; and Robert C. Price, Notes to Kim Huber, April 23, 2007.
5. www.merriam-webster.com.
6. Robert C. Price, Notes to Kim Huber, April 2, 2007.
7. Bill J. Harrison, *10 Questions to Ask after Your Special Event*, www.iteachfundraising.com/articles/10questions.html (June 13, 2007).
8. Devney, *Organizing Special Events*, 22.
9. Carter McNamara, "Basic Guide to Program Evaluation," adapted from the *Field Guide to Nonprofit Program Design, Marketing and Evaluation, 1997–2007*, www.managementhelp.org/evaluatn/fnl_eval.htm (June 7, 2007).

CHAPTER 9

Education Online

TIM GROVE

> Museum educators need to be keenly attuned to their audience. Having only a matter of seconds to engage their viewer, they must be unique, concise, and expedient in order to create continued interest and exploration to deeper levels of educational understanding.
>
> —*Larry Warner, museum curator, Pueblo Grande Museum and Archaeological Park*

When the Internet burst into public use in the mid-1990s, museums and other cultural agencies joined the rest of the world in trying to figure out the nature of this new technology and whether it was around for good. The technology landscape is ever changing, and there is never a guarantee that the public will embrace a new innovation. The first Museums and the Web Conference was held in 1997 and brought together a group of visionaries who already foresaw that this new medium was unique and would bring big change for museums.[1] Today, more than a decade later, no museum, whatever its size, can afford to ignore the Internet. In the minds of younger generations, if your organization doesn't have a presence online, then it doesn't exist. The Internet is here to stay.

From its outset, the Internet has raised many questions and challenges for museums. From initial questions of how the availability of online materials would impact on-site visitation, to questions of who has the responsibility for online operations within an organizational chart, to the complex issues of online copyright and permissions, there will always be issues to ponder. And as technology matures, it changes. Like all media, the Web medium, even in its short life span, has already seen trends, and change is guaranteed. The current popularity of Web 2.0, discussed later in this chapter, is raising more questions, and Web 3.0 is on the horizon.

The responsibility for online efforts varies greatly from organization to organization. Smaller museums may contract with outside firms to design and maintain their websites. Most larger organizations have dedicated staff to develop and produce their websites. The Web staff is usually focused on the technical aspect and rarely produces content. The direction of an organization's website is often set by the director or top administrators. Within an organization there can often be tension over whether the site is a tool for marketing or education or research. Whatever its major focus, a museum's website should be seen as an extension of its on-site presence. Most of the major functions of a museum are usually represented online. To the extent that museum education staff members contribute to these varied functions, they can and should also contribute to these efforts online.

Generally the evolution of websites has followed a basic pattern, though sometimes the pattern involves several phases at once. First, museums want to establish an online presence—a marketing tool to essentially say, "We are here; come visit." The marketing stage is followed by efforts to share the collections with constituents. This stage has resulted in the abundance of online databases and search tools. From libraries to archives to museums, organizations are in the process of digitizing collections. The next phase seems to focus on education. Once the collections are available, the educators work with content experts to develop materials and tools to provide greater understanding of the collections. Museum educators should have knowledge of the Web medium, its strengths and limitations. They should keep current on Internet trends and, as always, know the audience.

DEFINING THE AUDIENCE

With the Web, knowing the audience is not as easy as one might think. While it is readily apparent who comes through the doors to view an exhibition or participate in a program, the Internet audience can seem like a faceless unknown. In face-to-face environments, educators can respond to various cues about the learner's knowledge, interest, and ability. We do not have that luxury when designing online learning components, so we must find other ways to anticipate how learners will respond to our materials. This is one of the challenges that educators face.

Just as many different audiences visit a museum on any given day, the same is true for a museum's website. Thus certain components of the site will be targeted to different ages, different interest levels, and different agendas. Teachers may expect curriculum materials, researchers may want access to a database with specific information about your collections, families may want information to plan a visit, or children may be looking for something fun to engage in online.

Who is using the Internet? In 2007 the Pew Internet and American Life Project reported that 71 percent of Americans use the Internet, and the number is increasing every year. Not surprisingly, 87 percent of people ages 18–29 use the Internet versus 32 percent of people ages 65 and older.[2] According to the Pew Project, "The Web has become the 'new normal' in the American way of life; those who don't go online constitute an ever-shrinking minority."[3] Beginning in the mid-1990s, there was a big push to provide Internet access to every student across America. The United States Department of Education statistics reveal that 100 percent of U.S. schools provide Internet access.[4] Does this mean teachers are using the Internet? Early on in my experience with developing Web activities, it became clear from talking with teachers that access to the Internet was not their challenge. Instead, the challenge was having the time to learn about the medium and finding time to fit it into the curriculum. In the 1990s many teachers were frustrated by pressure from their schools to use the Internet, with little training in how to do this.

By now, the Internet has become a staple in the classroom. Yet, the question is no longer "Are people using the Internet?" but "How are people using the Internet?" Evaluating Web use even on the most basic level has proven a challenge. How do people use the Internet and why? There are quantitative tools to track use—page "hits" and downloads are two examples of numbers that are easy to tabulate. There are programs such as WebTrends that can do this. While quantity is a helpful statistic to obtain, quality is even more helpful but more elusive. If your specific interest group is teachers, it is important to know how they are using the Internet. If your goal is to produce Web activities that are useful to teachers and students, you need to know how people learn online. A recent study looked at the influence of learning style, gender, and age on preference for computer-based educational activities. It concluded that Web developers need to consider the spectrum of learning styles when designing online materials. It also concluded that children place great emphasis on a Web activity's "play" value—whether role-play games or those where the user designs or creates something.[5] Studies like this that measure user preference are valuable to those of us who create online materials. More studies that assess actual learning are needed, and museum professionals should take the lead in conducting their own research.

THE UNIQUE QUALITIES OF THE WEB

In order for museum educators to develop effective online learning materials, they need to have an understanding of the qualities of the medium. What are the Web's strengths? It is important to understand the Internet medium for what it is and is not. It is a unique medium that is not a book, an audiovisual or film, or exhibition. Not unlike an exhibition, it can combine text, images, film, and audio into an engaging presentation. But a virtual exhibition is very different from a physical exhibition. In 1998 Janet Murray wrote that "the computer presents us with the spatial mosaic of the newspaper page, the temporal mosaic of film, and the participatory mosaic of TV remote control."[6] She continued by saying that the computer—and I would add specifically the Internet—offers new ways to master fragmentation. Fragmentation refers to the ways the information chunks are organized and the user's ability to direct paths through the information. At its essence, the Internet is both a communication tool and a seemingly limitless source of information. But its structure allows the user to access information in a different way. It allows for a layering of information and linking of information unlike other media. The user can construct his own learning by going exactly where he wants to go, staying as long as he wants, and often getting sidetracked for the sheer enjoyment of "surfing the Web." You go online with the intent to find out how to build a birdhouse, but you end up researching vacation villas in Tuscany and buying a sofa on craigslist.

One of the best features of the Web is the degree of flexibility it offers. In many ways the nature of the Web is fluidity. Staff can update or change information at any time. They can do technical changes (substitute a better image or updated video), text changes (use a different phrase or update information), and add new features to an existing site—like updates on conservation efforts, podcasts of public programs, or visitor/user feedback. There are numerous ways to keep users returning to the site. An online exhibition can be changed to reflect recent research, add a new acquisition, or highlight a special program. The virtual record of an exhibition usually outlasts the physical component. Often when a museum develops a substantial online exhibition, it will keep it online long after the physical exhibition has closed. Thus the Web can extend the life of an exhibition, especially one that is temporary due to short-term loans from other institutions.

ONLINE EXHIBITIONS

An example of an online educational component is the online exhibition, now a standard feature of most museum websites. Educators who have been on an exhibition development team should stay involved in the development of online materials. As with the physical exhibition, the educator plays an important role in stressing active rather than passive experiences, the inclusion of Web activities, accessibility to users with a variety of technology capabilities, and the layering of information. The educators should lead the team in a discussion of the intended audiences. If teachers are included in the list of audiences, it is necessary to clarify how you envision teachers using the site. Will you develop special materials for them?

An effective online exhibition takes advantage of the strengths of the medium. Some online exhibitions are based on physical exhibitions; some are created solely as a virtual exhibition. Developing an online version of a physical exhibition provides an opportunity to think about that exhibition in a different way. For exhibitions with extended periods of development, the online work usually happens after the team has completed the physical exhibition planning. For exhibitions with short development time, the work often happens simultaneously. The most important point for the team to recognize is that because the Web is a unique medium, team members must think very differently about the online version.[7] Not only is it possible to change or add content, but it is possible to increase both physical and intellectual access. Additional content can include images, objects, video footage, or other materials that got cut from the physical exhibition because of space limitations. This does not mean that the space becomes a dumping ground for everything the physical space could not contain. Links to scholarly articles or a historian's notes used to form the interpretation are other ways to provide deeper layers of information. With careful planning and design, the online version can both enhance and supplement a visit to the physical space.

An exhibition can face many limitations that do not apply to an online exhibition. These include the challenges of limited space, low light levels due to conservation concerns, and barriers that limit close inspection due to security concerns. There are numerous ways to increase access to online sources. Web designers are taking advantage of zoom tools and are creating sites that allow the user to examine primary source materials and art in amazing ways. For example, the site www.dohistory.org features Maine midwife Martha Ballard's diary from the late 1700s and early 1800s. A "magic lens" feature on the site allows the user to read the diary's challenging script through a lens that transcribes the words into type. A map that may be hard to read in the low light of an exhibition can be totally accessible online. It makes no sense to put images of objects or documents online unless they are readable and can be studied. I once received an e-mail from a person in another state in reference to an online exhibition I had developed. She was very complimentary about the site, but two lines caught my attention: "I am a lover of museums and art and never thought of how much I could see by going onto the various Web sites. The pictures are better than being there." She followed that statement by writing that she would definitely visit the exhibition when it traveled to her city. This statement showed how the Internet can enhance the study of a museum's collections at home and also drive traffic to the museum itself.

An online exhibition allows the team to think outside the limits of a physical space and create a totally different layout. The strongest online exhibitions provide multiple entry points and layered information. Recognizing the differing interest levels that users will have in a given topic should impact the way designers present the information. One way to organize information is to provide layers targeted to different

I worked on the online version of Lewis & Clark: The National Bicentennial Exhibition. The site features three main layers: a layer with entry points through the physical exhibition's nine themes (women, trade and property, language, and others), a map-based narrative layer for people who want to follow the expedition in chronological sequence, and a database of all of the objects and documents in the exhibition—for researchers and those people with a deep interest in the topic. The site ended up including much material that did not fit into the physical version due mostly to space limitations. The team collected some thought-provoking film footage of our Native American advisors talking about the impact of Lewis and Clark on tribal nations today. This footage is peppered throughout the website, making for an enriching online experience. We also created a component called "connections to today," a series of interviews with different people today who discuss issues related to each of the major exhibition themes.

—Tim Grove

audiences. The amount of detail per layer will differ. For example, every topic will have an audience that wants to know detailed information while some people may be interested more in images and less information. One layer could organize information around themes. These themes may or may not reflect the conceptual organization of the physical space. Thus, the best online exhibitions take a layered approach, where users can go deeper into more extensive information if they choose.

Another strength of the Web is its ability to illustrate multiple perspectives and change over time. The capability of providing unlimited links to additional information makes the Web very suitable for historical and cultural sites especially when they want to provide several perspectives on a historic event or even an artwork. Information about a piece of art can include the artist's perspective of why she created the work, the collector's perspective of why he collected the work, the curator's perspective of why it's important, and other perspectives such as that of a teacher or student. A zoo site can feature video footage of an animal such as a polar bear in the wild, sketches of the animal, audio clips of the animal, and textual descriptions from field notes describing behavior. Change over time can be illustrated effectively by layering visual information, whether maps or photos or illustrations.

OUTREACH POTENTIAL

The Internet has the power to affect outreach in ways unlike other mediums. Anyone with Internet access around the world can view your website at any time of day. While an online presence does not automatically guarantee traffic to your site, it is the potential that is important to consider. The staff of a historic site with enduring interest, such as Thomas Jefferson's home, Monticello, can reach millions of people who may not be able to travel to Virginia but will visit the website. Every American student at some point in his study will learn about Thomas Jefferson. This potential audience provides an opportunity for Monticello educators to present the latest research about Jefferson to people across America and around the world. All historical societies and sites have stories within their collections that connect to broader themes in American history. If you find a story that resonates beyond your general audience, the Web increases your potential audience greatly. Sometimes a movie or television show with widespread release may feature a topic that connects with your museum or site. If you can anticipate this and create related content for your website, the result may be a teaching moment with wide impact.

REACHING YOUNG AUDIENCES

Younger generations have been raised with computer and video games and are used to having access to information at the touch of a button. In order to engage these audiences we must find ways to connect to them. Museums have been developing online educational activities since the beginning of the Internet. I remember developing the Smithsonian National Museum of American History's first Web activity, "You Be the Historian," in 1997. We called it an "activity" rather than a "game" to avoid diminishing it as an educational tool. We wanted to see if it was possible to adapt what was designed as a hands-on experience in the museum's Hands On History Room to the Web medium. Would the experience lose its appeal without the tactile component? We studied other online activities and held a teacher focus group to discuss how such an activity could be used and to critique examples of what was currently available. There were obvious changes that we had to make. We substituted photographs for the objects. Our questioning strategies changed somewhat, and we ended up adding a layer of text and images. We also tested it with visitors to the museum. The effort taught us a valuable and enduring lesson that educational activities are adaptable from one medium to another, but it requires a different way of thinking and an understanding of how the Web medium is different.

In the past ten years online educational games and activities have evolved into much more sophisticated and visually engaging experiences. Museums of all kinds have experimented with online activities targeted to younger audiences and designed to deliver content in a fun way. Most Web developers understand that if you don't draw the user into an activity in a few seconds, he will quickly move on to another page. Dave Schaller, an educational media developer, reports that "digital games have become a primary preoccupation for most young people and many adults, making this an exciting arena in which museums can develop new audiences."[8] Schaller explains that, "In a digital game, we can re-create the rules of nature and society in a virtual world that puts artifacts back in their historical context. Such games let the content drive the game play, in contrast to the simple games that populate many museum Web sites." Many museum educators already use traditional games as tools to teach younger audiences in their galleries. Educators should assess the pedagogical tools they are already using and consider adapting them to the digital world.

Schaller notes the research of Thomas Malone and Mark Lepper and the distinction they make between games that are placed in a specific context and thus require the player to have a knowledge base in order to successfully play versus games where the context is irrelevant to the player's ability to play the game. An example of the former is a role-play game like *The Oregon Trail*, because the player's success in navigation requires knowledge of the time period. Examples of the latter include popular games like crossword puzzles, memory, or hangman. Plug in words or images related to your collection and you have an instant activity.[9]

It is important for museum educators to understand the parameters of quality and effective online learning. It is also important to be aware that funding sources are available. Most federal funding agencies for the humanities and sciences recognize the value of funding educational Web projects and thus make funds available for such projects. New technology is also making digital games more affordable.[10]

USABILITY

Just as visitor testing is absolutely necessary when developing interactives for exhibitions, testing is also crucial when developing materials for the Web. Because of the complex layering of information online, navigation can be a major challenge for the user. Usability testing is a term that refers to assessing how "user-friendly" a site is. This kind of testing is easy and fun to do. Here is a tried and true process as demonstrated year after year at the Museums and the Web Conference.

1. First determine a list of items you want someone to find on your site or tasks you want him to complete. Items to find could include information about hours, school materials, a specific artwork, publication or program, or a historical fact presented somewhere on the site. Tasks to complete could include registering for a particular program, planning a school visit, or finding information about a specific item in the collection.

2. Next, recruit users and ask them to locate the items on your list, talking out loud as they think through their process of searching for the items. The key is to make sure you hear what they are thinking as they navigate the site. This think-out-loud approach reveals a wealth of information and often results in changes to the site. The bottom line is that not all people think like the site's designer, and what is intuitive to one person is not necessarily intuitive to another person.

As always, museum educators should advocate for accessible website design. It is important to encourage Web programmers and designers to think about all audiences and especially those using older technologies. There are a variety of websites that provide suggestions for how to make sites accessible.[11]

NEW TRENDS

Time magazine's Person of the Year for 2006 was "You"—the many Internet users in the world who are transforming the fabric of the Web into personal social commentaries, online communities, and personal collections to share with fellow Internet users. The magazine called this social media trend a "revolution."[12] Web 2.0, according to Wikipedia, "refers to a perceived second generation of web-based communities and hosted services . . . which facilitate collaboration and sharing between users."[13] It gives users more opportunity to create their own Web content and offers greater potential to interact with others in the digital world. Wikipedia, the online encyclopedia, is a good example of this new social medium. It is written collaboratively, and anyone with access to a computer can contribute to entries. Created in 2001, Wikipedia has grown into one of the Web's largest reference sites. Other examples of social media include MySpace, Facebook, and YouTube.

What does the emergence of social media mean for museums? There seem to be two main challenges. One is amateur involvement in content, and the other is protection of digital content. A 2001 American

Association of Museums survey on public trust and various information sources revealed that Americans trust museums over other sources of information such as books and television news. The dilemma for museums becomes one of weighing that public trust with the addition of amateur voices. Matthew MacArthur, web director at the Smithsonian's National Museum of American History, asks these questions: "How is that trust impacted if users are allowed to have a greater voice on our websites and even in our galleries? What is the proper relationship between professional experts and amateur enthusiasts?"[14] We will need to carefully consider how much involvement with content production we are willing to give to our visitors and website users. With more users than ever creating their own website and blogs, and borrowing images and music from other sites online, should museums be concerned with controlling their online digital content? The proponents of this increased online self-expression see many advantages and the potential for greater online learning in new ways. Of course other Internet trends will follow, and ultimately it is crucial for museum educators to stay aware of such trends.

ELECTRONIC OUTREACH

An increasing number of museums are using the Internet and other technologies to extend their programming reach. *Distance Learning Education* is an umbrella term for content-driven programs delivered via the Web, satellite, or videoconference and designed to offer students or other audiences learning opportunities they would not otherwise experience.

Several types of programming generally fall into this category.[15]

WEBCAST The delivery of live or delayed sound or video broadcasts using web technologies. The sound or video is captured by conventional video or audio systems. It is then digitized and streamed on a web server.

- Strengths: Can be accessed at any time
- Limitations: Not usually interactive

ELECTRONIC FIELD TRIPS (EFT) Live, interactive, satellite broadcasts in which students interact with presenters through live demonstrations, phone calls, and e-mail.

- Strengths: Can be interactive, provide focal point for big topic, or event—can be broadcast to a wide audience

- Limitations: Cost makes these extremely prohibitive; requires classroom to tune in at a specified day and time

VIDEOCONFERENCING Video monitors connected by telephone wires, satellite technology, or ground wires, which allow individuals to meet "face-to-face" from almost anywhere in the world. A videoconference can also include graphics, video clips, and transmission of data or documents.

- Strengths: Usually includes a limited number of venues, so can feel more personal; flexibility in scheduling to coordinate with curriculum
- Limitations: Can be complicated to foster effective interaction if more than one group is involved.

Various Smithsonian museums have experimented with all of these formats and have used technology to send programs around the world. The Smithsonian American Art Museum was closed for renovation for six years and took the opportunity to develop a videoconference program series using a studio in its office building. The Smithsonian Environmental Research Center on the Chesapeake Bay in Maryland has the technical capability to offer videoconferences on environmental research from the water's edge and even from a boat. The National Air and Space Museum offers videoconferences direct from the Museum's galleries. The best advice museum educators at these institutions can give is to do your research first before you begin planning for any distance education programming. Talk to museum educators who have experience with the medium. Find out their challenges. Talk to teachers and find out what their specific challenges are. And talk to students to find out what engages them. Make sure you have an audience with the technical capability your programming requires.

CONCLUSION

While the Internet and other forms of technology offer new ways to reach museum audiences, the museum educator's approach to technology should not be very different than his approach to other media. He should:

1. know the audiences and how they use the medium
2. understand how the medium is unique
3. study trends
4. test materials with users before making them public

There are many available tools to help museum professionals understand new technology. The best place to go for inspiration and guidance is often the Internet itself. By discovering what other organizations have produced, you can track trends, compare designs, analyze organization, and test usability. Whatever direction the Internet heads in the future, the medium is now well established as an information and communication tool, and no organization can afford to ignore it.

Textbox 9.1. Discussion Questions

1. Ask several middle school, high school, and college students what different Web programs they use on a social basis. (Examples may include flickr.com, youtube.com, myspace.com, facebook.com.)
   - Visit those sites and consider their purpose.
   - What are their strengths?
   - List possible ways that your institution or a specific museum could use them within the broader mission of the institution.

2. Visit an exhibition and its online version. Compare the experiences. Discuss the following:
   - Were the experiences different or similar? In what ways?
   - What components were the same or different?
   - What did the online version accomplish that the physical space did not?
   - What are the strengths and limitations of the Internet in regard to online exhibitions?

3. Try conducting a usability test on several websites that you are familiar with. Follow the procedure outlined in the chapter. Ask several people who are not familiar with the sites to test them. Make a list of several questions you want them to answer about information included on the site (e.g., What are the current exhibitions? What school programs are available?). Ask your users to verbally articulate their thoughts as they navigate the sites. Observe and listen as they look for the specific items on your list.

NOTES

1. Museums and the Web is an international conference held annually. More info at www.archimuse.com/conferences/mw.html.
2. www.pewinternet.org/index.asp.
3. "Internet: The Mainstreaming of Online Life," *Trends* 2005. www.pewinternet.org/pdfs/Internet_Status_2005.pdf.
4. Department of Education statistics. nces.ed.gov/surveys/frss/inc/displaytables_inc.asp.
5. D. T. Schaller et al., "One Size Does Not Fit All: Learning Style, Play, and On-line Interactives," in J. Trant and D. Bearman (eds.), *Museums and the Web 2007: Proceedings*, Toronto: Archives and Museum Informatics, published March 31, 2007, at www.archimuse.com/mw2007/papers/schaller/schaller.html.
6. Janet Murray, *Hamlet on the Holodeck: The Future of Narrative in Cyberspace.* Cambridge, Mass.: MIT Press, 1998.
7. Ideas in this section have been presented in my column, History Bytes, in *History News* 59, no. 3 (Summer 2004).
8. David T. Schaller and Susan E. Edwards, "The Name of the Game: Museums and Digital Learning Games," in Herminia Din and Phyllis Hecht (eds.), *The Digital Museum: A Think Guide* (Washington, D.C.: American Association of Museums, 2007), 97–108.
9. David Schaller, History Bytes, *History News* 62, no. 3 (Summer 2007).
10. Schaller, History Bytes.
11. The Web Accessibility Initiative offers extensive information on this topic: www.w3.org/WAI/ and its quick tips page at www.w3.org/WAI/quicktips/Overview.php.
12. Lev Grossman, "Time's Person of the Year: You," *Time*, December 25, 2006, 40.
13. *Wikipedia*, s.v., "Web 2.0," en.wikipedia.org/wiki/Web_2.0 (June 28, 2007). *Wikipedia* is a prime example of a Web 2.0 function.
14. Matt MacArthur, "Can Museums Allow Online Users to Become Participants," in Herminia Din and Phyllis Hecht (eds.), *The Digital Museum: A Think Guide* (Washington, D.C.: American Association of Museums, 2007), 57–66.
15. These definitions were written to inform discussion at a Smithsonian Educators Exchange program in December 2006.

CHAPTER 10

Evaluation

Nancy Cutler

At their best, the role of museum educators is to facilitate visitor interaction with artifacts, which can and should take a variety of forms. As staff that has considerable public contact, they also need to be visitor advocates, reporting on what visitors seem to want or need and helping to plan/execute visitor studies as needed.

—*Maria Quinlan Leiby, museum historian, Michigan Historical Center*

The question for museum evaluation is always: What is it you are trying to learn from or about your visitors, your exhibits, or your programs?

Evaluation carries a scary connotation. People often feel threatened by evaluation, assuming that its goal is to look for and point out failures. Yet, nearly every chapter in this book has made reference to evaluation, and it becomes clearly apparent that every phase of museum education can benefit from evaluation. What, then, is evaluation in the museum environment? Kathleen McLean, in *Planning for People in Museum Exhibitions*, says this:

> Evaluation is the careful appraisal and study of something to determine its feasibility and effectiveness. In museum[s] . . . , it is the systematic collection and interpretation of information about the effects of exhibitions and programs on visitors for the purpose of decision making.[1]

WHY DOES EVALUATION MATTER?

Museums should continually assess how their programs and exhibits impact their constituents, and work toward improving their products. Why? First, because fiduciary responsibilities to constituents and funders require it; second, because AAM/ICOM (American Association of Museums/International Congress of Museums) both say that it is an important function of museums as institutions held in trust for the public; and third, because museums must compete for visitors, not only with other museums, but with all other leisure time attractions. Evaluation of their programs and exhibits informs decision making and results in more effective, better quality products. Museums feature unique and significant collections with documented information, and they tell great, real-life stories from history, art, science, and national and international heritage, but why should anyone choose to visit a museum over going to a ball game or a theme park?

Actually, many studies have been done to determine people's motivation for visiting a museum compared to doing something else. In a well-known study of visitor behavior, Marilyn G. Hood identifies six main criteria by which individuals choose their leisure time activities:

1. Being with people or social interaction
2. Doing something worthwhile
3. Being at ease in one's surroundings
4. A challenge or new experience
5. An opportunity to learn
6. Participating actively[2]

According to these criteria it behooves museums, as Hood says, "to promote themselves as places for families and friends to explore, discover and enjoy each other's company in relaxed settings."[3]

Museums have wonderful factual stories to share through their collections. Whether the collection is the art of Monet, fabulous rocks and gems, a historic home, archaeological artifacts, or animals from around the world, by enticing visitors to participate in those stories through their unique presentations to the public, museums can provide opportunities for exploration and discovery, and inspire learning. The programs and exhibitions that are most appreciated by visitors are those that create experiences that are enjoyable, interactive, informative, and socially welcoming. How do we know? When asked (or observed), visitors will tell. That is why it matters! That is the point of visitor evaluation.

The scope of evaluation techniques and resources extends beyond what can be said in a chapter. This chapter will, however, demonstrate the value of doing visitor evaluation and of using evaluation results to improve the visitor experience. We will also share some ideas of evaluation techniques and a lot of resources that you can refer to for additional assistance.

WHAT IS VISITOR EVALUATION?

Visitor evaluation, as suggested earlier, gathers visitors' input, via a variety of methods (see Figure 10.2 on page 121), in order to assess the impact of an existing or proposed program or exhibit, in view of its stated goals and objectives. Evaluation can suggest that changes would improve or enhance the project, or it can validate the impact. Through visitor input, data can be collected to answer specific questions, to develop suggestions on how to make improvements, or to determine if the institution is meeting its community's needs. Any program that involves a visitor, volunteer, member, donor, or funder can benefit from evaluation.

Projects that benefit from evaluation include:

- Exhibits and signage
- Programs and events
- Outreach and technology
- Volunteer programs
- Docent tours and presentations
- Docent and volunteer training
- Teacher training and school programs
- Summer camp or children's programs
- Adult education programs

Many funders of projects (and certainly all government funding agencies) require organizations to document the results of grant activities to demonstrate that the funding makes a vital contribution to the museum and to the community it serves.

BUT IS VISITOR EVALUATION REALLY IMPORTANT OR VALUABLE?

Let's do a little exercise to determine the answer to that question. Consider for a moment a memorable experience you have had as a visitor at a museum or an interpretive site. Consider some aspects of why it is memorable. Did you feel valued as a visitor and a person, or were you just another warm body, or worse, did the experience leave you feeling lost, confused, or frustrated? Were the staff and volunteers friendly, welcoming, and informative? Were the exhibits engaging and enlightening, or boring, or frustrating? Was your overall experience enjoyable, informative, and socially welcoming? Would you want to return? Why? Would you recommend it to others?

As a visitor, your reactions, along with those of potentially thousands of other visitors, will determine the success of the institution. Isn't it, then, in a museum's interest to continually learn about its visitors' wants and needs; and to use that information in exhibits and program development? Staff should be constantly aware that (for most museums) visitors are not only the primary audience but also an important source of support.

- Audience support includes visitor, member, and volunteer *attendance*; attending workshops or events; and important word-of-mouth marketing.
- Financial support includes admission fees, membership fees, fees for attending events or workshops, money spent in the gift shop, donations, and return visitors to the museum bringing along other visitors.

Therefore, understanding what brings visitors through the doors and entices them to return is of paramount importance and value to an institution. Without an understanding of the importance of visitors, visitor evaluation of exhibits and programs has little meaning. In this process we do not mean to override the mission and goal of the institution, or dumb down the exhibits and programs to pure entertainment. Doing visitor evaluation we seek to discover how to engage the visitor with the wonderful stories embodied in the museum's collection.

STAGES OF EVALUATION FOR EXHIBITS, PROGRAMS, AND SUPPLEMENTARY MATERIALS

We will first look at the four stages of visitor evaluation learned from the Visitor Studies Association (VSA). I will then share the process that was used for developing exhibits at the Desert Botanical Garden, which

Stages of Visitor Evaluation	Explanation
Front-end Analysis	A needs assessment (could also be a marketing analysis). What types of experiences do your visitors expect? What are their perceptions of the institution? Do these agree with either the reality of the institution or with the ideal (optimal)?
Formative Evaluation	Collecting visitor data while developing an exhibit or program in order to make improvements before it is finalized.
Summative Evaluation	A report on overall effectiveness after the project is established. Usually used to evaluate the value or success of the project and either make final decisions or apply information to decisions about a new project.
Remedial Evaluation	What needs to be fixed to make it work better? This is different from summative evaluation because it presumes an expectation of making modifications.

Figure 10.1. Stages of Visitor Evaluation
Courtesy of Nancy Cutler

was easily adapted for development of programs and supplementary materials such as gallery guides, trail maps, and so forth.

The following case study showing examples of the four stages of evaluation are from my experiences with the Desert Botanical Garden's project in the 1990s, "Developing a Comprehensive Desert Exhibit: An Innovative Model for Informal Science Education in Outdoor Museums." This project was funded in large part by the National Science Foundation, and the summative evaluation and outside critical appraisals found it to be highly successful in meeting its stated goals and objectives.

How Do We Begin?

The first step is a front-end analysis—a needs assessment. Features of a front-end analysis include:

- learning public perceptions about your institution
- determining what is the "reality" (actual)
- determining what is the "ideal" (optimal in the user's view)

- identifying the gaps between them

Focus groups are often used to help determine what the community wants—what they see as the current reality, their ideal, and sometimes who the community members are.

So, front-end analysis is the first step to learning how your institution can become, as Marilyn Hood suggested, "a place for families and friends to explore, discover and enjoy each other's company in relaxed settings."

CASE STUDY AT THE DESERT BOTANICAL GARDEN: FRONT-END METHODS Visitor surveys and interviews (see Figure 10.2 on page 121) were used to gather basic information about the Desert Botanical Garden experience. In addition to this information, the staff and volunteers were asked to gather and report input from visitors. This was to help them understand the visitor perspective and to build their support for the visitor experience at the Garden. Docents, admissions staff, gift shop staff, horticulture, security, receptionists, and any volunteers who interacted with visitors were asked to make a list of the most common questions, suggestions, or complaints visitors had over several months. This served two purposes: (1) the staff and volunteers had a better appreciation of the visitor needs and of their understanding of the desert environment, and (2) the Garden began to form a picture of what would be the "ideal." This front-end evaluation told not only about comfort issues that were important to visitors, like drinking fountains and shady places to sit and rest, but also some of their preconceptions, misconceptions, and expectations about the desert, which were then to be addressed in the project. Common questions that visitors had about the plants were used to develop signs and trailside exhibits, which answered those questions and shared other information about the desert plant collection in a manner that visitors had already demonstrated curiosity about.

Staff and volunteers were also polled as an interested focus group as to how they thought the Garden could be improved. Using this valuable front-end information, the Garden learned what the "reality" of the former displays and trails was missing for visitors, and used the stage set by those visitors to develop and design trailside exhibits that could respond to their "ideal."

Development Phase

Formative evaluation follows front-end analysis and consists of collecting data during development of an exhibit or program in order to make improvements before it is finalized. First, determine your goals and

A Rubric as a Model for Front-End Evaluation

When I was in graduate school, I took a course on critical thinking. The class was made up primarily of secondary (junior and senior high school) teachers. One technique that teachers use in grading something that is somewhat subjective (like a paper) is to write a *rubric* for the assignment. A rubric lays out the standards, and in this case it is a way of defining an A paper, B paper, C paper, and so forth, by listing main points that need to be included and identifying the impact of grammatical errors on the grade. So, a rubric is a way of evaluating a piece of work.

In this class we each had to do a presentation, so I decided that this was an excellent opportunity to ask teachers to define what they want in a history museum by creating a rubric for a history museum. Here is what they identified:

- Life-size replicas
- Suggestion box
- Physically comfortable: room to move, places to sit, moderate temperature
- Docents—more personal information
- Reenactments
- Actors
- Recorded messages
- Written supplemental materials
- Involves all senses
- Visually stimulating displays
- Problem solving
- Handicapped accessible
- Displays should answer or stimulate questions
- Appeals to *all* ages

During this same time, I asked the staff of a history museum to create a rubric for a history museum. Here is what they included in their rubric:

- Fascinating artifacts
- Real artifacts
- Direct link to the past
- Personal identification with something
- Different from the ordinary (things we don't normally see)
- Learn something new
- See something in different light
- Air conditioning
- Good gift shop
- Interaction with some of the exhibits
- Social interaction
- Identification with the story
- Human impact
- Engaging
- Tell a story (a story that is of value to people)
- Setting
- Involve all the senses
- Entertainment—fun

Note: In explaining to each group how to do a rubric, I used an ice cream sundae example. The A grade sundae would include 2 scoops of ice cream with 2 warm sauces, whipped cream, nuts, and a cherry on top. The B grade sundae would include 2 scoops of ice cream, 1 warm sauce, whipped cream and a cherry, while the C grade would be 1 scoop of ice cream, 1 sauce, and whipped cream. As you can see, the sundae became less fancy as the grade dropped. However, I wanted the groups to think in terms of the biggest and the best, and the sundae was a good way to get that point across. After the rubric was explained with the definition above, we brainstormed what was needed to make an outstanding sundae. Then we applied that same thought process to making a rubric for an outstanding history museum. Try this in your next staff meeting, docent meeting, focus group, or other interested group. People are willing to share information without feeling intimidated.

—Anna Johnson

objectives, that is, what do you *most* want to know from the visitors? Be specific—these will drive your evaluation. Evaluation instruments can collect information in a variety of ways. Methods include the following.

Both quantitative and qualitative procedures should be used to determine whether a specific exhibit or program is successful and which characteristics are successful. For example, for exhibits you want to know how many people stopped to view the exhibit, how much time they invested (quantitative measures), and what impact the exhibit had as measured by their comments and actions related to the exhibit (qualitative measures). There are many resources to consult for details of these methods. Some will be found in the bibliography.

CASE STUDY AT THE DESERT BOTANICAL GARDEN: FORMATIVE EVALUATION Using formative evaluation, the Desert Botanical Garden in 1993 inaugurated a then-innovative approach to developing trailside exhibits and signage that was truly visitor-centered. The *goals*, as an informal science education center, were (1) to develop exhibits that would increase visitors' understanding of science and desert plant ecology, (2) to foster excitement that would lead to further exploration of the subject, and (3) to encourage learning as a social interactive experience. The *objective* was to create exhibits and supplementary information that truly engaged visitors of all ages, interests, backgrounds, and motivations. The visitors, then, rather than the curator or educator, were final arbiters (as indicated through formative evaluation) of whether or not the trailside

Evaluation method	User	Kind of information it provides
Surveys/questionnaire	Written by trained personnel; filled out by visitor; used by an interviewer	Qualitative—open-ended questions provide descriptions or opinions—harder to compile Quantitative—scaled ratings for numerical analysis—easier to compile
Interviews	Conducted by trained personnel	Usually used for qualitative information —Previsit —Postvisit —Communication value
Observation—clearly defines what is to be observed and recorded.	Conducted by trained personnel	Usually used for quantitative information—for example, time spent in exhibition or at an interactive, which exhibits were visited and by how many people. Qualitative in reporting of comments and actions.
Focus group	Conducted by trained personnel	Often used for qualitative information—such as communication value
Previsit and postvisit tests for communication value	Written by trained personnel; filled out by visitor	Ask a few content questions of visitors before an exhibit is designed and installed to learn the level of general knowledge and again after it is installed, and compare. Did visitors learn things from the exhibit they had not learned before?

Figure 10.2. Methods Used for Evaluation
Courtesy of Nancy Cutler

exhibits were informative and engaging. Those two museum authorities, however, the curator and the educator, did review and ultimately approve each exhibit as accurate and communicating the message. Some prototypes had to be revised and retested with visitors to ensure this.

Here is how this process went. Carefully structured teams of staff and volunteers were put together; each team had specific sets of skills including a content specialist, an educator, and a novice to represent the visitor view. The teams received (1) some special training (a few easy group exercises in creative thinking, and how to use the evaluation tools), (2) specific goals for information along with researched content information (in the form of starter packets), and (3) consistent reemphasis on the importance of the visitors. They were then challenged with creating and testing with visitors an interactive (or sensory) paper prototype for each trailside exhibit. The challenge for each exhibit (which focused on a plant that demonstrated a desert concept) was to attract visitor attention and to hold their attention long enough to read the message, examine the exhibit, *and* convey the scientific message/story that met the goal of the exhibit. A large order, but the synergy of the teams and the visitor observations resulted in some amazingly creative and effective exhibit prototypes.

When a prototype design was completed (see Figure 10.3 on page 122), it was taken with an easel onto the trail to an appropriate location (near the plant that was the focus of the prototype) and set up for visitors to view. Team members had been trained in the use of the observation tools (a stop watch and a form to fill out) to record how visitors responded to the prototype exhibit. (See examples of observation and summary forms, Sample Forms 10.1 and 10.2, in the appendix). Secreting themselves a short distance from the exhibit, team members observed and recorded whether a chosen visitor stopped to view the exhibit or not (its attracting power); the amount of time that a selected visitor spent reading and examining the exhibit (usually 20 seconds to 3 minutes); and any comments or other reactions by that visitor (the exhibit's holding power). (See the sidebar "Attracting Power and Holding Power.") If less than 50 percent of the visitors met the goals and objectives for engagement, then the prototype was returned to the creative center for a remake of the design.

When an exhibit prototype reached its goal for over 50 percent of the visitors (over several observation periods), some visitors who were engaged with the exhibit were then interviewed (following a specific format) about the communication power of the sign to see if (1) they thought that other people could understand the message (slyly representing

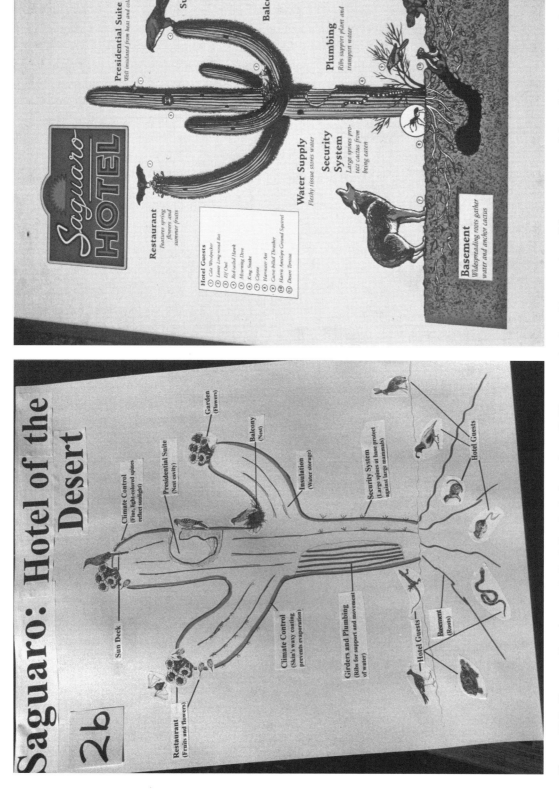

Figure 10.3. Signage Development. A visitor-tested mock-up (left) was revised and retested until it was successful, and the resulting final interpretive sign (right) was then created by the designer. Visitors enjoyed learning from the mock-up and giving their input on its effectiveness.

Photos courtesy of the Desert Botanical Garden

whether or not they understood it), (2) they had any questions about the information, and (3) they had any suggestions for the exhibit. All were recorded, summarized, and analyzed and, if appropriate, applied to the prototype. (See the sidebar "Testing for Communication Power" and Sample Form 10.3.) Interviews were also conducted with focus groups, which included a class of museum studies students, for each exhibit in order to assure that the intended message was being transmitted.

This team process for exhibit development, designed by Kathleen Socolofsky and Ruth Greenhouse (a relatively new concept for exhibit development in 1993—see Chapter 12), was based on the sound principles and guidelines found in visitor studies literature. It incorporated creative and accurate scientific input from staff and volunteers from all departments. And most important, it relied on visitor evaluation as the main indicator for success.[4] Through this process the staff and volunteers learned the power and value of testing their ideas with visitors, and as a result the Garden became a venue that is truly visitor-centered.

Attracting Power and Holding Power

Attracting Power
A report of the percentage of visitors who *stop* at a specific exhibit. It is the fundamental measurement of whether an exhibit captures visitor attention. If visitors do not stop at the exhibit, there is no chance that the exhibit will deliver its message.

Holding Power
An exhibit's ability to *hold visitor attention* long enough to deliver the message. This is often expressed as a fraction of the total time the average visitor would take to "get the message."

In the End
Summative evaluation is the final report on overall effectiveness (degree of success) in achieving the goals of the project. It is based on additional testing after the project is in use.

CASE STUDY AT THE DESERT BOTANICAL GARDEN: SUMMATIVE REPORT A summative evaluation report by an outside evaluator for this project stated, "All components of the new exhibit, especially the interactive interpretive signs, but also the guidebooks, directional signs, hands-on activities and school programs were field-tested with visitors and improved using formative evaluation." "One of the unique features of the process was using the findings of ongoing evaluation activities

Testing for Communication Power
This is a different objective than testing for learning!

Communicating Important Messages—How well does this exhibit explain our objectives to visitors? Does it

- have a clear and meaningful teaching point?
- have text and graphics that are clear and understandable to visitors?
- have scientifically or historically correct information?
- encourage people to think—using comparisons or connections or correcting misconceptions?
- foster social learning?
- avoid confusing visitors or leaving them with the wrong conclusion?

Attitudes and Feelings—Are visitors gaining the experience we intended or something else?

- Do visitors enjoy their interaction with this exhibit?
- How do visitors describe their experience (open ended)?

[during the development]." In comparative surveys and interviews of visitors prior to installation of the new exhibits and after, "visitors perceived the Garden as significantly more dynamic after exhibit installation, and tended to rate it as more exciting, academic and inspiring." Visitors often "named the displays and signs as among the aspects they most enjoyed from their visit," and indicated overwhelmingly that they would like to return to the Garden.

There was a serious concern, especially in a botanical garden, that visitors would shift their focus from the plants to the exhibits or that the signage would detract from the beauty and serenity of the Garden. Those fears proved to be unfounded. "Most visitors both before and after installation, still named plants or particular plants, such as cacti or desert wildflowers, as among their favorite aspects of the Garden and as among the features they learned the most from." In a comment book at the exit, visitors said, "The educational stuff . . . provides challenges for all ages" and fosters "interaction between all ages" (one of the goals of the project). A volunteer concurred, saying, "the new exhibits make the Garden more meaningful." Docents also noted that visitors asked more specific questions or for more extended information after viewing some of the exhibits.[5] This summative report demonstrates the power of applying formative evaluation during exhibit development in order to achieve the goals of the project.

Corrective Measures?
An additional step is the remedial evaluation: What needs to be fixed to make it work better?

CASE STUDY AT THE DESERT BOTANICAL GARDEN: REME-DIAL Due to the extensive formative evaluation done during development there were few items that demanded remedial attention. According to the same summative report, "As final exhibit components were completed, visitor evaluations and observations were again conducted to test their effectiveness as installed." A few changes were made in some areas, for example, "a few signs and exhibit locations were changed as a result of remedial evaluations."[6] On one exhibit the hardware needed to be redesigned, to make it function properly. There also were still a few areas where staff, volunteers, and visitors felt the Garden could make improvements, having to do with comfort features and even more information.

As stated before, remedial evaluation presumes an expectation of making the modifications. Few museums actually budget for this in their exhibit development plan. According to some visitor studies experts, 10–20 percent of the development budget should be reserved for evaluation and improvements.

CASE STUDY AT THE DESERT BOTANICAL GARDEN: VISITOR EVALUATIONS Doing visitor evaluations is empowering and very enlightening! Through evaluation observation, staff and volunteers developed a real sense of what factors would attract and engage visitors with the trailside exhibits. This activity was so powerful, in fact, that the head of the Garden's research department, Joe McAuliffe, became a real convert to the visitor perspective. As an academic his tendency for exhibits was to explain the whole story with a large amount of text. During testing he saw visitors turn away from text-heavy signs, and watched them engage with exhibits that included a sensory learning component, a labeled graphic (where you can sneak in a lot of information), a commonly asked question with a challenge, and other clever means to convey meaningful information. He became a real believer in visitor evaluation as a driver in exhibit development. If visitors don't read the information, how can they learn anything from it?

Another believer:

> After attending your workshop session at the 1998 Museum Association of Arizona Conference, I hightailed it back to my museum and reported on your success with "new" methods of developing signage. We implemented some of your methods and to our delight, our clientele responded . . . by reading our interpretive material in a way they haven't ever done!!"—Rebecca Akins, curator, Arizona Museum for Youth

A Few Things We Discovered

- The evaluation process following the model described above worked successfully for the NSF project and for other projects as well. The critical appraisals indicated that the outcomes closely matched the goals and objectives for the project.

- Evaluations for museum exhibits or programs do not always need to be strictly scientifically formal. Basically you just want to know if it is working with most visitors and how well. Statistical analysis is often helpful when combined with qualitative (observed) information such as visitor comments and expressions that indicate some engagement with the exhibit information.

- Front-end and formative evaluations are enlightening and empowering, and although a great deal of hard work, the work can be fascinating, fun, and well worth the effort.

ANOTHER EXAMPLE OF MUSEUM EVALUATION

Again, the question to ask is always: *What am I trying to learn from or about the visitors or the programs?* To answer this question there must be clearly defined goals and articulation of the intended impact. The evaluation tools must then be designed to reflect whether the desired outcomes are being achieved. For example, the school tour survey in Figure 10.4 was done back in the classroom. The goal was to learn what information the students took away from their visit to the Garden (general content learning) and how they *felt* about the visit and the Garden (affective measure). Not scientific, but it served its purpose.

Although there are several studies and models for looking at what visitors take away after a visit (and much research has described various aspects of that topic), in truth, evaluating visitor "learning" in museums is exceptionally difficult. The reason is that museum visitors are not in a structured learning environment like a classroom, where they can be tested; and they come from a variety of backgrounds, knowledge levels, interest levels, and ages. The impact of a museum exhibit or program on its visitors, as voluntary learners in an informal learning environment, often tends to be indirect, subtle, and even cumulative over time. It is nearly impossible to assess the impact of subtle elements unexpectedly picked up on a tour or from an exhibit that are taken away with a visitor and can surface later in life.

Stephen Bitgood, psychologist and visitor studies expert, suggests that when people are exposed to an unfamiliar concept they become "sensitized" to it, and when they encounter the concept again they may have more of an interest and may even pursue learning some further information on the subject. The impact of the museum visit thus surfaces at a later time.

Learning in museums is generally no longer viewed as simply being on the receiving end of the transmission of information. Being "taught" or "educated" often has a negative connotation; but providing "learning opportunities" where the learner has choices is seen as much more positive. However, this flexibility makes testing for learning more difficult. The best learning requires the participation of the learner (is interactive)—and people approach it with a variety of different learning styles and interests. Most museum educators now view the museum as a place where a variety of teaching methods are used to offer free-choice learning opportunities. So, how can all these aspects be measured? The aspects you choose to evaluate depend on how you expect to use the information. Are you using it for marketing, or to meet school standards, to appeal to members or volunteers, to validate your programs to your administration and board, to attract funding, or report to funding agencies? According to visitor studies experts Barbara Butler and Marcella Wells, the goal of the evaluation instruments is to find or create the most effective tool for gathering the most appropriate and useful data. Evaluators must decide what questions to ask and what decisions to make about the information collected.[7]

ENTER OUTCOME-BASED EVALUATION (OBE)

State and federal government funding agencies, in particular, are looking for a specific measure of the impact their funding provides for the museum and the specific benefits to people in the community it serves. What value does the museum or program provide for the public? How does it manage its resources to provide that value? These agencies require performance goals and annual reports on the progress of the projects they fund (to satisfy the requirements of the Government Performance and Results Act of 1993); and their focus is on whether the nonprofit programs they fund are really making a beneficial difference. Outcome-based evaluation looks at the direct impacts, changes, or benefits to clients during or after their participation in the programs. It has changed the way state and local agencies measure success and has influenced how foundations and nonprofit organizations measure their performance.

Basic Components of Outcome-based Evaluation and How They Are Helpful

In 1995, United Way of America revised its evaluation approach and reporting guidelines for organizations it funds. It looked at specific inputs and activities of the potential program as well as the outputs and outcomes, which are not the same things. Outputs are quantitative measures while outcomes show qualitative results. Some form of the following adapted model has been adopted by many funding agencies for developing programs and reporting on the process.

- *Inputs.* Dedicated resources: materials and resources (supplies, equipment, facilities, money, staff, volunteers, etc.) used in the activities.
- *Activities.* How input resources fulfill the program mission: teaching, feeding, sheltering, counseling, tours, classes, etc.

A student evaluation for school tours at the Desert Botanical Garden asked students to answer specific questions in order to *gather specific information*:

1. My favorite part of the visit was . . . . (*Did they like it? This also requires a mental review of the trip to evaluate their favorite part.*)
2. I saw. . . . . (*What did they remember most?*)
3. I was surprised to find out that . . . . (*What new information did they learn?*)
4. I didn't know that . . . . (*Another new thing they learned?*)
5. Desert plants are important because. . . . . (*Information retained and value judgment.*)
6. I would like to learn more about. . . . . (*Did the Garden pique their interest? Where could/ should we go from here?*)
7. If I could grow a desert plant I would grow . . . . (*Did they bond with anything? Demonstrates a value and ownership—affective measure.*)

Figure 10.4. Student Evaluation
Courtesy of the Desert Botanical Garden

- *Outputs.* Products of the activities counted as units of service: number of people who went through the program, number of gallery guides published, number of schools or students served, etc.
- *Outcomes.* The actual impact or benefits for participants, such as content knowledge (can identify five species of butterflies), attitude changes (deserts can be beautiful and useful environments), values or conditions changes (using or promoting desert landscaping to conserve water).
- *Outcome Targets.* The number and percentage of participants that you want to achieve the outcome.
- *Outcome Indicators.* Observable and measurable milestones toward the outcome target.[8]

Specifying all the above pieces in your project helps to design and examine the components of any program and forces you to establish goals and objectives to measure the impacts. Outcome-based evaluation looks for observable changes (e.g., learning) or benefits to clients during and after their participation in your program, and can examine these changes in the short term (knowledge and skills—as in learning to read or to draw), mid term (behaviors—such as reading a how-to book or creating artistic pieces), or long term (values and conditions—e.g., a better appreciation of art museums). For more information on outcome-based evaluation, see resources for this chapter in the bibliography.

CONCLUSION

Evaluation is the key to excellence. Visitor evaluation allows museums to monitor the impact of their efforts and make adjustments as necessary. It is valuable on many levels: Gathering input from your clientele (or potential clientele) can help determine how the community views your institution and what your institution can do to entice visitors to your doors; doing formative evaluation in development of your programs and exhibits can help ensure that you develop the best product possible and can achieve your set goals and objectives (and visitors *love* to share their input); summarizing and reporting results is useful for validating the project—for your own information, for the funder, and/or for the administration (for making decisions on future projects); remedial evaluation (and funding for improvements) can help better the product. Outcome-based evaluation is a blending of all this and also looks specifically at the resources allocated and some specific measurable results of the impact or benefit of the program.

Evaluation for ongoing programs should be conducted regularly, as well. Evaluation surveys are easily distributed, filled out by participants, and then collected at the end of each public class and volunteer training or tour. Don't be afraid to use volunteers as focus groups. Teachers and students should also receive evaluation surveys (and incentives to return them), in order to assess if your school programs and teacher trainings are meeting their intended goals.

Docents also need to do some form of assessments in order to ensure that their tours and programs are up to date and accurate. This can be a particularly touchy subject, because people often feel threatened by having their personal presentations evaluated. However, it is necessary for ensuring excellent programs, and good docents do want to put their best foot forward. (See Sample Form 10.6, "Guided Tours Evaluation/Feedback"; also see Chapter 3 for additional information.) A simple and quick overview evaluation for visitors to do following a tour is easy to design. Sample Form 10.4, "Visitor Tour Survey," asks visitors short-answer questions following a tour. Compiling the answers on tour surveys such as these will help to gain a sense of how people are reacting to the tours in your museum. You can ask more specific questions about content; just keep the survey short and easy to answer. (Field test it to ensure the questions give the type of feedback you are looking for.) Sample Form 10.5, "Immediate Program Evaluation by Docents," from the Tempe Historical Museum is answered by docents following a school tour. It provides a docent's evaluation of the school's behavior. (It also gives docents a place to vent if frustrated by a particular group.) Over the years it becomes evident if a particular school's classes are an ongoing problem or if the behavior (good or bad) is an isolated incident. Docents might also suggest things the museum could do to improve the visit.

Outreach programs can and should have a survey for participants who use the programs, and they, too, benefit from front-end and formative evaluation. For example, have a teacher advisory council or task force to help develop teacher training, school tours, or traveling trunks. Gather their experienced input and then test the products in development with them (as a focus group—they, too, love to share their input) as well as with others who will use it. (See teacher and student evaluation forms for traveling trunks in Chapter 7.)

Used appropriately, evaluation should not seem threatening or "scary." To put it in a positive light, learning which aspects of your museum are not the "ideal" can be very useful, and can provide promising opportunities! Without knowing where programs can be improved, how can we possibly offer the best product? Doing evaluation and using its results truly is the key to having excellent programs. Proceed with confidence!

NOTES

1. Kathleen McLean, *Planning for People in Museum Exhibitions* (Washington, D.C.: Association of Science Technology Center, 1993), 70.
2. Marilyn G. Hood, "Staying Away: Why People Choose Not to Visit Museums," *Museum News* 64, no. 4 (April 1983): 50–57.
3. Hood, " Staying Away," 50–57.
4. Kathleen Socolofsky and Ruth Greenhouse, "Developing a Comprehensive Desert Exhibit: An Innovative Model for Informal Science Education in Outdoor Museums," National Science Foundation final report and technical information (July 1997), 2.1
5. Wilhelmina C. Savenye, *Summative Evaluation Report*, "Developing a Comprehensive Desert Exhibit: An Innovative Model for Informal Science Education in Outdoor Museums," National Science Foundation final report and technical information (July 1997), 5.1–5.4.
6. Savenye, *Summative Evaluation Report*.
7. Barbara Butler and Marcella Wells, "A Visitor Centered Evaluation Hierarchy," *Visitor Studies Today!* 5, no. 1 (Spring 2002): 5–11.
8. Carter McNamara, "Basic Guide to Outcomes Based Evaluation for Non-Profit Organizations with Very Limited Resources," 1997–2007, www.managementhelp.org/evaluatn/outcomes.htm (July 15, 2007).

PART III

WORKING WITH OTHERS

Illustration by Larry R. Warner

CHAPTER 11

Financing Museum Education Programs

KIMBERLY A. HUBER

> **The role of a museum educator is: To advocate for the public, fostering accountability and accessibility, so that museums can fulfill their public service mission.**
>
> —*Carol Stapp, director, The George Washington Museum Education Program*

Throughout *The Museum Educator's Manual: Educators Share Successful Techniques,* the authors have discussed docent training, teacher training, outreach, and website development, along with other education-related programs. Internal funding is common for many of these activities, and financial assistance can sometimes be found in self-supporting programs or event fees. But from where does the funding come for special programs and events? Can we expect all museums to have additional activities in their budgets, as part of their internal funding? If not, where do educators get money and how do they get external funding for new programs that enhance the museum education experience for visitors? Unfortunately, there are no universal answers to these questions; however, I offer museum educators some options for growing their programs. This chapter will briefly address internal funding, which tends to be more dependable. But the chapter focuses on external funding for projects or programs to supplement the educator's budget, in the form of grants (private, public, corporate), bequests, sponsors, and gifts.

INTERNAL FUNDING

Educators should expect that a portion of the museum's ongoing operating expenses, which I will refer to as "internal funding," will finance the staff, supplies, and materials needed to run the museum's primary educational programs. According to *Excellence and Equity,* museums must make a commitment to financial resources "to strengthen the public dimensions of

museums. . . . Exhibitions, programs, and other activities that enable museums to fulfill their public responsibility need financial backing if they are to reflect high standards and engage a diverse audience."[1] Most successful museums have reliable sources of funds from governmental agencies (like many Canadian museums), interest from endowments, membership dues, admission fees, and gift shop and food sales, along with other revenue sources. These resources provide the funds for the entire museum's annual operating budget.

Even with an expectation of internal funding, this does not absolve the educator from planning, providing input into the budgeting process, and presenting justification to support the enhancement of the overall education program. Educators are responsible for preparing a well-planned proposal for their department's activities each year as well as a long-term strategy for the following three to five years. These activities and programs should support the institution's mission, collections, and exhibits. Evaluations, survey results, and attendance records can provide the documentation that reports on the success of previous programs and activities, verifies visitor interest in future programs, and demonstrates a need for continued as well as additional internal funding for the education department. Purposeful evaluation is a great tool for providing useful data about programs. The responses let the education department know what programs work well, what additional programs are needed, and how best to reach your intended audience. (See Chapter 10, "Evaluation," for more information about how evaluation results can be used.)

If educators are new to the planning and budgeting process they can benefit by reading any number of works on strategic planning or visiting some of the museum websites and resources listed below. The Institute of Museum and Library Services website includes a project planning tutorial.[2] Although this website was designed to assist museum and library professionals with planning projects for grant application purposes, it is also useful for project planning in general. The American Association of Museums offers information to its members about mission and institutional planning.[3] Focused on history, the American Association for State and Local History offers a technical leaflet bundle (BNDL005) on how to fund your organization.[4] These are just a few possible places to begin your search for overall planning, budgeting, and funding information.

During the planning and budgeting process, educators should work with collection, exhibition, administration, public relations, and other department staff members to ensure educational activities support all the areas of museum operation. If your institution has a development officer (DO, someone responsible for writing grants and bringing in additional funding), the educator and director should consult with the DO to plan and prepare the education department's funding plan. Once this plan is in place, decide what can be funded from the operational budget and what additional monies are needed, as well as where you might get them. Effective educators view themselves as part of an overall museum team committed to the success of the organization. Collaboration is essential for a cohesive and comprehensive museum education program. (For a more extensive discussion about internal and external collaboration, see Chapter 13.)

Self-supporting Programs

Developing self-supporting programs may be one of the easiest ways to fund activities. In other words, the fees charged for the special event, class, workshop, film, or lecture cover all the expenses for the program. Huber and Johnson have described programs in detail in Chapter 8. They define a program "as an activity or series of related activities that present information or entertainment to the audience at a specific time and place, for a specific purpose." Examples of programs are lectures, forums, seminars, films, puppet shows, storytelling, or workshops. They can be targeted to any age group or any size audience. When planning self-

supporting activities, the educator must itemize all related expenses so she or he can establish the minimum number of attendees needed to determine an appropriate admission or class fee. This might be more easily done if the educator has some experience or begins by planning smaller programs so that she or he knows everything that must be considered, such as promotion, materials and supplies, staffing, food, equipment, and all additional expenses. (See the Chapter 8 checklist to help you determine program categories.) Before you finalize the price of your program, a little "comparison shopping" is recommended. "Shop" for similar educational activities at other institutions by phone, online, or through program flyers to verify that the price of your program is comparable to similar programs at other museums.

EXTERNAL FUNDING

After you have prepared your budget plan, when should you seek outside funding? What types of external funding are available? There comes a time in any organization's growth where more money will be needed to fund special programs, activities, projects, or events and all the necessary costs that accompany them. At these times, educators will need to look beyond the institution's annual budget to outside sources, or "external funding." Because many good articles and books have been written about fund-raising and grantsmanship, this chapter will not be another "how to" for planning fund-raisers or writing grants; rather, I intend to present a wide variety of other funding options for educators to consider.[5]

Grants

What are grants? Grants award financial assistance, often competitive in nature, to fund a particular activity, project, or facility. Generally, grant awards do not need to be paid back, although many require the organization to provide some cash or in-kind match up front. Grants are commonly offered through governmental agencies, corporations, and foundations for various reasons. They can be public funds in the case of government grants, or private, from foundations and businesses. Most granting organizations identify who is eligible, what they fund, and what the requirements are for the application and award process. Although you may occasionally find grant funding for operations, development, buildings, and staffing, the majority of funders only support projects or programs.

The grant application process is generally formal and is structured by the granting agency. The process

I have used self-supporting programs, especially for children's classes (ages 8–12), although these types of programs are not limited to this age group. In the late 1980s I managed the Sirrine House, a historic home museum that was part of a larger city museum. There was no budget for the home's education program. I worked with a local education consultant to offer classes relevant to the era of the home. The consultant taught a variety of classes at museums in Arizona. After looking through her list of available workshops, she began with a Victorian Valentine's Day card-making program. I calculated the program costs, including her fee, and determined the minimum number of registrants we would need for the class to proceed. Fortunately this educator understood my dilemma—no program budget—and agreed to schedule her workshop knowing that if the required number of children were not confirmed, I could not afford to hire her. The instructor, the parent museum, and I promoted the workshop at every opportunity. She announced our class at her other programs. I advertised in the members' newsletter, posted flyers at the local library and both museums, and contacted the local paper, and we used every free or inexpensive way we could think of to advertise the class. As a result, we had no problem filling the class. With the success of this first self-supporting program, I contracted with this educator and others to run additional workshops. Due to active and timely publicity, we were able to fill every class we offered.

This self-supporting process worked well again when I was the assistant director at the Deer Valley Rock Art Center, a petroglyph site and museum. I had a very small and inexperienced staff and group of volunteers. Our part-time educator was a master's degree student at the university. There was no funding to support her salary over the summer, so we developed an archaeology summer camp program for children that she could run. Once again, using a program checklist to determine costs, we identified the minimum number of children needed for the camp to be self-supporting. The museum offered several all-day, one-week programs throughout most of June, July, and August. The camp taught program participants about rock art, archaeology, and preservation. In this case we looked at school schedules and holidays and considered parents' commute times before we selected the weeks and times we would run the camp. The only week that wasn't fully enrolled was the first one. However, because future weeks were completely booked with at least the minimum number of children, I agreed to let the first camp proceed even though we were short a couple of kids. We more than made up for the extra costs of the first program in the other weeks, and the smaller first class afforded the student educator an opportunity to test her program under less pressure. Since then, this museum has continued its summer camp program, even though the educator and I no longer work there. This speaks to the success of the program in serving both the need for funding as well as a public program serving the educational mission of the institution.

—Kimberly A. Huber

may include a letter of intent, application, review, award, implementation, evaluation, and reporting. Grant recipients are generally expected to spend their funds in accordance with the granting agency's guidelines and are held accountable for fiscal and project reporting. Often the level of accountability is in proportion to the amount awarded and the nature of the granting agency. For example, large government grants (public funds) may require extensive applications, structured evaluation, and final reports, whereas smaller foundation grants might only require request and completion letters. Consequently, educators should seek to match their grant request to the appropriate agency or organization, taking into account the eligibility requirements and project guidelines along with the amount of time and effort involved in making the request and completing the reporting process. It just doesn't make sense to request small amounts of money for very simple projects from large governmental agencies, unless the granting process is a relatively simple one. In these cases the educator would be much better served by applying to a local funder, such as an arts or humanities council or a local business, or even by asking the museum's guild for the money. To find out more about where to get grants go to your local library, especially if it has a foundation center or grantsmanship center. You can also search online under grants, foundations, or philanthropy; some useful websites are the Foundation Directory and First Gov for Nonprofits.[6]

FUNDING APACHE GAMING VIDEO DOCUMENTARY A personal example of project funding follows: In 1994, I produced a video documentary, *Apache Gaming: Betting on the Past*, to accompany an exhibit I curated on Indian gaming for the Mesa Southwest Museum, now the Arizona Museum for Natural History. The museum frequently ran short videos in its theater, which was adjacent to the large, changing exhibition gallery. Because the exhibit was going to take a unique look at the gaming controversy in Arizona, I wanted to include perspectives from two native cultures; the exhibit examined the Yavapai-Apache Indians at the Fort McDowell Mohave-Apache Indian Community (now the Fort McDowell Yavapai Nation), and the documentary focused on the White Mountain Apache Tribe. Although I was given a budget to curate the exhibit, no money was available when I also wanted to produce a video. After talking with the museum's director and assistant director, I prepared a simple request letter and presentation for the museum's guild, which awarded $30,000 for the video project. Although the guild's mission was to support the activities of the museum, it could have rejected the request or offered less money.

Throughout the project I sought additional assistance and funding through basic requests. A local airline granted free flights for the two-man video crew from California, and a national hotel chain provided free housing for us when we recorded in Tucson. In the case of the airfare I made several phone calls to identify who at the airline was responsible for reviewing these kinds of requests and what was required. A one-page letter explained the project and identified our needs. After following up with a phone call, in less than a month an award letter and coupons for airline tickets were received. The hotel request was even easier. I made one call, asked for the manager, explained the project, and made my request. He approved our complimentary housing on the spot, but asked for a request letter as well. I reconfirmed our reservation before leaving town. In both cases these organizations had an interest in supporting Arizona projects. They asked for nothing in return, but I promised to include their institutions' names in the credits of the documentary. The museum planned to promote the video to some television stations, and we hoped the documentary would be aired, but I specifically told both corporate funders I could not promise the program would be broadcast. Fortunately, *Apache Gaming: Betting on the Past* played on several Arizona and California television stations. I verified the spelling of each person's name and organization and sent them each a personal thank-you note, a copy of the video, and an invitation to the exhibition and documentary opening reception. I couldn't believe how easy it was to get goods, services, and money just by asking! Although it may be unusual to get such a large amount of money in such an informal manner, the point I am making is that I asked, and you can too.

MAKING SUCCESSFUL FUNDING REQUESTS Why was external funding for the *Apache Gaming* video documentary successful? Although we did not formally evaluate the fund-raising efforts, I believe we were successful for the following reasons. Foremost, I asked. This first step is surprisingly underrated. Organizations are not likely to come to you to offer free funding; you have to seek it out. If I hadn't gone to these organizations, they would not have known about the project or volunteered their funds and services. When making a

financial request, be prepared with the following information (also see Textbox 11.1 on page 139):

- Thoroughly understand your project and believe in its importance.
- Approach your request in a format the funders are comfortable with (phone call, letter, presentation).
- Prepare your request in a way that briefly outlines the project, goals, needs, and relevance to their organization.
- Be specific about what you need from them (money, tickets, or hotel rooms).
- Be specific and realistic about what you will offer in return. (Only promise what you can actually deliver.)
- Be professional and polite.
- After the money or service is granted, deliver what you promise and more. Credit their organization, send a thank-you letter, invite them to the program, and send complimentary materials from the project or program, if appropriate, such as a video, compact disc, an exhibit catalog, or something produced from their funding efforts.

Once the funds, free services, or supplies are awarded it is especially important to follow through with your plan. Complete final reports or send thank-you notes in a timely manner. Always acknowledge outside support unless you are specifically asked not to. The people who work at funding agencies have wide-reaching communication networks. You will quickly receive a bad reputation as a grant recipient if you don't follow the award process through to completion.

Individual Support

Although many people think external funding comes mostly from corporations, foundations, and governmental agencies, the truth is that individuals provide the greatest source of funding dollars. According to *Giving USA 2006: The Annual Report on Philanthropy*, "The majority of that giving came from individuals, $199.1 billion (76.5%) . . . . Giving by bequest was $17.4 billion, foundations gave $30 billion, and corporations donated $13.7 billion (AAFRC)."[7] What does that mean for the small, rural, or midsize museum and its education program? It means that educators should not only seek out grants, but also reach out to individuals and businesses in the community who have an interest or connection to their institution's educational needs. Board members, former staff, community leaders, teachers, family members, artists, or relatives of pioneers may be interested in supporting your institution's educational objectives. Museums should be integral parts of their community by enhancing formal education, providing family-friendly environments, offering hands-on activities, and including meeting spaces when appropriate. As institutions of informal learning, museums should have a local public presence that has some relevance to each community's needs. If the museum is recognized as contributing to the public, then staff should not be afraid to ask for support.

Individuals can be approached to sponsor projects and programs, make donations, and leave bequests that benefit the institution as a whole and the education program specifically. According to the American Association of Museums, museums and individuals benefit from a relationship. "Through museums, donors can reaffirm their commitment to the arts, sciences, history, and lifelong learning and to creating a stronger and more civil society by making objects and information accessible. In addition, individual donors often have family connections or other close personal relationships with the museums they support, adding to the importance and significance of that support."[8] Each institution must establish guidelines for how these requests should be made and by whom. Educators should not make personal requests on behalf of the institution without prior approval of the director and, in some cases, the board. AAM's publication "Guidelines for Museums on Developing and Managing Individual Donor Support" provides suggestions for getting started or revising your policies on dealing with individuals.[9]

BEQUESTS Probably one of the most complicated and sometimes controversial types of funding comes in the form of bequests. Bequests, planned giving, and many donations involve legal documents. Complications may arise from the legal portions of the bequest, will, and subsequent donation including authenticity, ownership, and appraised value. Legal knowledge and assistance should be of utmost concern with these types of gifts. Occasionally museums are caught unprepared by a bequest that they know nothing about until they are contacted by a lawyer. Some have been pleasantly surprised with generous remembrances, but others have been left wondering what to do with objects that don't fit into their collection. Therefore a museum benefits most when it is part of the bequest plan. When it is, the institution enters into the future gift and legal document with the knowledge that the financial or material gifts are something that will be welcome, useful, and in keeping with the institution's mission and future plans on the passing of the donor. Former employees, volunteers, local pioneers, families, patrons, or anyone interested in supporting the museum and its educational programs might be potential donors.

Bequests are somewhat controversial because not all institutions find it appropriate or comfortable to talk about gifts that result from a death. However, universities and museums as well as many other organizations have taken a much more proactive approach in asking and preparing for these types of gifts. The public has also become more accepting and open to discussions as they look toward their will preparation and estate planning. Some larger institutions have entire wings, libraries, or programs named after a benefactor. Even given the changing attitude, educators should leave the details of soliciting these types of gifts to the director, board, or whomever the institution has assigned this responsibility. However, all staff should be aware of the possibility of bequests, so they may encourage planned giving when appropriate and can refer potential donors to the designated staff member if they are approached about the subject.

Sponsorship and Corporate Funding

Sponsors are another important source of external funding. A sponsor is a person, corporation, or business that helps to defray expenses or pays for a particular program, event, web project, or exhibit, whereas donations can be cash, materials and supplies, services, or consumable goods.[10] (For additional information about program sponsors see Chapter 8.) Generally, sponsor support comes with an expectation that the sponsoring organization or individual will receive name recognition at the program and be credited in publicity materials. Recognizing the sponsor is a common practice, although on occasion sponsors request anonymity. Large corporations have sponsored traveling exhibits, especially those that emphasize curriculum materials, self-guides, catalogs, and other educational publications. Once again, the institution must be able and willing to follow through with sponsor's publicity requirements and provide a written agreement. I have seen many instances during my work as a grants administrator where the awarded museum has forgotten or omitted the required credit line in its publicity. Funders often have long memories when the conditions of the grant or gift have not been met, and may be unwilling to finance additional requests because of this oversight.

These days potential funders are expressing greater interest in education. They are attracted to educational products related to both small and large projects. They often want to know what educational components, such as curriculum materials or electronic field trips, will be included with an exhibition package. Or they are interested in funding smaller, stand-alone educational products that can be distributed with their name as funder—thus linking their name to an educational mission. Over the years the National Air and Space Museum education department has received private funding for a variety of teaching posters and educational web activities. One source for funds related to education is federal agencies. Many federal agencies have monies stipulated as funds for education. Sometimes these agencies look for other institutions they can partner with to accomplish this mission. They may fund an exhibition or teacher materials. Museum personnel, from directors to curators and especially development staff, are realizing the value of including educational components in funding requests.

—Tim Grove

As with individual donors, the American Association of Museums also offers suggestions for museums when dealing with businesses. "These guidelines are intended to help museums develop and implement policies and practices that address their relationships with business."[11] This online document includes general principles and guidelines that museum management can refer to when preparing their own policies within the ethical standards and best practices adopted by the AAM board of directors. Each museum must regularly review and revise its own policies in keeping with its mission, community focus, laws, and public trust responsibilities.

The smart museum educator is familiar with the institution's policies and procedures regarding grants, bequests, and sponsorships and takes these things into account before accepting any external funding. If the legal concerns are beyond the scope of the educator's responsibility and expertise, the appropriate level of legal counsel should be consulted. Many museums have no problem listing the sponsor or other funder in their publicity; however, not all corporate sponsors or donors may be a good match for the institution, project, or event that needs outside funding. If your museum is hosting a large family event you may not be willing to have a corporate sponsor that is linked to alcohol, tobacco, or even junk food. Many institutions are especially unwilling to take on the potential legal liability issues that come with serving alcoholic beverages. In some cases, even if the institution is willing to include a liquor-related sponsor, it may cost too much for additional liability insurance, making this type of sponsorship impractical.

Most large corporations are interested in giving back to their communities by giving a certain percentage of goods, services, or cash locally. Each state and likely each community will have businesses with similar objectives. In Arizona many businesses give regularly to local museums and other nonprofit organizations. For example, The Salt River Project (SRP), a large power company in the Southwest, is actively involved with Arizona's museums. SRP has a museum and history division that regularly participates in the statewide museum association and conferences as well as other community programs. This company has frequently printed, at no charge, the Museum Association of Arizona's annual conference brochures. It has provided signs and banners for many arts events and has sponsored exhibits for a variety of museums. SRP has a long history of providing power to the Southwest. Because much of its energy comes from water-related resources, it also has a speakers' bureau that offers presenters to various community groups interested in power, energy, water, and related topics. Savvy museum educators in Arizona have linked their projects to one of these subject areas and received funding from this corporation.

Before agreeing to accept sponsorship from businesses, make sure you know and can satisfy their publicity requirements such as logo and photo usage as well as the exact wording needed to recognize the organization. Each museum should have its own guidelines for use of its own name and logo. Many large corporations have structured giving and reviewing processes. You may need to plan at least a year in advance to take advantage of corporate and grant time lines. Some organizations only review requests once a year, while others may review requests monthly. Educators must review each organization's giving policies online, check funding directories at the local library, or call the appropriate person at the corporation to find out how and when to proceed.

Even if corporations have a commitment to the community, their business image may not be a good match for your institution or program. While I was working for a city-owned and operated museum we were involved with a nature-oriented changing exhibition that presented a preservation and conservation message. In order to present a balanced approach to politically charged issues such as grazing and water rights, the museum invited a wide variety of panelists to discuss these issues and opened up a forum for public discussion. Although a group such as the Sierra Club or PETA might have appeared to be obvious sponsors, a city-run museum may require less controversial perspectives in its programs. In the past some museums have come under unpleasant public and professional scrutiny when it appeared that the sponsor controlled the content of the event or exhibit. Keeping true to the museum's mission and following the institution's policies will help guide your sponsorship choices.

Museum exhibits may sometimes play an advocate role or present a topic from one point of view. Another example from my personal experiences follows. Referring again to the exhibit and documentary on Indian gaming, it was my feeling that this controversial topic was being covered in the media from economic and political perspectives, but wasn't being addressed from a native, cultural perspective. I did research and conducted fieldwork to find out what people from the White Mountain and Yavapai-Apache tribes thought of gaming and gambling from their cultural viewpoints. Although this approach led to some controversy, I made a point to inform the audience that the media had dealt extensively with the political and economic components of gaming in Arizona, but the exhibit was offering another point of view. As previously mentioned, the accompanying video received external funding from the museum's guild and corporations, but I did not seek any funding from the tribes. I felt it would have been a conflict of interest to ask either tribe to fund this project.

LOCAL BUSINESS SUPPORT Museum professionals should cultivate community relationships that will promote their interests and enhance their services. It is not uncommon for museums to work with local restaurants that are willing to cater events gratis or at reduced rates. Watch the business section of the local paper to see what new restaurants are opening. They may choose to use their community relations budget or take some of their publicity funds to provide food and promote their restaurant at a large museum function. If your event draws a diverse segment of the local community or a large crowd, you can let the restaurant know that supporting your event would be a great way to "kick off" its grand opening. In some cases it may be willing to cater a reception the first time for free in the hopes that the museum will ask it to cater future events. In other instances restaurants can be charged to participate as vendors at large-scale programs. For

example, the food vendor pays a fee to the museum to be represented at the event. The restaurant promotes itself through signs, banners, or business cards to a large and diverse audience and it profits through food and drink sales.

Other likely support for the small or rural museum is the local hardware store, printing/paper company, and local newspaper. Educators frequently need materials and supplies for programs and advertising. Even small businesses are interested in community support and free publicity. Donating or discounting supplies or printing services to the museum may be a good match with their business plans. The press needs information for its papers. Even though you may not get financial support from a print medium outlet, you should develop a relationship with the cultural arts reporter to garner their attention. Good media relations can provide your organization with invaluable in-kind advertising and free publicity opportunities. Send press releases when you have news of interest to the paper or offer information about upcoming programs for its community calendar section. Advertisements are generally paid, but some press outlets may donate their services for special events. In some communities the newspaper may agree to a limited number of free ads of a specific size, including the layout and design. Any option is possible when working together. But, you must ask them for their support, respect their deadlines, and invite them to your events. It is not likely that these local business groups will approach you.

What to Know before Making Your Funding Request

As you can see, corporate, business, and individual sponsorships come with conditions and responsibilities. Museum educators must always follow the policies of their organization and have the permission and support of the director or board before considering any form of external financial support. You must also weigh the pros and cons of sponsorship. Before seeking external funding, here are some useful questions to ask:

- Do I have the approval and support of the museum administrator or board to pursue external funding?
- Do I understand all the museum's policies with regard to giving and grants?
- Is my project clearly defined?
- Do I have a clear understanding of what I will need for the project?
- Does the sponsor have a community image that is consistent with our project, program, or event?

- Do I know who should approach the sponsor and how?
- What will the sponsor require from us?
- Can we deliver what the sponsor requires and commit to the terms of the agreement?
- Will it cost us more to accept this financial assistance than we can afford or will receive in return?
- If there are any profits for this project or program will the funder expect or require a percentage?
- Are the political implications of accepting funds from this group or organization acceptable to the museum administration?

Once you know the answers to these questions and any others that are relevant to your institution, you can prepare to make a request for support or financial assistance. Keep these things in mind:

- Clearly define your program or project.
- Research and contact appropriate funders or sponsors.
- Briefly identify your institution, yourself, and your project in a professional manner.
- Be specific about what you want.
- Don't get greedy. Only ask for what you need or what they can give.
- Don't take advantage of the sponsor or funding agency by asking them too often. Spread your requests to a variety of individuals, businesses, or organizations.
- Satisfy all the funders' requirements.
- Thank them in the manner in which they want to be thanked.

Donations and Volunteers

Donations are most often thought of in the museum field as gifts to build or enhance the collections area. However, gifts can come in many forms and should not be ruled out as a form of assistance for museum education programs. When I managed a historic home museum's education and volunteer program, the education department received many gifts. In the early stages of building the interpretive program, guides were asked to make their own costumes. They were provided with historic information, resources, and costume patterns to guide their choices of fabric, style, and color. Volunteers adapted their outfits to a particular character or type of character relevant to the period, in our case a middle-class family whose home was built in the Southwest, circa 1895. Volunteers took their sewing and design tasks to heart, and many made

more than one dress, added a hat, and even styled their hair in a historically appropriate manner. No museum funds were available for these costumes, yet all the volunteers had them and no one complained about making or buying them. Technically their historic attire were not really gifts, because they didn't donate them to the museum. However, their outfits did not cost the museum anything. The clothing enhanced the interpretation program, so that is certainly a gift in my view. Without the generosity of these volunteers, no one would have had costumes at that time.

The docents at this historic site also became interested in contributing more than their time. We met monthly to update the program, discuss issues, and interact. At these meetings the volunteers would offer suggestions about hands-on activities or objects that would enhance the tours. Often an item would be suggested, such as a rug beater, and at the next meeting someone would arrive with one. Curators might be cringing after reading the previous sentence. Having also been a curator I know the complicated issues surrounding accepting gifts, accessioning objects, and caring for collections. I understand these concerns and am sensitive to these curatorial needs. But, I am not talking about educators accepting unrestricted gifts for the collection. Instead, we were seeking educational materials that could be used during tours or activities, not collection artifacts. Although these teaching materials were period specific, they were not accessioned. In this case it was appropriate for me to receive gifts for educational purposes. Once again, educators must check with their institutions' policies before accepting any educational donations.

Sometimes items would come in that weren't appropriate. I respectfully declined them, and there appeared to be no hard feelings from the volunteers. It quickly became obvious to me that our volunteers wanted to give, so I worked with other museum staff to create a list of items we would like to have donated for educational purposes. Occasionally we needed objects for special events, like a Christmas tree and related holiday decorations, at other times we needed signs or building supplies. As the list grew, we decided to expand our requests beyond the small volunteer base. The historic home was a satellite of a larger museum with a much larger support system. We reached thousands of people, including members and the guild, by advertising the list in the primary museum's newsletter. People were encouraged to call me before making purchases so that I could give them specific details about the items or could shop with them to make certain we had period-appropriate pieces that fit our project needs. We checked off many items from our list this way and found this technique very successful in meeting our needs. Educators could take this a step further by advertising in their local newspaper. It is essential to be very specific about your needs. Also, I strongly recommend that you encourage donors to contact the education department prior to making any purchases. Remember, when individuals provide a donation of money or objects they often have expectations: having a wing named after them, having their gift used for a specific purpose, seeing their object on permanent display, influencing educational content, or any number of things. Discuss the gift and gift process with the donor, make sure that the museum has clear title, and require unrestricted giving, and, if there are restrictions, they are ones that the organization can comfortably and legally accommodate.

VOLUNTEERS SHARE TIME AND EXPERTISE The services of dedicated volunteers may be the biggest gift a museum can receive. Volunteers have performed nearly every function in museums, and their contributions cannot be understated. Nearly every museum relies on volunteers to do something; even if they are not involved in the daily activities, they may serve on the board. Guilds, docents, boards, tour guides, and auxiliaries are just a few examples of the ways volunteers are commonly used. Volunteer management is discussed in Chapter 2, docent training in Chapter 3, and teaching tour guides in Chapter 4 of this text. Other works discuss nonprofit boards, but docents and boards are not the focus of this discussion. What I want museum educators to consider is using some volunteers in ways you may not have previously considered.

Many communities have volunteer organizations whose purpose is to provide small and emerging institutions or businesses with free expertise from those in the field or from businesspeople who have retired but seek meaningful community involvement. A group that might be of assistance to you is DOVIA, Directors of Volunteers in Agencies (www.dovia.org). To locate a volunteer center in your state check this website: www. pointsoflight.org/centers/find_center. Volunteers from these groups can be tapped to help with planning, special projects, and mentoring, but they generally are not likely to be good sources for finding docents, long-term volunteers, or board members. Many corporations and businesses have community services divisions that send employees to do special, limited projects. They can be used to paint and remodel, staff

event booths, aid in parking, take tickets, or for many other short-term jobs that require minimum training. Using volunteers in these ways helps museums "fund" large-scale programs and projects they would not be able to otherwise support using their own staff and budget.

CONCLUSION

I hope I have given you some new ideas about funding and different types of donations along with some examples you can use or adapt in your work. Museums and other nonprofits should rely on operation funds for the bulk of their educational programs. But educators are often forced to look outside their organizations for external resources if they want to enhance their programs and continue to engage their communities. Educators cannot sit back and wait for internal funding to support all their activities. They must be creative in looking for other ways to bring in money, staff, gifts, materials, and supplies. Grants, self-supporting activities, individuals, and businesses can provide alternative opportunities to do more, but volunteers can be one of your best resources of all. When educators successfully use external assistance to build more and better public programs, they can use their results to bolster future internal funding by demonstrating that the museum's audience desires special programs, projects, and events. Use your imagination to find your own local, state, and national resources to enhance your museum's educational programs.

Textbox 11.1. Tips for Making Successful Funding Requests

- Know what your project is about and believe in its importance.
- Conduct research to match your project to the correct funder.
- Prepare your request in a way that briefly outlines the project, goals, needs, and relevance to the funder's organization.
- Make your funding request in the format the funder requires and pay special attention to instructions and deadlines.
- Be specific about what you need from the funder.
- Be specific about what you would offer in return.
- Be professional and polite.
- Always correctly cite and publicize the funder.
- After funds or services are awarded, deliver what is required, what you promise, and more.
- Thank the funder, publicly if it is appropriate.

NOTES

1. American Association of Museums, *Excellence and Equity: Education and the Public Dimensions of Museums* (Washington, D.C.: AAM, 1992), 24.

2. Institute of Museum and Library Services, "NLG Project Planning: A Tutorial," IMLS 2007, www.imls.gov/Project_Planning/index1.asp (Jan. 21, 2008).

3. American Association of Museums, "Mission and Institutional Planning," AAM 2007, www.aam-us.org/login.cfm (Jan. 21, 2008).

4. American Association for State and Local History, "AASLH Homepage: Technical Leaflet Bundles," AASLH 2007, www.aaslh.org/leaflets.htm (Jan. 21, 2008).

5. For more detailed information about grant writing, grantsmanship, and fund-raising, see Foundation Center, "Foundation Center Homepage," Foundation Center 2008, www.foundationcenter.org (Jan. 21, 2008), or go to your local library.

6. These websites are available at foundationcenter.org/find-funders/fundingsources/fdo.html; www.tgci.com/; www.firstgov.gov/Business/Nonprofit.shtml, www.grants.gov/; and www.grantsmart.com/.

7. AAFRC Trust for Philanthropy, *Giving USA 2006: The Annual Report on Philanthropy* (Glenview, Ill.: Giving USA Foundation, 2007).

8. American Association of Museums, "Guidelines for Museums on Developing and Managing Individual Donor Support," AAM November 2002, www.aam-us.org/museumresources/ethics/indiv_support.cfm (June 18, 2007).

9. AAM, "Guidelines for Museums on Developing and Managing Individual Donor Support," 2002, www.aam-us.org/museumresources/ethics/indiv_support.cfm.

10. Merriam-Webster, Inc., "Sponsor," *Merriam-Webster Online Dictionary*, 2008, www.m-w.com/dictionary/sponsor (Jan. 21, 2008).

11. American Association of Museums, "Guidelines for Museums on Developing and Managing Business Support," AAM November 2001, www.aam-us.org/museumresources/ethics/bus_support.cfm (June 18, 2007).

CHAPTER 12

Educators on Exhibition Teams

TIM GROVE

> **Museum educators combine knowledge of content with creativity of presentation in order to spark the imagination and inspire their audience.**
>
> —*Brenna Holzhauer, The George Washington University Museum Education Program, class of 2008*

The production of an effective exhibition, whether small or large, requires a team effort. The team is usually made up of members who each bring a specific knowledge and skill to the group, and thus each member plays a certain role. While there is no magic formula for the structure of an exhibition team, there are roles that are necessary. It is this group of people who will conceptualize the exhibition and develop the plans that will lead to the production of the exhibition. Many museums today recognize that educators can contribute to the exhibition development process in more ways than traditionally thought. An educator was often brought in when planning was finished to develop programming, tours, and curriculum materials. This chapter discusses the benefits of including an educator on the team from its formation and the expertise and skills that educators bring to the team.

TEAM MEMBERS

Exhibition teams should generally include a content expert, a designer, and an educator. A project manager is also important, especially if it is a large exhibition. Some teams may also include a registrar or conservator, a writer, or a researcher.

The content expert, the person who knows the subject matter and artifacts the best, is often a curator, historian, or scientist. This person has researched the topic and is usually the person who provides the initial vision for the focus of the exhibition. This person also has researched the artifacts and documents and other sources that will be the backbone of the exhibition and takes the lead in selecting which sources best illustrate the interpretive themes. The group relies on this person's scholarly knowledge of the subject.

The designer is skilled in both the 3-D and 2-D world of exhibitions and is the person who will guide the overall look of the exhibition. This person can visualize the proposed space and help team members see where ideas would and would not work. The designer draws concept (bubble) plans, floor plans, and case layouts, creates 3-D models, determines exhibition colors, and the graphic design of labels, and oversees the quality of the final built product. He or she may also design interactive components including prototypes for testing purposes. It is important for the designer to understand universal design principles so that the exhibition is accessible to as many people as possible regardless of age, ability, or circumstance.

The educator is sometimes called the exhibit developer or interpretive planner. This person contributes knowledge of how people learn in informal learning environments. He or she also has a good understanding of the typical visitor to the institution. This person understands accessibility, both physical and intellectual, and thus advocates for components such as tactiles, interactives, and layered label hierarchies. The educator helps the team think about learning objectives. The educator usually takes the lead in evaluation as well, recommending what needs to be evaluated and guiding the process.

My experience has shown that most projects, larger ones especially, benefit from having a designated project manager. This person's responsibility is to keep the project moving forward, to manage the budget and schedule, to facilitate interactions with outside contractors, and ultimately to ensure the steady progress of the project toward completion. It is usually in this person's best interest to avoid involvement in the interpretive planning process. When conflict arises between team members, the project manager can moderate disputes, and thus it is best that this person be seen by all parties as an unbiased observer. Smaller organizations may be able to assign someone from the administrative staff for this function.

Collaboration Is the Key

Every team member wants to produce an excellent exhibition of which he or she can be proud. Yet, excellence to one member may not be excellence to another member. In the end, exhibition development is all about negotiation and collaboration. Team members rarely achieve the exhibition that they all think is ideal. Often each member's ideal exhibition is different from the rest of the team's. Think about the various agendas.

CONTENT PERSON The content person has done amazing research and analysis and she has found powerful artifacts to illustrate her points. She wants an exhibition that will showcase this research. She also has become attached to the artifacts she has spent time tracking down.

Caution: There can be too much text and in-depth analysis of an argument, too many artifacts that do not specifically connect to main points, and text written for a peer audience.

DESIGNER This person uses creative tools to develop exhibitions that are aesthetically pleasing and engaging. She wants to create a space that generates an emotional response.

Caution: Sometimes the design can overpower the artifacts or artwork; bad design can make text hard to read; some designers find it difficult to marry accessible design with stimulating/immersive design.

EDUCATOR This person understands how people learn and wants to find the best ways to engage them with the content. He wants to provoke thought and stimulate the desire for extended learning beyond the exhibition.

Caution: There can be too many interactives; too many bells and whistles, which can overshadow the message; too much focus on entertainment and/or technology rather than learning; and text that is too simplistic and loses its main message.

CONSERVATOR/COLLECTIONS MANAGER This person's job is about preservation. Her concern is the safety and well-being of the objects, which requires consideration of temperature, humidity, and mounting.

Caution: Low lighting levels are usually the challenge here. If the visitors can't see it, how can they learn anything or even appreciate an artifact's beauty?

By working together to accomplish agreed-on goals, the group can support the bigger picture instead of just individual concerns.

Conflicting Agendas Case Study

My work on the Lewis & Clark bicentennial exhibition team serves as an example of mixed agendas. The curator had spent years researching the topic and had traveled to collections across the nation finding the most interesting and powerful objects for the exhibition. Her ideal exhibition would feature as many of those objects as possible—so that visitors could see the amazing objects that she had found. The designers and educator cringed at the thought of cases and wall space filled with hundreds of objects—visual overload for visitors. The designer was concerned with aesthetics and wanted to keep the design clean. The educator was concerned with creating an environment that was conducive to learning and feared that making the visitor work too hard would ultimately affect the learning. The registrar, working closely with the conservator, was responsible for the objects and the many loaned artifacts coming from outside institutions. She was sensitive to light level requirements, seen by both the curator and educator as too low. Both the curator and educator wanted the visitor to be able to see and examine the artifacts. With space as a major issue, the educator proposed various large components like a map of tribal lands that he thought would help visitors understand the topic, recognizing that the exhibition's interpretation of the cultural landscape was different from the one visitors might be expecting. The curator, again, wanted space for more objects. Ultimately the curator and educator found compromise and proposed interactives that would engage visitors and provoke thought. Both wanted to provide visitors with an engaging experience that would make visitors want to stay in the exhibition. The administration soon became concerned that visitors might want to stay too long in the space. They saw this as a revenue generating opportunity and were concerned with throughput—again, a conflict from another agenda.

—Tim Grove

Education-driven Exhibits—A Perspective

Beginning in the 1980s, exhibit development at the Desert Botanical Garden in Arizona originated in the education department. Prior to that time there were minimal labels and no attempt to provide interpretation within an exhibition context. In the 1980s the Garden obtained an Arizona Humanities Council Grant to develop an educational interactive exhibit featuring ethnobotany of Sonoran Desert peoples. The new trail was designed as a teaching vehicle, thus the hands-on exhibits, signage, and docent touch carts focused on learning in an immersion setting. The hands-on exhibits and human focus of the trail made it wildly popular with visitors, and it became an important place for fourth-grade students to study about Arizona.

In 1992 the Garden received a National Science Foundation Grant to go a step further and develop outdoor visitor-centered exhibits to create a "Comprehensive Desert Exhibit: An Innovative Model for Informal Science Education in Outdoor Museums." The grant funded 60+ interactive trailside interpretive signs, and five trailside "investigation/discovery stations" to be staffed by docents. Because the funding was education-focused, staff understood from the beginning that all exhibits needed to have educational messages based on the goals of each trail. Development teams included staff and volunteers from every department at the Garden. Formative evaluation data was collected for each exhibit prototype. Exhibit prototypes were then reviewed by education experts for educational messages and intellectual accessibility and by content experts for accuracy.

The funding also paid for supplementary educational materials like new trail guides, handouts, a new children's guide, teacher training, new plant labels, and more. All this was included in the grant proposal as a complete educational package. Having education-driven exhibits has not been the norm in most museums, but if educators are included in designing the exhibition or the grant proposal, education could be a primary driver or a very important one rather than an afterthought.

—Nancy Cutler

FOSTERING COMMUNICATION

Within almost any group of people with a range of concerns and agendas, conflict will arise. Often exhibition team members have some experience in several discipline areas. The educator must have good research skills and a sense of how design contributes to or detracts from accessibility. The designer should recognize the accessibility concerns and should have some evaluation experience. This skill overlap is good and should be encouraged when it aids collaboration. However, sometimes it can result in the perception that boundaries have been crossed. "Everyone thinks he is a designer" and "Everyone thinks he is an educator." The key to avoiding conflict is communication and recognizing the other person's expertise. It should be clear who has the final say in a conflict. Opposing viewpoints should be articulated with solid reasoning. Sometimes it is helpful to bring in an outside voice of experience, someone who has struggled with similar issues. Often the team is more receptive to the thoughts of an outside person when members are dug in on opposing sides of an issue. A project manager who has stayed neutral can be helpful, too. In many organizations it will be the director who has the final say. In the end, with all the viewpoints, the collaboration and even compromises will produce a richer product.

The Educator and the Curator

The curator-educator relationship is perhaps the most important among team members because the educator will be working with the curator's research and may even do some of the research. Sometimes educators feel that curators either don't see the value of the educator's contribution to the team or don't understand the educator's role. It is in the educator's best interest to work well with the curator. An educator needs to be familiar with the content and to understand the research process, be it historical, scientific, and so on. An educator can be most effective when he or she has an excellent grasp of the exhibition content. The curator should help with this by answering questions and recommending reading materials. If the educator shows an interest in the curator's research area, it strengthens the relationship. The educator serves as a translator in some regards. He or she is taking scholarly research and interpreting it in multiple ways to reach a variety of audiences. Some curators are better writers than others, and some understand diverse audiences more than others. The educator can help the curator think about the many audiences. It is crucial for educators to request curator review of materials that they produce, whether they are family labels, a family guide, text for interactives, curriculum materials, or docent materials, because this validates the curator's role as content expert. The curator should always be recognized and respected as the content expert, while the educator should be respected as the audience research expert.

ORGANIZING THE CONTENT

Several different team members may take the lead in defining the conceptual focus for the exhibition. Often the curator fills this role. Sometimes the educator does. Ultimately it is the entire team's responsibility.

The starting point should be crafting the big idea: a central focus that unifies the exhibition's many parts. In her book on exhibit labels, Beverly Serrell writes that "good labels are guided by a strong, cohesive exhibit plan—a theme, story, or communication goal—that sets the tone and limits the content. Not just the labels, but all of the interpretive techniques and the elements designed for the exhibition will be driven by this plan."[1] The next step should be writing take-home messages, the main points of the exhibition. Take-home messages provide focus for the exhibition text and help ensure a smoother development process.[2] The process of writing them is a valuable exercise for the core exhibition team. They should be stated simply. Even for large exhibitions, one main message should be central. For Lewis & Clark: The National Bicentennial Exhibition, the main message was:

> When they encountered each other, Lewis and Clark and the Indians made discoveries about their respective worlds.

This broad message conveyed the overall theme of cultural exchange. Ultimately the team wanted visitors to learn that Lewis and Clark traveled through a peopled landscape and that the various cultures that interacted influenced each other. Under that main message were primary messages and secondary messages. These are a little more specific.

- Primary messages
  o The encounters between the Indians and Lewis and Clark demonstrate the difficulties and the rewards of cross-cultural exchange.
  o Lewis and Clark traveled through a land inhabited by established cultures that were rich, diverse, and complex.
- Secondary messages
  o Lewis and Clark helped shape America's view of the West, a view that did not include the Native perspective.
  o How we view history changes over time.
  o Historic objects can be interpreted in diverse ways, and each object conveys a cultural message.

THE INTERPRETIVE PLAN

While the take-home messages help organize the content, an interpretive plan defines the overall exhibition experience. The plan outlines target audiences, provides a framework for how the various sections fit together, defines the visitor experience, and describes the types of media that will convey the messages. The team should consider pacing, layout, circulation flow, and other concepts that create the overall visitor experience. For example, don't put objects that will draw a lot of attention in a corner that can't accommodate a crowd. If using a narrative approach, where will the climax of the story go? Questions to consider include:

- Why is this topic important?
- What are the main components of the story?
- What objects will the story be built around?
- Is the exhibition visitor-centered or curator-centered?
- Who is the target audience?
- How do we want the visitor to feel or react?
- What should be the overall feeling (loud/playful/contemplative, etc.) of the exhibition?
- Will there be a specific route through or free-flow?
- Is some kind of orientation experience needed?
- Will we include interactives? What type—mechanical or computer?
- Will we include video?
- Will an audio tour be part of the experience?
- Will docent-led tours be available?
- Is space for programming needed?

INTERACTIVES

Another major way that educators typically contribute to exhibition teams is to guide the development of interactive components. The recognition that people learn in different ways leads to the need to find ways to make the exhibition visit a more active experience. It is important for the educator to have an understanding of learning theory and the ability to explain how people process information. A good interactive will provoke thought and increase both physical and intellectual accessibility.

Interactives can be high-tech or low-tech, mechanical, electrical, or computer-based. The term *interactive* has many different meanings, depending on who is using it. Generally, an interactive is an exhibition component that requires action on the part of the visitor. It requires a thoughtful response, and as Kathleen McLean has said, "Interactivity is about being reciprocal." The term *interactive* "puts more emphasis on the exhibit component's ability to *react* to visitor stimuli, to reciprocate."[3] Hands-on and interactive are not the same. Something can be tactile but not interactive. Some people might define a flip-book as an interactive experience; it's tactile and participatory, but doesn't usually require a response other than turning the pages. One way to understand it is that a good interactive requires a mental response such as a decision, not just a physical response. An example of this is an interactive that requires the visitor to put items into a specific order and then provides the visitor with a positive or negative response.

Interactives come in all shapes and sizes, and thus their budgets vary greatly. An important point to consider is that a good interactive does not have to cost a lot of money. There has been much debate in some circles as to whether or not computer interactives are the most effective way to reach younger visitors. My experience and observation have shown that this is not necessarily the case—one theory is that computers are such a major part of a child's everyday life that a mechanical interactive can be more effective in attracting and keeping the attention of a student because of its novelty.

Developing interactives requires creative thought and the willingness to prototype, test, and listen to visitor feedback. One should never develop an interactive just for the sake of having an interactive experience. Most important: Every interactive should have a clear learning objective. What do you want visitors to learn? There should be a compelling reason for the interactive—it expands on the interpretation or presents an interpretive point in a way other methods could not, or it reaches an age group the rest of the exhibition format does not reach. Another key point to remember is that the more simple and intuitive an interactive, the better. Complexity usually confuses visitors. If the directions are complicated or if the task requires many steps, visitors are more likely to move on. Directions must be clear. A payoff or reward for correct completion is not always necessary, but welcomed.

Not all ideas translate into a good interactive. History-based interactives are generally harder to develop than science-based interactives. They are often not about process or testing theory but about narrative or comparison. Interactives work well when you are trying to demonstrate phenomena, illustrate a process, show change, or compare and contrast.[4]

Qualities of a good interactive:

- Focused—one clear learning objective
- Requires a thoughtful response
- Provides an outcome based in visitor input
- May ask the visitor to:
  o Conduct activities
  o Gather evidence
  o Select options
  o Form conclusions
  o Test skills
  o Provide input
  o Alter a situation based on input
- Simple directions
- Clearly relates to and reinforces exhibition themes/concepts

Developing an Interactive—Around the World

Educators working on an exhibition about the history of commercial aviation at the National Air and Space Museum sought ways to infuse the exhibition with the stories of historical people. The story of the reporter H. R. Ekins came to their attention. Ekins decided to investigate the status of commercial aviation in the world and set off to try to beat the time record for traveling around the world. His adventure became a race when rival newspapers heard about it and sent reporters to race him. The trip is well documented in period newspapers and in a book that Ekins wrote about his experience. Ekins's story represented an opportunity to tell the status of commercial aviation around the world in 1936. Ekins's trip showed that there were no commercial airlines flying across the Atlantic yet (he traveled via the *Hindenburg*), that many foreign airlines were flying American-made planes, and that commercial service was available over the Pacific Ocean. The challenge was how to turn this story into an interactive experience.

The educators came up with a map-based activity focused on a large and colorful 1936 map. Visitors are challenged to find out if Ekins beat his competitors. Visitors track Ekins's trip by placing five "tickets" in the correct sequence based on his trip. Tickets included destination information and a brief fact about the mode of transportation. When the tickets are correctly placed, an LED strip lights up Ekins's route, and brief quotes by Ekins describing his experience on that particular aircraft also appear. When visitors have successfully placed all five tickets, they see Ekins's entire route around the world and learn that he did indeed beat his challengers (the payoff).

Primary source materials incorporated into the interactive include Ekins's portrait, an image of the front page of Ekins's newspaper with a banner headline about his race, an editorial cartoon about Ekins's trip, and photos of him in several countries. Text includes several tips from Ekins about traveling by airplane and a quote describing his feeling of disorientation—what today we call jet lag.

Formative testing showed that visitors connected to the topic and wanted to complete the task. They tended to focus entirely on the information on the tickets and sometimes failed to look up at the map, thus missing the quotes. The fabricators ended up adding a bell sound when a ticket is correctly placed—this makes the visitor look up at the map.

—Tim Grove

Interactive Examples

Trading with Lewis and Clark

The exhibition team working on the Lewis & Clark bicentennial exhibition wanted to find a way to demonstrate the challenge faced by Lewis and Clark in attempting to establish a trading relationship with the Chinook Indians during their winter on the Pacific Coast. It was a complex concept.

The team came up with a low-tech interactive that placed visitors in the shoes of Lewis and Clark. The visitor is placed in a role-based scenario where he must establish a relationship with the Chinooks in hopes that when he is ready to travel again in the spring, the Chinooks will sell him a canoe. The visitor is presented with three different scenarios from the Lewis and Clark journals and given two choices for how to respond. One is the way the explorers responded. The scenarios demonstrate that there is no right answer. After the visitor has responded to each situation, he finds out if the Indians would sell him a canoe—if he had established a good trading relationship. He also finds out that the Indians would not sell Lewis and Clark a canoe because they failed to establish a good relationship.

Wring-o-meter

Educators at the National Museum of American History wanted to show the hard labor involved in doing laundry by hand in the late 1800s. They devised an interactive they called the wring-o-meter where the visitor grasped two handles and turned a piece of laundry to simulate the wringing process. A meter featured an arrow that moved on a scale and showed the success or strength of the movement and told the visitor how successful he would be at wringing many loads of laundry in a day.

Price Meter

Educators wanted to show the complexities of the airline ticketing structure and emphasize that the airline industry is a challenging business. They came up with a computer interactive called the price meter that gives the user a budget of $300 and challenges them to purchase a ticket for that price or under. The interactive takes them through a series of questions that relate to factors affecting ticket cost—such as direct flight or layovers, how many amenities the user requires, whether the ticket can be purchased in advance, and other factors. The user learns that much sacrifice is necessary to obtain the right price.

—Tim Grove

EVALUATION

The educator on an exhibition team should also guide the visitor evaluation process. It has been my experience that often other team members do not recognize the usefulness of evaluation. Evaluation can be useful to learn many types of information at all stages of the development process. See Chapter 10 for more specific information about evaluation. In brief, the following questions inform the interactive or exhibition development process.

Front-end evaluation is done when considering a project or at the very start of the project.

- Does this title interest visitors and make sense?
- Do people understand this specific term?
- What background knowledge do visitors have of a topic?
- What questions do visitors have about this topic or object?
- Which topics resonate most with visitors?

Formative evaluation is gathered during the development.

- Do visitors understand the directions of the interactives as written?
- Do visitors "get" the basic concept of the interactive?
- Is this too challenging?
- Is this font readable?
- Does this quote make sense?

Summative evaluation is done at project's end.

- How much time do visitors spend at this specific component?
- Does the exhibition influence visitor attitude about this specific topic?
- Did this component reach this specific intended age group?
- Did families find this guide useful?
- Did visitors learn the take-home messages?

Evaluation is most successful as a tool when the entire team understands why it is being done and how it informs the development process. Ideally all team members should be involved in some part of the evaluation process. Curators and designers learn much when observing visitors and talking with them. It can change their minds about the volume of text or design features. Educators should have knowledge of evaluation techniques and should be able to draft a questionnaire and visitor surveys. They should be able to articulate why evaluation is important to the exhibition development process. And, when possible, educators should advocate for including funds in the budget for all stages of evaluation. It has been my experience that funds for summative evaluation, if even present in the budget in the first place, usually get cut from the final budget or are used up along the way. Sometimes team members or museum administrators will argue that there is no money left to make any changes even if remedial or summative evaluation recommends making changes to strengthen the exhibition. The best counterargument to this point is that summative evaluation almost always reveals information that will help inform future exhibitions and thus ultimately helps the museum produce stronger projects. Many educators, though, would argue that front-end and formative evaluations are most important.

WRITING FOR THE EXHIBITION

The task of writing the exhibition script, and sometimes audio and video scripts, has traditionally fallen to the content expert—the curator or historian. In some ways this makes sense since this person usually has done the original research and should know the material better than anyone. Curators are scholars and most often write for their peers—learned professionals with much experience on the topic and an expectation of a scholarly language. Some find it a challenge to write at a level accessible to different age groups, levels of interest, or types of visitors. Attempts by others to revise the text with shorter sentences and fewer large words can be perceived as an attempt to dumb down the material. Sometimes the educator on the team might be given the responsibility of writing the script. In some ways this makes much sense because an educator usually has a better understanding of the various audiences and their needs. A team may include a writer who takes on this responsibility. Ultimately it seems that the practical solution is that the best writer on the team should work with the curator to write the labels. In all cases, however, the writer should involve the educator in the writing. The educator should look for jargon, words that the average visitor will not understand, and at the basic reading level of the sentences. Often the standard reading level is eighth grade. Psychologist Stephen Bitgood has written about the challenges of motivating museum visitors to focus on labels and objects. He lists three general factors that help increase focus: Minimize the perceived effort to read, provoke interest in the subject matter, and minimize distracting factors.[5]

Writing an exhibition script is not easy because it requires both content and audience knowledge and skill in guiding the visitor. An exhibition reaches more people if it:

- is active rather than passive
- engages the variety of learning styles
- helps the visitors to make personal connections with the content

In recent years label length has become shorter as writers begin to understand that most visitors do not want to read a lengthy treatise on the wall. The developers of the Price of Freedom exhibition at the National Museum of American History used the following standards:

- Each main label had a single summary sentence (per Smithsonian Accessibility Guidelines) that was 150 characters (not words).
- "Body" text for primary labels was 630 characters, letters, and spaces.
- Secondary labels were 600 characters, letters, and spaces.
- Extended IDs were 430 characters, letters, and spaces.

—Tim Grove

- directs the visitors to look at specifics of the objects or artworks

Unfortunately, inquiry is absent in most exhibition scripts. I have heard one curator say that questions within text are for kids. Thus, it becomes the educator's role to advocate for layered text, questioning strategies, directed-looking at sources including artifacts, and, generally, a more active role for the visitor. Consider using the following strategies for a more active approach.

- *Layered Text.* Write information in chunks with the most important information stated as a single sentence at the beginning and more detail in smaller text below.
- *Questioning Strategies.* Look for places to pose questions that ask visitors to ponder a question, examine a document, compare two artifacts or images, relate content to their personal lives, and promote discussion among family members.
- *Directed Looking.* Write statements that direct visitor attention to specific features of objects, encourage comparison between objects, and ask visitors to take a closer look at the items on display

The challenge of writing for different ages and visitors with differing education levels and comprehension of the English language can be daunting. There are various ways to approach this challenge, and the team must decide on an approach from the beginning of the project. There are strengths and limitations to every approach.

- *Family Labels.* A different track of labels, in addition to the standard labels, that is specifically targeted to a younger audience o Strengths: Through design, the audience will learn to look for these labels; they highlight or supplement standard labels; if well written, they will attract all ages. Techniques might include: questions, directed looking at objects, compare and contrast, and a more relaxed writing style.

o Limitations: They are perceived as "for kids," and a result is that sometimes the curator will think that all inquiry and directed looking should be confined to these labels.

- *Family Guide.* A separate publication for use by families visiting the exhibition that focuses their attention on specific artifacts/documents of interest to younger ages.

o Strengths: Allows kids to take something home; if space is extremely limited, this enables the team to target an audience that might be ignored otherwise.

o Limitations: It becomes crucial to ensure that your audience knows that the guides are available. Also, a study at the National Air and Space Museum revealed that visitors would rather read text on the wall than have to carry around a publication.

- *Integrated Text.* The ideal exhibition text will be layered and clearly written to include questioning and directed-looking statements.

o Strengths: A layered approach with excellent design will draw each audience into the exhibition.

o Limitations: Can require more space since it includes a variety of strategies to reach many audiences.

- *Family Sections.* A separate area or areas within the exhibition that are targeted to a younger age group.

o Strengths: Provides an area where families can react in a way different than in other parts of the exhibition.

o Limitations: May encourage the curator to think that any inquiry, tactiles, and directed looking should be confined to this area. Requires additional space and may draw visitors away from the main exhibition.

REACHING FAMILY GROUPS

We know that a large percentage of museum visitors come in a group on a social outing. Whether a group of family members or friends, they are there to enjoy

---

Combining It All—A Case Study

I recently worked on the development of an exhibition about the history of American commercial aviation. The exhibition's main themes were policy, technology, and passenger experience. The team attempted to show how changes in the first two areas affected the passenger experience, thinking that the passenger experience was what the majority of visitors would most readily relate to. Yet the educators were bothered by the fact that the exhibition did not seem to ultimately answer the "so what?" question. They did not want visitors to leave the exhibition without a basic understanding of how air travel has impacted everyone's life.

A large wall underneath the nose of a 747 jet was available space. The team debated how to illustrate the ways that air travel impacts daily life. A wall of images might work, but ultimately the space was used to illustrate a different point. Its images showed how deregulation and other events changed the passenger experience.

But the educators were still bothered by the original problem—how to make air travel relevant to each visitor, regardless of cultural background and age.

They led the team in a brainstorm session to think of the many ways we are all impacted by air travel. The list was very diverse and intentionally included many areas of life—from health and medicine to grocery shopping to sports to politics to the nuclear family. Gradually an idea took form that would become a key area of the exhibi-

tion. Affectionately called the "luggage pile," the concept was transformed into an exploratory, interactive area located around the wheel supporting the nose of the 747. A lifesize 3-D figure of a TSA officer stands in the middle of a horseshoe-shaped pile of luggage in a simulated baggage claim area. The colorful pile of assorted shapes and sizes immediately attracted attention. Visitors of all heights and ages could open various doors and windows and see the contents inside. The main label read: "Air travel affects your life, even if you don't fly. Can you imagine a world without airplanes? How does it affect you? Explore the baggage to find out some of the many ways."

With this invitation to explore, visitors could discover "live" lobster in transport from Maine, vegetables and fruit from South America, a kidney en route from a donor, a vial of vaccine to address the negative aspects of potential spread of disease through air travel, a suitcase with mementos from Hawaii, a family reunion photo showing family members coming from all across the country, a politician's calendar page showing extensive travel in just one day, sports team paraphernalia to show distant rivalries, and retails items purchased online. Brief questions asked them where their food came from, where they travel, who is their favorite team's big rival, and so forth. The ultimate design encouraged discussion between visitor group members and reinforced how air travel impacts everyone, even if you don't fly.

—Tim Grove

1. Listed below are people who have a vested interest in the success of an exhibition. Describe how each might define a successful exhibition. Discuss where agendas might differ.

> Curator/Historian/Scientist (content person)
> Designer
> Educator
> Registrar/Conservator
> Administrator/Director
> Public Relations/Marketing
> Special Events

2. Should the exhibition team try to engage every visitor for every exhibition? Why or why not?

3. Discuss the following scenario. What would you do and why?

The designers on your exhibition team want to include a series of life-size 3-D human figures throughout the exhibition to provide photo opportunities for visitors. Having seen them in other exhibitions, the designers believe in their capacity to attract visitors. The educators advocate for a series of life-size 2-D photo prints of people taken from actual historical photographs. They argue that photos are primary sources and that they would better foster learning than a monochromatic 3-D figure. The photos feature real people. The educators also argue that 3-D figures are best used if placed in a context—which often requires much space. Space is at a premium. In addition, figures are expensive to create. Neither side can convince the other. How should the team proceed?

4. Which of the following interactives do you think are the most compelling and follow the definition of *interactive* given in the chapter? Why? Describe an effective interactive that you have seen in an exhibition. (*You may also draw from examples in this chapter.*)

Contact Flying Interactive

Educators working on an exhibition about the history of commercial aviation wanted to find a way to explain the concept of contact flying crucial to the success of early airmail pilots. They found a hand-drawn sketch of a section of the transcontinental airmail route showing various landmarks along the route. The sketch matched the directions published by the Postal Service for airmail pilots. These sources provided an opportunity to get visitors to analyze primary source materials. The challenge was to find a way to simulate contact flying using the sources.

The team came up with an interactive based on the map of the airmail route. Given a series of five color aerial photographs of landmarks listed on the map, visitors place the photographs in the correct order they appear on the map, having to follow the pilot's route. Clues from the published pilot's directions serve as another layer of information if necessary. Successful placement of the photos results in a blinking LED light showing the route. Accompanying information includes a portrait of the pilot who drew the sketch.

You Be the Ethnographer

Lewis and Clark attempted to understand the native cultures around them. Part of their mission was to document these cultures, and they tried. But their job was not easy. Is there a way to convey this challenge through an interactive?

One interactive idea that got cut from the final plan was called "You Be the Ethnographer." It placed the visitor in the shoes of Lewis and Clark in their role as ethnographer by providing a glimpse at a Native culture. Looking at a very short video segment of a Native dance or ceremony, the visitor would be challenged to interpret what is going on. The visitor could learn what was happening by a follow-up video that featured a Native American describing the meaning and symbolism behind the segment.

Stewardess Qualifications

Would you have qualified to be a stewardess in the early 1950s? This simple question was designed to draw people into a basic interactive that features a large newspaper ad from the 1950s recruiting women for stewardess positions. It encourages them to apply if they meet the qualifications listed. A series of eight flip panels highlight the qualifications, which include gender, age, weight, height, appearance, marital status, education, and race. Visitors soon realize that a very small number of women met the qualifications, yet a large number of women applied for what was considered a prestigious job.

Trade Network

The exhibition team working on Lewis & Clark: The National Bicentennial Exhibition wanted to find a way to show visitors the vastness of the trade network that expedition traveled through during its journey down the Columbia River. The team could easily have featured a large map with all of the information on it. Yet, they ended up turning it into a simple interactive.

A large map of the trading area—the entire West Coast—has minimal information showing raw materials and finished products. Visitors are challenged to match a column of five tactile raw materials—abalone shell, buffalo hide, goat wool, whalebone, and sheep horn with images of finished products made from the raw materials. The actual finished products are in a case next to the interactive. With a correct match, lights on the map show the origin point of the raw materials and the finished products they made. So the visitors can see the vast distances goods traveled.

each other's company and, therefore, often want to learn together. How does recognition of this evidence change the way an exhibition is designed? An educator should attempt to create places within the exhibition that promote group discussion. They might present a historical or scientific problem to solve, a puzzle to put together, or a question that promotes interaction between generational members of groups.[6] Specific examples relating to intergenerational learning can be found in Chapter 6.

RESOURCE FOR ACCESSIBILITY

Another role for educators on an exhibition team is accessibility resource. The goal is an exhibition that is accessible to as many people in the target audience as possible regardless of age, ability, or circumstance. People often think in terms of physical accessibility, but intellectual accessibility is just as important. The term "universal design" is perhaps a better phrase to use and may have a less negative connotation. While the designer on the team should be a strong advocate for physical access, the educator must provide solutions for intellectual access. Many of the examples in this chapter are aimed at intellectual access for those visitors with cognitive disabilities, reading challenges, or limited command of the English language. Universal design means including tactile reproductions or models for visitors who are blind or have low vision, ensuring that main messages are provided in audio format, or simply providing information in multiple formats. The major point to make when arguing for access is that we are all only temporarily able. Age eventually sets in and then we appreciate larger fonts and seating with arms. Universal design should not be an afterthought. The initial budget should have line items for various components relating to diverse audiences. No doubt you will hear the argument that your institution gets very few blind visitors. Usually the reason is because you have not made your exhibitions attractive to their needs. The trite saying "If you build it, they will come," is true . . . but only if you market it. The most important argument for universal design is that by making an exhibition more accessible for one group, in most cases you are making it more accessible for other groups as well. Hands-on learners will appreciate tactile components as much as visitors who are blind. The Smithsonian National Postal Museum was working on a project for the deaf community. Its surveys revealed that deaf visitors love tactile components. Many of them did not learn English as a first language so exhibits that rely heavily on text are difficult to understand. Also, the language they do speak, American Sign Language, is spoken with their hands, so the best way to communicate is through tactile exploration. People who speak ASL as their first language process content very effectively through their hands.

CONCLUSION

Educators can greatly contribute to every phase of the exhibition development process. They offer insight and knowledge of the visitor perspective, and their involvement undoubtedly enhances the final product. However, their job is by no means finished when an exhibition opens. Other responsibilities include related outreach programs, teacher materials, docent training, and online components. All of these are mentioned in other chapters.

NOTES

1. Beverly Serrell, *Exhibit Labels: An Interpretive Approach* (Walnut Creek, Calif.: Alta MiraPress, 1996), 1.
2. Kathleen McLean, *Planning for People in Museum Exhibitions* (Washington, D.C.: ASTC, 1993), 55. McLean expands on take-home messages.
3. McLean, *Planning for People in Museum Exhibitions*, 93.
4. Some items on these lists are from McLean's book.
5. Stephen Bitgood, "The Role of Attention in Designing Effective Interpretive Labels," *Journal of Interpretation Research* 5, no. 2 (2003): 31–45.
6. www.familylearningforum.org is an excellent resource with recent research on this topic.

CHAPTER 13

Collaboration

KIMBERLY A. HUBER

> **Engaging the public is the No. 1 goal at the Autry National Center. Much of the Autry's work is organized around exhibition projects. Museum educators are the voice of our patrons on every exhibition team. It is important that museum educators work closely with curators and exhibit designers to ensure the quality of the visitor experience.**
>
> —*Michael Duchemin, senior curator, Autry National Center*

Collaboration is not a new concept. Traditionally museum staffers collaborate internally as they work with other staff members, and externally with other institutions on traveling exhibits, with other professionals at museum conferences, and with sponsors who contribute to educational programs, among others. Museum collaborations have expanded in number, variety of types, and the diversity of organizations with whom they collaborate. Incentives in the form of grants or economic necessity often drive contemporary collaborative projects. The American Association of Museums recognized the financial impact collaboration has on museums: "The joint acquisition of equipment and use of facilities are partnerships motivated by economics."[1] The International Council on Museums (ICOM) lists on its website "joint action with partner organizations, and projection of ICOM's work and values internationally" as a core value for museums and museum professionals.[2] However, collaboration may or may not come naturally to museum educators, as it is often difficult for them to see the immediate value of additional meetings and alternative perspectives when working with others. A major roadblock for many is the "it is just easier for me to do it myself" approach to getting work done. In this chapter I discuss collaboration, likely partners, types of collaborations, examples from my experiences, how collaboration can benefit you, and "Keys to Successful Collaboration."

DEFINING COLLABORATION

What does it mean to collaborate? According to the Merriam-Webster online dictionary, to collaborate means "to work jointly with others or together especially in an intellectual endeavor; to cooperate with an agency or instrumentality with which one is not immediately connected."[3] Where these definitions fall short is that they do not elaborate on the reason or reasons to collaborate. Because collaboration takes more time and effort, it should be done for a reason, and have a purpose. I modify and add "in order to" to the definition because collaboration should accomplish something. I think of collaboration as people working together in the spirit of cooperation, often with another organization to which they are not normally connected in order to achieve individual and shared goals that solve a problem, serve a need, or create opportunity. In my experience it is the "in order to" or goal portion that seems to be lacking in unsuccessful collaborations.

Those who collaborate can and should reach their goals, but they can only have a chance of doing so if the goals are clearly articulated at the beginning of the partnership and then are measured at the end using thorough evaluation. (Evaluation is addressed in Chapter 10.) Successful collaborators consider what unique attributes each partner brings to the project and articulate what benefits each partner will receive. Every institution needs to seriously examine what it is getting out of the collaboration. If you find that you are participating solely for the sake of collaboration, there will be little motivation for sustainability.

Internal Collaboration

Educators should expect to collaborate both internally and externally. Internally they will work with other museum staff to produce programs, interpret exhibits, run events, negotiate budgets, develop strategic plans, and participate in any number of projects that their institution is involved with. A portion of any job involves working with other people in the organization. Because this type of collaboration is part of the daily working environment and the skill set is similar, the focus of this chapter is external collaboration, or working with people outside your organization.

External Collaboration

The dictionary also includes "to cooperate with or willingly assist the enemy of one's country" in its definition of collaboration.[4] Although museums may not perceive other arts and cultural institutions as enemies, they may be viewed as competitors for grant dollars, visitors, and programs. So, why collaborate? According to *Excellence and Equity: Education and the Public Dimension of Museums*, "Museums cannot operate in isolation in a world of shifting boundaries. Collaboration today has expanded possibilities for ensuring that museums use their collections, programs, and resources effectively. It is a way to invite more participation from outside the museum in shaping ideas and making decisions and to augment the personal experience and professional expertise of a museum's staff."[5] The Commission on Museums for a New Century recognizes collaboration as not only a societal trend, but an economic necessity for museums and the business community while recognizing that museums are just beginning this process.[6] The commission established collaboration as one of sixteen recommendations to guide museum, business, and community leaders in working together to find solutions and serve the public.[7]

WHY COLLABORATE?

AAM's suggestion that collaboration is necessary for museums to be successful in this changing world may seem worthy, yet lofty to staff who face impending deadlines and countless daily activities. Educators may want specific reasons why collaboration is a good idea for their institution or project. Some common reasons to collaborate are:

- To reach a broader audience.
- To maximize resources (staff, expertise, funds) and reduce duplication.
- To solve a problem, reach a common goal, or unite overlapping interests.
- To open up new and creative opportunities for funding sources.
- To serve a political purpose.
- To build alliances.
- Because outside sources may dictate that collaboration is necessary.
- You may have other reasons to collaborate, but if you do, first consider why you are collaborating and follow my "Keys to Successful Collaboration" (included as Textbox 13.1 on p. 157), which ultimately come down to people and principles.

MUSEUM PARTNERS

Who are potential collaborative partners? *Museums for a New Century* urges museums to collaborate with other museums, schools, media, businesses, and so forth.[8] *Excellence and Equity: Education and the Public Dimension of Museums* adds arts and historic organizations, libraries, state and governmental agencies, and social service groups as potential collaborators.[9] I would add anybody your organization feels will enhance its institutional and educational mission. *Excellence and Equity* also encourages a variety of potential collaborators in the report's plan for action. It includes as its sixth principle: "Engage in active, ongoing collaborative efforts with a wide spectrum of organizations and individuals who can contribute to the expansion of the museum's public dimension."[10]

Collaboration Goal

Sometimes the goal of collaboration can be as basic as an increased visibility due to one partner's high profile. If one organization wants to get a message out there to a large audience, but doesn't have the visibility, it can partner with an organization that has the visibility and needs the content. For example, the Missouri Historical Society (MHS) collaborated extensively with the Circle of Tribal Advisors put in place for the national Lewis & Clark bicentennial commemoration. Tribal members wanted their stories told, their voices heard, and MHS wanted to include their stories in their interpretation of the exhibition. The tribes gave us advisors and a small exhibition written from Native perspectives. We gave them the highly visible national platform of a traveling exhibition, website, and exhibition catalog.

—Tim Grove

Schools as Partners

One of the most common partners museums work with is schools. In a 1998 survey the Institute of Museum and Library Services (IMLS) collected statistical data "that confirms that museums and schools are working together to better educate students at all grade levels."[11] In fact, IMLS 1996 *True Needs True Partners: Museums and Schools Transforming Education* reports that 88 percent of all types of museums provide K-12 programming, including guided field trips, staff visits to schools, lessons for pre- and post-museum visits, and traveling exhibits.[12]

Schools partner with museums because museum programs offer creative and informal learning experiences and enrich school learning. However cost and location also impact a school's decision to use museums. Museum survey respondents felt their directors are responsible for deciding to offer programs to schools, and teachers primarily decide whether to participate, but many people influence the process.[13] Identify decision-makers early and work with them as you begin the collaboration process. In the future school-museum partnerships need to be more thoroughly documented in order to measure the success of their contributions to each other[14] and to justify their continuing relationships.

Museum-Museum-Teacher Collaboration

As the education specialist working on the Lewis & Clark bicentennial exhibition, it was my responsibility to produce an extensive curriculum to complement the exhibition. The goal was to produce a curriculum that both social studies and science teachers would want to use. I was working for the Missouri Historical Society, and my background is history. The exhibition was traveling to three science institutions on its five-city tour. They wanted to make sure the curriculum was useful to their constituents. We decided to collaborate with the Academy of Natural Sciences in Philadelphia, the second stop on the national tour. We ended up with two teams of nine teachers, one in St. Louis and one in Philadelphia, who wrote lessons. Working with the science advisors at the academy ensured that our materials were strong in science content, and that the academy would want to promote the curriculum to its many school audiences. We also had residents of Philadelphia help produce the section that related to Lewis's research trip to Philadelphia. It was a winning collaboration for all involved.

—Tim Grove

Some of the things the IMLS study reveals are:

- Museums collectively spend millions of dollars to provide instruction and resources to schools.

- All types of museums offer a variety of educational programs to students of all ages all over the country that support school learning objectives and curriculum standards.
- Significant expertise and support are needed for school-museum partnerships to be successful.[15]

Museum educators must work with the schools to match their offerings to the school's needs, state's standards, and federal mandates.

Museum-School Collaboration

The National Air and Space Museum has a public annex located in Virginia. The education staff there includes two full-time teachers in residence in collaboration with two local school districts. The school districts pay the teachers' salaries. The teachers gain experience working in an informal learning environment, produce and present programming, and provide direct feedback on materials and programs that the education staff produces. The teachers are able to use their contacts in the school systems to help recruit teachers and students for focus groups and spread the word about special events. The program is competitive, and there is a term limit of two years.

—Tim Grove

Other Partners

Collaborative partners for museums are not limited to public schools. The Commission on Museums for a New Century reported, "We found a natural link of purpose between museums and performing and visual arts organizations, libraries, elementary and secondary schools, universities and colleges, continuing education programs, parks and recreation departments, and preservation groups. Collaboration among cultural and educational institutions can make them a more effective force and bring recognition to the value of their contribution to community life."[16] "Collaboration with community organizations serves museums well because it fortifies the notion that they have a serious service function, that they indeed meet a human need."[17]

TYPES OF COLLABORATIVE PROJECTS AND PARTNERS

On what types of projects can you collaborate? AAM recommends that museum leaders work together and share staff, programs, ideas, and resources at all levels.[18] Examples of collaborative projects follow. The first discusses joint docent training, the second spotlights two professional development training programs, and the third shows museums partnering with a department store chain.

Museum-Library Collaboration

The museum where I worked was located right next door to the local library. Both the museum and library were departments in the city community services division. From time to time, the children's librarians would come over to do special story times in our exhibit, and we would occasionally do a special presentation at one of their programs.

From that beginning, we decided to develop more programming together. Both of us wanted to increase our teenage visitors, and we chose that as our connection. The woman who headed up the children's division liked to write mysteries, and we asked her to write a murder mystery that would be staged at the museum. Once the mystery was written, then we created the scene of the murder, and together with the librarians we developed a series of clues. Some of the clues were visual and others required research. Then we developed a *Crime Detection Notebook* describing what had happened, and including directions for the visitors, outlining steps for them to take in attempting to solve the crime, and including a place for them to state their solution as to what happened and who was the guilty person.

To advertise the program, we used the museum and library newsletters as well as the local newspaper. We ran the program from 4 to 7 p.m., hoping that time slot would attract more teens and possibly some parents for the teens who could not drive yet. We also provided prizes of a large chocolate candy bar to those who correctly solved the mystery.

Well, you guessed it—the program was very popular! We had over 500 people within the first hour. The librarians were there to facilitate the research, and we had docents in the hall acting the parts of some of the mystery people and answering questions. We continued working together through that program for a number of years.

We tried several formats and learned a few things in the process:

- Because of a large turnout, scheduling became a major concern. We ultimately had to have people call and make reservations at set times in order to handle everyone.
- We tried having part of the mystery in the museum and part in the library. While the buildings are right next to each other, we found visitors would go to one site or the other and then leave rather than visiting both locations.
- We struggled with telling the visitors who was guilty because then they would tell the people coming in to solve the mystery. Finally, we announced the solution in the last half hour of the program, and gave away the prizes then.

This was a very successful collaboration for both the museum and library, and it was fun for the staff to work together on the project.

—Anna Johnson

As a novice educator, I was responsible for developing the docent training program for a historic home museum. Volunteers needed information about the unique features of the site as well as tour training techniques. Through membership in the Museum Educator's Council of Arizona I became acquainted with a fellow historic home museum educator in an adjacent city. Both homes were built in the 1890s in the Queen Anne Victorian style. Because they were built at approximately the same time in the same area, we decided to offer a joint training program on Victorian architecture for all staff and volunteers.

Another overlapping continuing education need was to teach the volunteers about tour techniques for special-needs visitors. The other educator had acquired an instructional video on this topic produced by the Smithsonian Institution, which she agreed to share. So we also decided to offer this video in a second joint training program. Both sessions provided detailed information that was not available to the volunteers through their regular training, but the additional information could be incorporated into public tours.

We considered many factors in order to make these joint sessions successful. Of primary concern was the scheduling of the two classes. Docent training occurred at different times of the year and on different days for each museum. After discussing the options with the volunteers we scheduled the programs in the evenings on different months, at times with the fewest conflicts. (Evening programs can present challenges for people accustomed to attending day programs, and therefore give consideration to transportation, parking, and security.)

Publicity and marketing to promote the training sessions were carefully planned. Flyers were designed and distributed to all staff, volunteers, and guild/society members. Other programming details included the selection of speakers, speakers' fees, refreshment funding, and transportation. Fortunately, the commitment displayed by the participating institutions made these concerns easy to resolve. Initially I hosted both programs, and the other museum educator provided the refreshments. We alternated the responsibilities the following year.

Following each program we evaluated the training. We provided the attendees and presenters with written evaluation forms and we also sat down together to discuss what went right and what needed to be improved. The overall response was very positive. Areas that needed to be improved in the first year included marketing and topic selection. We agreed that docent involvement in topic selection could improve future attendance.[19]

If you do not partner with another museum for programs or exhibits, consider professional development opportunities. I recommend that museum professionals network with others in their field through local, regional, national, and if possible, international museum associations. Collaborating with people who understand your work and who have experienced some of the same kinds of stresses and successes can be very useful, especially to the new educator. Some of the strongest professional relationships I developed resulted from serving on museum organization boards, committees, and conference planning teams. I made real friends, learned a lot, and gave back to the profession. I can honestly say I got much more than I gave, and that seems to be a common sentiment.

An example of museum associations working together involved an Institute of Museum and Library Services (IMLS) Professional Services Program grant that I wrote and administered, Project SMART (Small Museums of Arizona: Resource Training). Project SMART offered six professional development workshops to staff and volunteers of small, culturally specific, and rural museums. The Central Arizona Museum Association (CAMA) applied for the grant and partnered with the Museum Association of Arizona (MAA), Museum Educator's Council of Arizona (MECA), and an informal collections group. Discussions with and evaluations from each of these groups provided me with a list of workshop topics, potential speakers, and suggestions for possible activities and materials. At each workshop I observed and fostered networking by introducing new museum staff to association leaders, offered collaborative project suggestions, and paired regional professionals with others from their area who could offer support, information, and/or mentoring services.

The success of Project SMART inspired a partnership between MAA and the Arizona State Library, Archives, and Public Records Agency. I worked for The State Library at that time, and it agreed to expand its annual Library Professional Development Institute to include museums for the first time in 2002. The Library Institute is an annual one-week intensive training program for managers and directors of libraries who do not have master's degrees. Because of the agency's focus on collaboration and the success of project SMART, along with other collaborative efforts, we offered a joint institute that would include

museums. Marketing, strategic planning, and exhibit design were class topics. All participants rated the joint venture highly. One student said, "There are so many areas where our [library and museum] missions blend and complement each other that it just makes sense to collaborate and partner as often as we can."[20]

Businesses can also be partners with museums for promotion and funding. While I served as a committee member to the Central Arizona Museum Association, we worked with Robinsons-May department stores. They promoted local museums each May, by offering a museum pass, which included a two-for-one entry price into many museums or free entry into others. The local department store chain also paid $10,000 annually to CAMA to produce brochures listing the over fifty participating museums in the Phoenix metropolitan area. The link CAMA made to Robinsons-May was International Museum Day, May 18. Because May was part of its company name, it seemed to be a logical connection. This collaborative effort has benefited both organizations for over 15 years. Throughout the month, Robinsons-May promotes the museum pass in the press. It draws thousands of people into their stores just to pick up museum passes. The benefits to CAMA are obvious: money to print brochures, free promotion, and increased visitation to valley museums, although some museums were so inundated with discount passes during the month they opted out of the promotion. Robinson-May demonstrated its community support through the partnership with local museums.

BENEFITS OF COLLABORATION

From 1998 to 2003, I spent much of my time working for the State of Arizona helping the museum, library, and archives communities build partnerships that led to grant funding and in some cases long-term collaborations. One of the first things I addressed when talking with people from these institutions was based on a recurring question, "Why should I collaborate?" Based on experience, observation, and research, I responded with a number of benefits: resource sharing, strengthening of cultural alliances, maximizing dollars, increasing public awareness, bridging gaps in knowledge, and developing better understanding in order to serve the public better.

Although my museum work in Arizona began in 1979, I do not recall a strong history of collaboration among the state's cultural institutions. In fact, the State Museum Association was not established until 1982.[21] Certainly there were examples of libraries and museums working together and instances where cultural organizations partnered, but as far as I know, that was only on an intermittent basis. This changed in 1997, when GladysAnn Wells accepted the director's position at the State Library in Phoenix. As the head of the agency she oversees four library divisions, as well as archives, records, and museum divisions. During her initial trips around the state to meet library, museum, and archives professionals, Ms. Wells observed duplication in collecting and preservation priorities, in particular, an early Arizona territorial map. After being shown the same map several times, she realized that Arizona's cultural communities were not sharing information and resources. In her early years as leader of the State Library, Wells established four goals for the agency. One of the goals was to build collaborations between Arizona's arts and cultural organizations.

Under Wells's direction the Arizona State Library created several statewide programs including The Arizona Cultural Inventory Project (CIP) and the Arizona Convocation. CIP is a statewide inventory of the collections in libraries, museums, and archives. It provides a collection-level inventory of materials housed at these various institutions for the purposes of sharing information and maximizing resources. Wells established The Arizona Convocation in 1999 to allow diverse professionals a reason and a place to come together with the hope of building a statewide collaborative network. The Arizona Convocation allows people to share information about their collections and programs and promotes public access to the books, records, and objects of Arizona's past. Each event includes speakers, breakout sessions, presentations, and resource materials. The convocation is the state's only annual gathering of librarians, archivists, museum professionals, genealogists, and others responsible for and interested in preserving Arizona's cultural heritage.

The Cultural Inventory Project and convocations have been successful at a number of different levels. The fact that people continue to participate is an obvious measure of success. Evaluations indicate that shared information is relevant and timely, and relationships have been formed or renewed. Another indicator that collaborative efforts are working was an award given to Wells in 1999. She received the Museum Association of Arizona's award for Distinguished Service "for her efforts to increase museum and library collaborations."[22] Although Wells may have had the desire to build collaborations, we all know this cannot be accomplished alone. Luckily others were receptive

to cultural partnerships at that time too. Many people and institutions helped to make collaborations happen in Arizona, and many continue to do so today.

Collaborations among museum professionals are also beneficial for educational programs. Just as the historical community can be overly saturated with territorial maps, an abundance of similar museum programs targeted to the same audiences can result in an oversupply of services. Museum education professionals have collaborated with theater groups, other museums, and recreational facilities to host summer camps, school tours, and lecture series in order to expand learning and reduce competition for audiences. It is important to work with fellow museum colleagues to keep abreast of potential partnerships that will enrich participants' experiences. Such collaborations can occur when all museum staff are active in national and state professional development organizations.

Museum-Museums across the State

There are a variety of digitization projects going on in many states around the country. Two of the more extensive ones are the Maine Memory Network (www.mainememory.net) and the Ohio Memory Project (www.ohiomemory.org). Both are led by staff at the state historical society. They collaborate with any institution around their state that wants to contribute to the overall website. The project results in a rich centralized location for primary source materials from around the state. The states usually provide funding and training to help the smaller institutions digitize their collections.

—Tim Grove

OBSTACLES OR CHALLENGES TO COLLABORATION

Although collaborative efforts can be very rewarding, they do not come without their share of obstacles and challenges. External collaboration takes more planning, time, and effort, so not all projects or programs are worth the costs of the collaboration. As I have previously mentioned, some arts and cultural professionals view other institutions as competitors. They have not been encouraged to recognize the benefits of collaborating, or their administration may expressly discourage it. People who work in different types of organizations may have differing terminologies, missions, and goals. For example, libraries want to provide extensive public access to all their collections, whereas museums and archives share their collections in limited ways. Another example involves the different bottom-line perspectives between for-profit and not-for-profit groups. Businesses are interested in making money, while nonprofit groups want to educate or provide services. As a result it can sometimes be challenging to handle bills and other financial concerns. I have found that one of the biggest challenges museum educators face is not knowing how to successfully collaborate. But these obstacles and challenges can be overcome with a willing spirit, some effort, and a few suggestions to help you through the collaborative process.

To overcome some of the aforementioned obstacles and challenges, it may be more useful to view other arts and cultural organizations as allies rather than competitors. By working together, organizations can combine financial, intellectual, and structural resources to achieve a synergistic outcome. It is worthwhile to take the time to learn new terminology, methods of operation, and attitudinal differences when building a

---

Textbox 13.1. Keys to Successful Collaboration

People

1. Seek supervisory and institutional support and approval for collaborative projects.
2. Be clear on what strengths each partner brings to the collaboration.
3. Identify decision-makers and get input from everyone who will be involved or has a stake in the outcome.
4. Identify similar needs/audiences/problems.
5. Select a project director.
6. All partners must have specific roles and responsibilities; put them in writing.
7. To expedite communication, identify one contact person for each institution. Have all information relayed through this person.

Principles

8. Be open to overlapping and creative solutions.
9. Determine as a group how final decisions will be made and by whom.
10. Determine as a group how disputes will be resolved and by whom.
11. Define clear goals and record what success will look like.
12. All partners must benefit.
13. Use evaluation to assess the success of the program as well as partners' satisfaction.
14. Evaluate the project, document the results, make modifications, and repeat the process as necessary for long-term projects/programs.
15. Promote the success to the public, supervisors, funders, and officials.
16. Use the project as a model for other collaborative programs or projects.
17. Consider additional future partners.

---

long-term relationship. Discuss these differences and how you will resolve them in the early stages of the partnership, and then you can begin to uncover shared topics of interest and find relevance for a more diverse audience. Weigh your choices and assess the benefits before you opt to collaborate on any project.

Museum Education Program

While working on the Lewis & Clark bicentennial exhibition, I wanted to find a way to spread the exhibition's content to a national school audience. The curriculum materials that we produced did that, but another collaborative opportunity presented itself. The Missouri office of the Newspapers in Education (NIE) program was seeking an opportunity to tell the Lewis and Clark story to both a state audience and a national audience. My employer, the Missouri Historical Society, ended up collaborating with the Newspapers in Education program to produce an eight-part series about Lewis and Clark in Missouri and a 16-page tab about the entire expedition. I wrote the text and supplied the images, together we hired a designer, and NIE promoted the project and handled the orders and printing. Since NIE was part of a national program, the project had a much broader reach.

—Tim Grove

SUSTAINING COLLABORATIONS

The Museum and Library Services Act was approved by Congress in 1996 and was implemented by the Institute of Museum and Library Services. In 2007 museums could apply to IMLS for competitive grants in several categories including community engagement, public programs, professional development/continuing education, formal and informal learning, and partnerships that encouraged and in some instances required collaboration. Partnerships have been encouraged through funding by Congress along with many state and federal granting agencies, so it is likely that this focus on collaboration will continue for some time.

I have seen a substantial change in the climate of the cultural communities throughout Arizona and the nation in regard to collaboration. Perhaps part of that is more accurately a reflection of my knowledge and personal experiences, but not totally. As a direct result of the Museum and Library Services Act, I began working for the State of Arizona in 1998 as a liaison between the museum and library communities. I know that there is now a much stronger awareness between museums, archives, libraries, and other cultural organizations and a statewide acknowledgment of the value of collaboration. Many groups and individuals still need help in finding reasons and ways to collaborate, and they need the tools and techniques to help them do it effectively. Certainly funding opportunities that bring people together are a good initial enticement, but in order for collaborations to really succeed, they must be relevant and sustainable rather than just a means to get funding. Although an act of Congress precipitated a changing national attitude, it is ultimately up to everyone who is interested in natural sciences and cultural arts education to participate if collaboration is to be truly successful.

CONCLUSION

Collaboration with people from other institutions has its pros and cons. It can provide an opportunity to meet new people, share new ideas, develop new relationships, and explore other organizations. The most sustainable collaborations are built on the combined strengths of each partner and create a richer experience for museum audiences that could not be achieved by one institution alone. It can also slow the planning process and create additional burdens. As funding and other resources become increasingly scarce for all types of museums, creative solutions to common problems become necessary. The museum profession is looking for model projects to serve as examples of success. Use the "Keys to Successful Collaboration Checklist" (Sample Form 13.1) in the appendix to help you begin the process, document your tips, and share your stories with others. With committed professionals who are open to new ideas, many mutual interests can be resolved through collaborative means.

NOTES

1. American Association of Museums, *Museums for a New Century* (Washington, D.C.: AAM, 1984), 92.
2. International Council of Museums, "ICOM Strategic Plans 2005–2007," ICOM 2005, icom.museum/strat_plan_eng/intro.html#core (Jan. 21, 2008).
3. Merriam-Webster, Inc., "Collaboration," Merriam-Webster Online Dictionary, 2008, www.m-w.com/dictionary/collaboration (Jan. 21, 2008).
4. Merriam-Webster, Inc., "Collaboration."
5. American Association of Museums, *Excellence and Equity: Education and the Public Dimension of Museums* (Washington, D.C.: AAM, 1992), 20.
6. American Association of Museums, *Museums for a New Century*, 90.
7. American Association of Museums, *Museums for a New Century*, 89–96.
8. American Association of Museums, *Museums for a New Century*, 90.
9. American Association of Museums, *Excellence and Equity: Education and the Public Dimension of Museums*, 20.
10. American Association of Museums, *Excellence and Equity: Education and the Public Dimension of Museums*, 7.
11. Institute of Museum and Library Services, *True Needs True Partners: 1998 Survey Highlights* (Washington, D.C.: IMLS, 1998), 2.
12. Institute of Museum and Library Services, *True Needs True Partners: Museums and Schools Transforming Education*, (Washington, D.C.: IMLS, 1996), 4–5.
13. Institute of Museum and Library Services, *True Needs True Partners: 1998 Survey Highlights*, 6.
14. Institute of Museum and Library Services, *True Needs True Partners: 1998 Survey Highlights*, 8.
15. Institute of Museum and Library Services, *True Needs True Partners: 1998 Survey Highlights*, 2–3.
16. American Association of Museums, *Museums for a New Century*, 94.
17. American Association of Museums, *Museums for a New Century*, 95–96.
18. American Association of Museums, *Excellence and Equity: Education and the Public Dimension of Museums*, 25.
19. Kim Huber, "Docent Training and Institutional Collaboration," copied and adapted from *Museum Association of Arizona Newsletter* 9, no. 2 (Fall 1991): 4.
20. JoAnn Stuckey, director, Cave Creek Museum, Thank-you note to Kim Huber, LSTA consultant, Arizona State Library, following attendance at 2002 Library and Museum Institute, 2002.
21. Rebecca Ragan Akins, *Serving, Sharing, Saving: The First Twenty-Five Years of the Museum Association of Arizona* (Phoenix, Ariz.: Museum Association of Arizona and Salt River Project, 2007), 5.
22. Akins, *Serving, Sharing, Saving*, 83.

1.1. Strategic Plan
2.1. Assess Need for Volunteers (Desert Botanical Garden)
2.2. Volunteer Job Description Worksheet (Desert Botanical Garden)
2.3. Volunteer Application Form (Desert Botanical Garden)
2.4. Application to Volunteer (City of Tempe)
2.5. Volunteer Informational Interview (Desert Botanical Garden)
2.6. Docent Daily Tasks Schedule (Desert Botanical Garden)
2.7. Volunteer Hours Log (Desert Botanical Garden)
3.1. Tools of the Trade for the Docent
3.2. Example Schedule A
3.3. Example Schedule B
3.4. Docent Training Curriculum (Tempe Historical Museum)
3.5. Example of Special Training Information (Tempe Historical Museum)
3.6. Docent Presentation Evaluation Form
3.7. Docent Feedback on Training Classes
4.1. Museum Group Visitation Guidelines (Tempe Historical Museum)
5.1. Education Task Force Profile Worksheet (developed at the Mesa Southwest Museum)
5.2. "The Road Showdown" — A Sample Lesson Plan from the National Project Archaeology Guide, "Intrigue of the Past: A Teacher's Activity Guide for Fourth through Seventh Grades"
5.3. Staff Development Activity Evaluation
6.1. Summer Youth Institute Organizational Outline
7.1. Teacher Survey (Gilbert Historical Museum)
7.2. Teacher's Trunk Activities Evaluation (Gilbert Historical Museum)
7.3. Student Evaluation (Gilbert Historical Museum)
7.4. "Design Your Own Program" Proposal Worksheet
8.1. Program Design Pyramid
8.2. Event Planning Time Line/Checklist for Programs and Special Events
8.3. 10 Questions to Ask After Your Special Event
8.4. Event Budget Information
10.1. Sign/Exhibit Observation Tool (Desert Botanical Garden)
10.2. Observation Summary: Attracting/Holding/Involvement Power (Desert Botanical Garden)
10.3. Exhibit Communication Power: Visitor Interviews Tool (Desert Botanical Garden)
10.4. Visitor Tour Survey (Desert Botanical Garden)
10.5. Immediate School Program Evaluation by Docents
10.6. Guided Tours Evaluation/Feedback (Desert Botanical Garden)
13.1. Keys to Successful Collaboration Checklist

Sample Form 1.1

Strategic Plan

Current activities:	Person to do task and time required:	Audience:	Budget:	Expansion possible only with additional resources:	Needs to be eliminated:

Assess Need for Volunteers

Need: _____

Questions 1 - 5 gauge current use of volunteers by staff

1. **What duties are the volunteers currently performing?**
   (No volunteers? Look at the staff person's job description and determine where volunteers could be used.)

2. **How many volunteers are active in your job now?**

3. **How long has your most seasoned volunteer (or volunteers) been doing this job?**

4. **How often is the volunteer needed to do this job?**

5. **What is the best time of the year for a new volunteer to begin working?**

Questions 6 - 8 illustrate basic information volunteers will need to know

6. **Which staff person will actually oversee volunteers?**

7. **What kinds of interests or skills should the volunteers have to do this job?**

8. **What kind of training do you give your volunteers for this job?   Who trains them?**

Questions 9 - 10 show basic needs & issues staff may have in working with volunteers

9. **What kinds of volunteer needs will you have over the next year?**
   o **Jobs needed**

   o **Number of volunteers per day**

   o **Hours needed per week**

10. **What kinds of issues are challenging you in supervising the volunteers?**

Sample Form 2.2

Volunteer Job Description Worksheet
(Information comes directly from the Assessment)

JOB TITLE: *Use one phrase to name the position* _____

STAFF MANAGER: **VOLUNTEER LIAISON:**
Who is the volunteer's staff supervisor?   *What Volunteer Chair oversees this position?* _____

JOB DESCRIPTION: *One sentence to describe responsibilities of the position, not specific duties* _____
_____

JOB OBJECTIVE: *What is the result or impact expected when this job is successfully completed?* _____
_____

QUALIFICATIONS: *What skills, knowledge, abilities, experience are you looking for?* _____
_____

HOW SELECTED: *New Volunteers: Volunteer Coordinator—Application, interview, and training process.*
"Seasoned" Volunteers: Volunteer Coordinator and Staff Manager—Interview and training. _____

TRAINING REQUIREMENTS: *What type of training is required and how will it be provided?* _____
_____

PLACE OF WORK: *Where will the activity take place?* _____
TIME COMMITMENT REQUIREMENTS: *What time(s) of day and day(s) of the week are the volunteers needed? Consider hours per week or total weeks or months required.* _____
_____

DUTIES/RESPONSIBILITIES/JOB ACTIVITIES: *What are the specific tasks involved? Spell out exactly what you expect the volunteer to do and be responsible for.*

1. _____   6. _____
2. _____   7. _____
3. _____   8. _____
4. _____   9. _____
5. _____   10. _____

Sample Form 2.3

Desert Botanical Garden
Volunteer Application Form
(You must complete all sections.)

Name:_____
       (Last)   (First)   (Middle Initial)

Street Address:_____ **City:** _____ **State:** _____ **Zip:** _____
Phone:_____ ❑ Home ❑ Work ❑ Cell **Email:**_____ **Fax:**_____

Availability: Please indicate when you are available to volunteer:
❑Monday ❑Tuesday ❑Wednesday ❑Thursday ❑Friday ❑Saturday ❑Sunday ❑Summer
❑Mornings ❑Afternoons ❑Evenings
Winter residents, please list months available:_____
Summer Address:_____
How did you hear about our Volunteer Program?_____
Date of Birth: _____ / _____ / _____ Place of Birth:_____ Garden member? ❑Yes ❑No

Emergency Contact Details: Please give the name of the person we should contact in an emergency:
(If you are under 18 this should be your parent or legal guardian.)

Name:_____Relationship to you:_____Telephone:_____
                                                        ❑Home ❑Work ❑Cell

Employment:
Are you currently: ❑Employed ❑Unemployed ❑Full time student ❑Retired ❑Other: _____
Employer /School/ (former employer if retired):_____
Does your company (or former company) support the following: ❑Time of Program ❑Donation Matching
If a student, do you need to complete community service hours? ❑Yes ❑No
If yes, hours required: _____

Volunteer Programs:
Please check any that apply to your interests or skills:
❑ I am a teacher   ❑ I'm an AZ Master Gardener ❑ I completed Desert Landscaper School
❑ I am bilingual   If yes, list language(s):_____
❑ I like working with people ❑ I like working with plants ❑ I like working with kids
❑ I like working behind the scenes ❑ I can walk distances of 2-3 miles
❑ I have database development experience ❑ Sales & Marketing
❑ Special events/Exhibits ❑ Data entry/clerical ❑ Other _____

Miscellaneous:
Have you ever been convicted of a felony or a felony that was reduced to a misdemeanor for
sentencing purposes, including DUI? (excluding minor traffic violations)
❑Yes ❑No (A convicted record will not necessarily be a bar to volunteering and factors such
as age, time of offense, seriousness and nature of violation, and rehabilitation will be taken
into account.)

Signature: _____Date:_____
If you are under 18 years of age, you must have a legal guardian sign below.

Guardian Name: _____ Signature: _____ Date:_____

In accordance with the Americans with Disabilities Act, we will not discriminate on the basis of
handicap/disability and will attempt to make reasonable accommodations in all volunteer programs.
Please return this form to the Registration Desk at the Volunteer Fair or mail <u>before</u> your first course
to Volunteer Recruitment Manager, Desert Botanical Garden, 1201 N. Galvin Parkway, Phoenix, AZ

 Used with permission of the Desert Botanical Garden.

Sample Form 2.4

Application to Volunteer

Name:_____Date:_____

Address:_____
                        Street   City   Zip

Home #:_____Work #:_____Cell #:_____

E-mail:_____   Birthdate:_____/_____/_____
                                                                                    (year optional)

Current Occupation:_____

School or Employer:_____

Supervisor's Name & Phone #:_____

Education Background:
Circle highest grade completed   **1 2 3 4 5 6 7 8 9 10 11 12 GED**

College_____Degree Received_____

Do you have transportation: Yes_____   No_____
Driver's License # and Expiration Date: _____

Skills and Interests:
Please list work and volunteer experience as well as any skills or interests that could be of use to the volunteer program.

_____

_____

_____

_____

_____

Please list type of volunteer work that would be of interest to you: _____

_____

_____

Is there anything that might limit your volunteer work:_____

_____

Continued on Back

Form supplied by Volunteer Coordinator, City of Tempe

Availability: Please indicate time you are available to volunteer with a check mark or specific times.

	MON.	TUES.	WED.	THUR.	FRI.	SAT.	SUN.
MORNINGS							
AFTERNOONS							
EVENINGS							

Have you ever been convicted of a **misdemeanor** or **felony** (other than minor/civil traffic offenses), placed on probation, fined, or given a suspended sentence (include military trial convictions)? *Note*: Reckless operation, hit-and-run, driving under the influence, excessive speeding, and similar charges are not considered minor traffic offenses. _____Yes _____No
If "yes," give details, including charges, dates, locations, etc.:_____

_____

Convictions will not automatically bar an applicant from volunteering. The relationship of the conviction to the volunteer job, as well as its severity and the passage of time will all be considered.

References: List two personal references other than family members:

Name:_____Phone:_____

Relationship:_____

Name:_____Phone:_____

Relationship:_____

In case of an emergency, please contact:

Name:_____Relationship:_____

Home Phone:_____Work Phone:_____

Do you have medical insurance? Yes _____ No_____

Name of Co. & Policy No._____

Signature:_____**Parent/Guardian:**_____
(IF UNDER **18** YEARS OF AGE)

For Staff Use Only:

SITE ASSIGNED:_____ENTERED IN COMPUTER:_____
SUPERVISOR:_____WELCOME SENT:_____

Form supplied by Mary Anna Bastin, Volunteer Coordinator, City of Tempe

Sample Form 2.5

Volunteer Informational Interview

Date: _____

Applicant's Name: Joe Volunteer

Interviewer: Jane Manager

Volunteer Program: **Please circle areas of interest**

Undecided	Ask a Gardener	Business Office
Butterfly Pavilion	Docents	Membership Sales (Envoys)
Garden Shop	Herbarium	Horticulture Aides
Instructor Aides	Music in the Garden	Propagation
School Guides (SAGES)	Seedlings (Preschool Assistant)	Seed Room
Special Events	Office Personnel (TOPS)	Scientific Plant Documentation (Voucher Program)

Question 1: Have you filled out a Volunteer Application form? (*If no, give them one to fill out.*)

Question 2: Have you ever volunteered before? What did you do and what do you feel you learned? If you haven't volunteered before, why have you decided to now?
(*Look for ability to make the time commitment to volunteer and attend training courses.*)

Question 3: What special skills or experiences do you think you can bring to this program?
(*Look for commonalities with the volunteer program skill set, from "Assess Need for Volunteers," Sample Form 2.1.*)

Question 4: Tell me about a time when you felt you were working at your best.... What was the situation? (*Look for individual's fit toward working in a group or if they are better suited for more autonomous work.*)

Question 5: Describe a "people problem" or a difficult situation you have had to deal with. How did you handle the situation and what was the outcome? (*Look for the ability to work closely with people; determine if individual can balance tasks with people and relationship skills.*)

Question 6: How do you handle changes that are out of your control?
(*Look for adaptability and good judgment skills.*)

Interviewer:
- **Do you feel this candidate would be a good DBG volunteer?**
  ____**Yes...Give candidate copy of Programs and Course Catalog**
  ____**Unsure...Please refer candidate to the Volunteer Office immediately for additional interview**

If Yes......
- **Go over volunteer job description, training courses, schedule of courses, and costs (if applicable)**
- **Answer any additional questions**
- **Enroll candidate in "How to be a DBG Volunteer" class**

Date of "How to be a DBG Volunteer" class:_____

Notes:

Docent Daily Tasks Schedule

DATE_____   10 A.M. TOUR_____
                             UNSCHEDULED TOUR_____TIME_____
                             UNSCHEDULED TOUR_____TIME_____
                             1:00 P. M. TOUR_____
                             BACKUP_____
♥*TIDY-UP DUTY*♥_____ BACKUP_____
FLOATING DOCENTS_____

DESERT DISCOVERY TRAIL STATIONS: *(items to carry to the station)*
Introduction to Deserts and the Botanical Garden *(Relief Map)*
9:00-10:30_____ 10:30-12:00_____ 1:30-2:30 _____

What is a Cactus? *(Saguaro Seedlings and Senita Cross Section)*
9:00-10:30_____ 10:30-12:00_____ 1:30-2:30 _____

Aloes and Agaves: Leaf Succulents *(2 Plants in Basket, Cut Aloe Leaf <u>and</u> Baked Agave Leaf from freezer)*
9:00-10:30_____ 10:30-12:00_____ 1:30-2:30 _____

Desert Birds *(Cactus Wren Nest, Verdin Nest)*
9:00-10:30_____ 10:30-12:00_____ 1:30-2:30 _____

Prickly Pear Cart *(Basket, Nopalitos, Candy, Toothpicks, Cut Fruit and*
    Prickly Pear Pad — Note: Jelly and Crackers are optional in place of candy)
9:00-10:30_____10:30-12:00_____ 1:30-2:30 _____

Butterfly Touch Cart *(Basket of hands-on items)*
9:30-10:30_____10:30-12:00_____ 1:30-2:30 _____

CENTER FOR DESERT LIVING:
Herb Cart *(Basket of hands-on items)*
9:00-10:30_____ 10:30-12:00_____ 1:30-2:30 _____

WILDFLOWER TRAIL:
Pollination Touch Cart *(Cut flowers in canister vase and honey)*
9:00-10:30_____ 10:30-12:00_____ 1:30-2:30 _____

PLANTS AND PEOPLE OF THE SONORAN DESERT TRAIL *(Requires <u>a</u> radio and <u>2</u> volunteers on the trail)*

	9:00-10:30	**10:30-12:00**	**1:30-2:30**
Ethnobotany *(Basket)*	_____	_____	_____
Saguaro *(Fruit in freezer)*	_____	_____	_____
Native Crop Garden	_____	_____	_____
Mesquite *(tea – optional)*	_____	_____	_____
Yucca	_____	_____	_____

 Used with permission of the Desert Botanical Garden.

Volunteer Hours Log - Desert Botanical Garden

Directions: **PRINT!** _Enter dates in top row._ _Enter hours per job in column below date. Enter totals at the· far right._ **Turn in** _to the Volunteer Headquarters notebook._ _Hour year ends on December 31._

Name   Month(s)

Area	Job	Dates →											Total Hours
Business Office / Facilities / Garden Shop	Business Office												
	Call Center												
	Facilities												
	Garden Shop												
Education Programming	Ask a Gardener												
	Butterfly Pavilion												
	Docent												
	Flashlight Tour												
	Instructor Aide												
	Kids Camp												
	SAGES												
	Seedlings Assistant												
Membership Envoy	Info Booth												
	Special Events												
Horticulture	Hort Aide												
	Plant Hotline												
	Propagation												
Leadership	Chair												
	Interviewer												
	Newsletter												
	Officer												
	Special Committee												
Research Programs	Herbarium												
	Library												
	Mapping/ Collections												
	Research & Field Work												
	Seed Room												

Sample Form 2.7 continued

Area	Job	Dates →											Total Hours
Special Events	Agave on the Rocks												
	Chiles & Chocolate Fest												
	Diá De Los Muertos												
	Dinner on the Desert												
	Flower Power Fest												
	Luminaria												
	Music In The Garden												
	Native American Recognition Day												
	Plant Sale												
	Pumpkin Festival												
	Teacher Open House												
	Teddy Bear Tea												
	Volunteer Fair												
Special Projects	Member Events												
	Photography												
	Planned Giving												
	Special Project (miscellaneous)												
Trustee	Trustee												
	Trustee Board Committee												
Office Work	Data Entry												
	Office Assistant												
	Web Design/ Maintenance												
Volunteer Training	Continuing Education												
	Course Facilitator												
	Instructor												
	Mentor												
	Team Leader												
	Volunteer in Training												

Tools of the Trade for the Docent

1. Make sure your information is accurate. If you do not know the answer, do not hesitate to say so. Instead carry cards (like note cards) and a pencil and give one to the visitor and have them write down their question on one side with their name, address, and phone number on the other side. Collect the card, and then find out the answer for them and follow-up with a letter or phone call to the visitor with the correct information. This shows the concern and interest of the docent as well as the organization about correctly answering the questions of the visitors and also satisfies the need of the visitor. It also gives the docent a recourse to just saying "I don't know," which feels more like "I don't care."

2. It is also important to correctly pronounce names, terms, and accurately explain cultural background of objects, and use of technical information.

3. Be able to provide information at several learning levels, considering visitors' age, knowledge, and preparation.

4. Know more about the objects than can be presented in one tour. This knowledge allows one a comfort level with the topic when answering questions as well as flexibility in responding to the interests of the group.

5. Be able to group and regroup objects together to serve a variety of objectives.

6. Consider a statement about the discipline. For example, remember history is accurate recording and time and context. It is necessary to explain objects in **their** time and context, not ours today.

Example Schedule A

DATE: Wed., July 5   TIME: 10:00-11:30   SCHOOL: XYZ School

Location & Activity:	Docent name & phone:	Docent name & phone:
Classroom: Games		
Exhibit Hall: 1990s		
Back of Exh. Hall: 1930s		
Video Theater: 1890s		

Note: This schedule is for a school program visit. It shows the date and time of the visit, the school coming and lists each activity in the program and its location in the museum. For the first two activities, two docents are required while the last two activities only need one docent each. This format can be easily created as a computer table, and copied for all booked programs. Keep a master copy, but also give the docents a copy as they sign up, so they can take a copy of the schedule home with them.

Note: Putting the year in the upper right hand corner of the page helped prevent mixing up schedules from one year to the next.   —Anna Johnson

	Example Schedule B	
DATE:	9:30 SCHOOL: ABC SCH.	11:30 SCHOOL: DEF SCH.
	10:30 SCHOOL: GHI SCH.	12:30 SCHOOL: JKL SCH.
	Docents come at 9:00	**Docents come at 11:15**
LOCATION:	**Docent name & phone:**	**Docent name & phone:**
KITCHEN:		
PARLOR:		
UPSTAIRS:		

Note: This is also for a school program, but it runs every hour. First it states the date, and then it lists the hour and what school will be there for that hour. It takes one docent to do each activity, but because the program runs for so long, they come in shifts. The top defines one group of docents to be there at 9:00 a.m. (The program starts at 9:30 a.m., but this allows set-up time). The second group comes to replace the first group at 11:15 a.m. (Everything is set up, and they will start at 11:30 with the new class. They will be responsible for teardown). It is helpful to ask the docents to include their phone number when they sign up. It is easier to contact them when the phone number is written down by their name if there are any scheduling questions or issues that arise before the tour, and it saves time from having to look up phone numbers. This form can also be created on the computer in tables and then copied.

—Anna Johnson

Docent Training Curriculum – Tempe Historical Museum

Session One: two-hour class
Educator: Welcome – 1 minute (Docent notebook at each seat for each class member)
Director: welcome, and how museum began – 15 minutes
Educator: Main hall tour – 20 minutes
Exhibits Coordinator: Explain exhibit design and take class into galleries for examples – 25 minutes
Curator of History: Introduction to Arizona history to 1912 – 60 minutes

Session Two: three-hour class
Educator: Welcome, docent training goals and objectives – 10 minutes
Introduction (each person – 1 minute on tape) – 30 minutes (Educator times & assistant films)
Educator: Tour and introduction to transitions – 30 minutes
Educator: Presentation techniques and how to use hands-on materials – 30 minutes
Break – 10 minutes
Education Staff: Transitions in exhibit hall – 15 minutes
Educator: What is interpretation? - using examples from our programs – 30 minutes
Education Staff: Game – 30 minutes

Session Three: two-hour class
Educator: video on historic site also managed by museum – 15 minutes
Curator of History: Arizona in the 20th Century – 75 minutes
Educator, Curator of History, Exhibits Coordinator: Interpretation – what's it all about? - 30 minutes

Session Four: three-hour class
Educator: Class does transitions in exhibit hall – 30 minutes
Educator: Being an effective docent means simple communication – 45 minutes (video exercise)
Educator: How people learn, and what do they want in a museum – 30 minutes
Break – 10 minutes
Educator: Learning through sensory activities and assessing your modality strengths – 15 minutes
Experienced docent: Presentation from current program – 30 minutes
Educator: Main exhibit hall tour – 30 minutes

Session Five: two-hour class
Curator of History: Tempe history – 60 minutes
Curator of Collections and Curator of Photographs and Archives: An explanation of what they do and collection policies. Lead a tour through their storage areas – 60 minutes.

Session Six: three-hour class
Exhibit hall exploration and presentation – 45 minutes (video taped exercise)
Educator: Docent procedures and scheduling – 15 minutes
Educator: ADA information – 15 minutes
Class does tour together (they take turns with the transitions) – 30 minutes
Educator: "Ask Me Docents" and why this is important – 15 minutes
Docents practice tour in the exhibit hall (often work with partner) – 45 minutes
Educator: Pass out take home test, state when due back, set graduation time and day, and sign up docents for their part in the graduation tour.

Note: The two hour classes were also used for all new volunteers to the museum and anyone who worked for the City (museum was part of City) as an introduction. Therefore, the three-hour classes were very focused on education.

Example of Special Training Information
Awesome Arizona Architecture (Elements of Design)

Goal: To recognize architectural elements in buildings

Activities:

1. **Use photographs of historic buildings to learn to identify different architectural features.**
2. **Use the pictures in the poster to identify architectural features about which the visitor has already learned.**
3. **Use the blocks to build different architectural features.**

This activity requires two people: one to relate with the photographs while the other works with the foam blocks. The presenters should take turns at each position. During the change between camps and/or groups of visitors, one person needs to tidy up the blocks (disassemble anything that has been built).

Photographs:

There are five photographs that will be used to show different architectural elements of each building. When each picture is shown ask questions like these: Who has seen this building? Who knows the name of the building? Has anyone seen buildings like it? What do you think happens in this building? Does someone live here? Is it a business? Why do you think that?

- The first photo is Hayden Mill. Point out the columns/towers, the flat roof and the circular chimney near the center of the picture.
- The second photo is the Andre building. Point out the Pilaster strip, the relieving arches above the windows, the pediment roof, and the frieze below the pediment roof.
- The third photo features Old Main in the center of the ASU campus. Elements to point out are the relieving arches above the windows, pediments, pilaster strips next to the upper windows, the palladium (three windows grouped together), and the cornice below the palladium. There are also finials on top of the pediment.
- The fourth photo is a classically styled bungalow located at Tempe Town Square and called the Cole House. Elements to mention are the sleeping porch, ionic columns, and broadside roof. This style of house was popular in Arizona, as well as the state of California, from 1905 through 1925.
- The fifth and final photo is of the Casa Loma Hotel building in downtown Tempe. This building contains a couple of elements already mentioned such as columns and relieving arches above the windows. This building also has two tiers of verandas with columns and arches, dormer windows on the roof, and fanlights above each door (arch-shaped windows).

Poster:

Using the poster, have visitors point out the architectural elements they see in the buildings. The presenter may have to point out some features to get them started.

Tempe Historical Museum summer camp, 2000, packet activity.

Form developed at Tempe Historical Museum.

Docent Presentation Evaluation Form

Presenter: _____ **Date:** _____

1. **Overall Effectiveness (Circle one) 1 = poor   5 = excellent**

Introduction	1	2	3	4	5
Content	1	2	3	4	5
Conclusion	1	2	3	4	5
Speaker	1	2	3	4	5

2. **Personal Qualities** – Enthusiasm, Empathy, Personality, Style of Presentation, Flexibility

3. **Vocal Qualities** – Volume, Rate, Pitch, Word Selection, Pronunciation, Enunciation, Tone

4. **Time** – Goal of 20 minutes

5. **Nonverbal Delivery** – Smile, Eye Contact, Gestures, Body Position

6. **Communicative Techniques** – Audience Involvement, Humor, Drama, Props

7. **The area the Speaker most needs to work on is:**

8. **The Speaker's greatest strength was?**

Docent Feedback on Training Classes

1. Was this course beneficial to you?

2. Have you been well prepared to do tours in the main exhibit hall?

3. Do you feel you have a good overview of the museum, so you can represent it in a professional manner to the public?

4. What are the strengths of this program? Explain.

5. What are the weaknesses of this program? Please include ideas on ways to improve them.

6. What programs would you like to see for the docents in the future?

7. Any other comments?

Form developed at Tempe Historical Museum.

Museum Group Visitation Guidelines

THE TEMPE HISTORICAL MUSEUM IS A CENTER WHERE THE COMMUNITY COMES TOGETHER TO CELEBRATE TEMPE'S PAST AND PONDER THE FUTURE

Welcome to the Tempe Historical Museum. We are pleased that you have decided to join us for a tour into Tempe's past. The following tour guidelines are designed to assist you in planning your visit, and to aid us in making your visit an enjoyable experience.

MUSEUM TOUR GUIDELINES

When arranging your museum visit please plan on spending at least one hour. We request that tours be reserved **at least two weeks in advance.**

Docent led tours. The focus of your tour will be the main exhibit hall with a brief introductory tour of our changing galleries. Our usual tour size is approximately 20 individuals per docent. Please divide your group accordingly.

 Check in. Upon arrival at the museum please check in at the Reception Desk and verify the number of people in your group.

 No food or drink is allowed in the museum. There is a common area outside, in front of the museum, where your group can eat. There are benches but no tables. Drinking fountains and restrooms are adjacent to the museum lobby.

 Photographs. Pictures may be taken in the Museum's exhibit hall, **but using a flash is not allowed.**

 Bus Parking. A large parking lot on the west side of the museum will accommodate your buses.

OTHER AVAILABLE ACTIVITIES

In addition to a docent led tour, the following activities are available and should be scheduled at the same time you schedule your tour.
- Scavenger Hunts on Tempe City Government or The Development of Transportation
- Mystery Artifact Challenge
- Timeline Activity

If you have any questions, please contact the Tempe Historical Museum. Your comments or ideas on how we can improve our tours are always welcome.

Sample Form 5.1

Education Task Force Profile Worksheet

Name	Professional Background				Subject					School District				Previous Visitation (Yes/No)
	Principal	State Dept of Ed	District	Profes-sional org	K-6	7-9	High	Soc. Studies	Science	Mesa	Tmp	Phx	Chand/Gilbert	Yes/No
GOAL#	2	1	1	2	4	2	3	3	3	6	1	1	2	Y = 10–12 N = 3–5

Note: Assumes the task force will consist of 12–15 members. One member could meet several criteria. Tempe (Tmp), Phoenix (Phx), Chandler (Chand), and Gilbert are cities within close proximity to Mesa.

Form developed at the Mesa Southwest Museum, 1997

"The Road Showdown" A Sample Lesson Plan from the National Project Archaeology Guide, "Intrigue of the Past: A Teacher's Activity Guide for Fourth through Seventh Grades"

THE ROAD SHOWDOWN

SUBJECTS:	Science, social studies, language arts
SKILLS:	Analysis, synthesis, evaluation
STRATEGIES:	Debate, role play, values clarification, decision making, writing, visualization, communication, problem solving
DURATION:	One to two 45-minute periods
CLASS SIZE:	Any; groups of 3 to 4

Objectives:

In their study of archaeological issues students will use a role play to:

1. Debate the viewpoint of four different interest groups regarding an archaeological site and a road construction project.

2. Formulate their own decision about the proper course of action.

Vocabulary:

cultural resources: a definite location of past human activity, occupation, or use identifiable through field inventory (survey), historical documentation, or oral evidence; includes prehistoric and historic sites.

land manager: an employee of a federal land managing agency (such as the Bureau of Land Management or U.S. Forest Service) with authority to decide how land under the jurisdiction of the agency and the resources on it will be used. Effects on cultural resources are among the factors weighed in a decision.

Materials:

Copies of "The Road Showdown" master for each student.

Background:

Many people care about the past, and for many different reasons. Sites and artifacts can provide meaning on several levels. Using the example of Stonehenge in England, we can list some values people hold toward the past. Archaeologists value Stonehenge for its **scientific** potential. Many people appreciate its **aesthetic** value. Druids, even today,

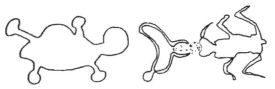

believe Stonehenge has **spiritual or religious** significance. In recent years, the English punk movement has held a large gathering there every year, to make **social and political** statements. The concessionaires and businesses around Stonehenge also value it for its **commercial and economic** value. To some people, Stonehenge has an **intrinsic** value, and to many Britons, it embodies **heritage** values (Chippindale, 1988; Project WILD, 1983, pp. 257-258).

We can examine these meanings by placing them in one of two categories, consumptive and non-consumptive. Consumptive uses are those that "use up" or deplete the past. Non-consumptive uses are those which do not deplete sites, artifacts, or the knowledge base.

To some people, places and things of the past are tangible reminders of their heritage and history. If a person experiences this by observing and being near certain sites or objects they are acting in a non-consumptive way. The thing or place will be there for them to experience again, and for others to experience. On the other hand, if a person takes an arrowhead, pottery sherd or old bottle, or writes his or her name on the wall of an historic cabin or rock art panel, they are consuming the past, and removing parts of it from others' experience. Other consumptive actions include collecting artifacts to sell or trade, and destruction by development projects, such as plowing and construction of buildings.

In a gray area between non-consumptive and consumptive use is site excavation done by a qualified archaeologist. The use of the site is consumptive, in that physically the site is no longer intact. It is non-consumptive in the sense that information derived from the site is obtained by scientific excavation and becomes public knowledge.

Archaeology is a rapidly changing field. New scientific techniques are developed every year that

allow us to learn more from sites and artifacts. Archaeologists have adopted the ethic of conservation, and laws concerning cultural resources also recognize that we need to conserve—to wisely use—sites. There will not be any more of them, and an archaeologist has to have a good reason to "consume" a site by excavation.

Archaeologists and land managers who make decisions about projects on public lands spend considerable time and energy analyzing how sites and artifacts are to be conserved. The issues surrounding use of the past are complex and often strike at the core of personal values. Responsible citizenship means being knowledgeable about these issues and taking informed and thoughtful actions.

Setting the Stage:

People often have conflicting ideas about what is the best use of a resource; and some uses preclude others. Brainstorm some examples. Possibilities include wildlife (hunters versus wildlife watchers), rivers (dams and energy versus river running and fish habitat), and fields (farming or housing development). These same kinds of conflicts affect archaeological and historic sites and artifacts as well.

Procedure:

1. Divide the students into four groups: archaeologists, American Indians, business owners, and recreationists.

2. Distribute "The Road Showdown" master to students. Ask them to read the story through the eyes of their assigned role—to adopt the viewpoint of that interest group. They will be presenting an argument for their viewpoint to a land manager who will make the final decision about the project. The manager can be the teacher, a student, or a panel of students. What should the land manager decide to do about the problem?

3. Give students 10 to 15 minutes to discuss in their groups. Each group appoints a spokesperson to present their arguments. They can propose solutions to the problem which they believe could meet the concerns of all parties, as well as their own.

4. Call the "town meeting" to order and establish two ground rules, (a) no interrupting another person, and (b) be brief and to the point with your arguments. You may also want to impose a time limit on presentations.

5. Each group presents their desired outcome to the manager(s), supporting their goal with solid reasons. General discussion and rebuttal follows.

6. Summarize the discussions by asking each group to choose one or two words which describe the value with which their group is most concerned. Examples may include science, heritage, religion, money, progress, fun.

7. Discuss how each of these values and concerns has validity, and that there is no absolute right or wrong answer to the problem. Point out that being a responsible citizen means understanding all of the viewpoints about an issue before making a decision or taking an action. Challenge the students to think of solutions to the problem that could meet everyone's concerns.

Closure:

Students abandon their assigned role and express in writing what they would personally decide if they were the land manager, and why.

Evaluation:

Evaluate students' group participation, the clarity and reasoning of their arguments, and their written work.

Links:

Section Two: "Introduction"

Section Three, Lesson 22: "Artifact Ethics"

Section Three, Lesson 26: "Archaeology—A Conservation Issue"

Extension:

The scenario and interest groups could be altered to fit a local situation. Students could write about the viewpoint of each of the interest groups.

References:

Chippindale, Christopher, 1988, "Telling Tales of the Past to the Public: The Stonehenge Experience." Paper presented at the Second Annual Presenting the Past Conference, Minneapolis, MN.

Western Regional Environmental Education Council, 1983, *Project WILD Elementary Activity Guide.* Project WILD, Boulder, CO.

THE ROAD SHOWDOWN

The state highway department is building a road connecting your town to a new reservoir. In compliance with Federal and State laws, a portion of the project funding has been budgeted for identification and excavation of archaeological sites. Archaeologists are excavating a site that will then be destroyed, because it is directly in the path of the new highway. They have used up all the money that the highway department budgeted for the excavation, but the site is much larger and more complex than they could tell when they first started. They say that the site is of tremendous scientific value and could help answer many questions about the state's past. They need $50,000 to finish the excavations.

Last week, the archaeologists uncovered some human burials. Following the law, they stopped excavating immediately and notified the nearby Indian tribe. Tribal leaders visited the site and told the archaeologists that the site included a cemetery of their ancestors, and that it had significant religious and heritage values to the tribe. Their wishes are that the site be covered up and left in peace . . . no further excavation, no road over the site.

The local business owners are concerned that the road will be delayed or not built at all. This affects their income significantly. If motorists aren't traveling through the town on their way to the reservoir, they won't be buying gasoline, food, or lodging.

Recreationists are also concerned. Water-skiers and fishing and boating enthusiasts all have been waiting for years for the chance to use the new reservoir. Some have even bought expensive new boats and fishing tackle. They will have to travel 60 extra miles on a dirt road, to get to the reservoir if the new highway isn't built.

Staff Development Activity Evaluation

Directions:
1. Complete the entire form.
2. To indicate the quality of the training according to the criterion listed below, mark "Yes" or "No"
3. In your written comments, cite specific information from the training/activity.

Your Name/Job Title/Building:	Date:	Location of Training/ Presentation:
Topic/Title:	Presenter:	

	Quality of Training/Presentation	Yes	No
Training/Presentation	Highly interesting and informative		
	Somewhat interesting and informative		
	Uninteresting and uninformative		
Usefulness	Very useful		
	Somewhat useful		
	Not useful		
Participant Involvement	Numerous hands-on activities and chances for involvement		
	Some hands-on activities and chances for involvement		
	All lecture with no chance for involement		
Questions/Answers	Numerous opportunities for questions and answers		
	Limited opportunities for questions and answers		
	No time for questions and answers		
Content	Very appropriate to the topic		
	Appropriate to the topic		
	Inappropriate to the topic		
Materials	Highly coordinated with presentation		
	Very useful		
	Somewhat coordinated with presentation		
	Somewhat useful		
	Poorly organized, lacked focus, hard to follow		
Pace	Optimal pace		
	A little fast		
	A little slow		
	Too fast		
	Too slow		

What have you learned that you did not know before?		
Will you be able to use what you've learned? Why/Why not?		
How will you measure the impact of what you've learned?		
What do you think will have the most positive impact?		
What would be appropriate follow-up for this training?		

The format for this form was adapted by Theresa Steinlage, KSDE Consultant, from: Project SAMPLE Training Evaluation, Flint Hills Special Education Cooperative, 9/2001.Courtesy of the Kansas State Department of Education.

Sample Form 6.1

Summer Youth Institute Organizational Outline

I. Recruiting
   a. Advertising in newspaper and at local high schools through history teachers
   b. Teens must apply by filling out an application and going through an interview process.
   c. Teens are placed at location that they choose and find interesting.

II. Training
   a. Mandatory two-hour training session during which they
      i. Receive a written packet of information about the summer programs detailing the goals of each activity and exactly what each activity includes
      ii. Observe demonstrations of what they will be doing for summer and practice some of the activities
      iii. Meet others who will be participating in the Institute
      iv. Receive scheduling information and choose the times they will be coming
   b. Friday sessions were required attendance for two hours every Friday morning
      i. First hour of this session is meeting with the curators, finding out what they do.
         1. I always began the first session, so that I could introduce them to their purpose in the exhibit hall and explain family night and their opportunity to develop activities for it.
         2. Curator of History was the presenter at the second session and as the content expert he could help the teens focus on ideas for topics for family night.
         3. Next two sessions were the Curators in Collections and Archives
         4. The last session was with the Exhibit Coordinator
      ii. Second hour of the meeting on Friday was focused on developing ideas for family night. We would start with brainstorming, and it would usually take two-three sessions to tie down what we wanted to do. Then students would divide into groups to take charge of developing different activities. The meetings with the curators also helped the students in gathering information on their topics and developing ideas. The exhibit coordinator and collections curators often played a key role in the development of the activities.

III. Scheduling
   a. Teens were scheduled for 3 hours and 15 minutes on Wednesday morning or afternoon and in a specific activity of their choosing.
   b. We were very accommodating regarding summer vacations. If someone needed to be gone during part of the summer, we generally had enough teens to cover that time period.

IV. Family Night
   a. The teens in the Institute ran the activities for this program. In addition, we hired a disc jockey to come and play dance music during the family night. We often had Dance Through the Decades, and would have adults teaching their children their favorite dances and vice versa. The event usually lasted from 6 pm to 9 pm. We also served refreshments, and we had prizes for those who completed all the activities in the exhibit halls. Usually some senior docents came in and helped with the activities and handing out the prizes.

V. Recognition
   a. The teens all received T shirts, and a badge. It was important that they look official in the exhibit hall, so the public viewed them as knowledgeable.
   b. At the end of the summer we had a big party for all the Summer Institute Members with pizza, certificates, and an invite to another bigger youth volunteer pool party.

c. If any of these students ever wanted reference letters to go with college applications, we happily filled them out.

d. We invited these teens to become part of our regular docent program and attend that training. We generally had one or two every year who went on to become year-round docents.

Note: An intern was hired every summer to oversee this program. It was very helpful to have someone in the exhibit halls with the teens to answer their questions, help with problems, and in general keep them focused on their tasks. My interns were generally graduate students, and the teens enjoyed working with them.

Teacher Survey
Gilbert Historical Museum

We are gathering ideas for the development of a plan to preserve, expand and improve the Museum's exhibits and educational programming. Your input will be extremely helpful. Thank you.

1. Which of the following topics do you think Gilbert School Children should learn about? Select the top 8 topics and rank them in order of importance.
   1 = most important; 8 = least important.

   ___ Gilbert's first homesteads
   ___ The role of farming in Gilbert history
   ___ The history of Gilbert's schools
   ___ Gilbert businesses 1900 – 1950
   ___ Gilbert businesses 1950 to present
   ___ The families that settled Gilbert
   ___ Cowboy life in Gilbert
   ___ Native American culture in Gilbert
   ___ Hispanic culture in Gilbert
   ___ Gilbert's soldiers and military history
   ___ Gilbert home life 1900 – 1950s
   ___ Gilbert home life 1950s to present
   ___ Religion in Gilbert
   ___ The growth of Gilbert 1970 to present

2. Please check (a) the topics that support your school curricula, and write down the study area (e.g., local history) if possible.

   Area of Study

   ___ Gilbert's first homesteads   _____
   ___ The role of farming in Gilbert history   _____
   ___ The history of Gilbert's schools   _____
   ___ Gilbert businesses 1900 – 1950   _____
   ___ Gilbert businesses 1950 – present   _____
   ___ The families that settled Gilbert   _____
   ___ Cowboy life in Gilbert   _____
   ___ Native American culture in Gilbert   _____
   ___ Hispanic culture in Gilbert   _____
   ___ Gilbert's soldiers and military history   _____
   ___ Gilbert home life 1900 – 1950s   _____
   ___ Gilbert home life 1950s to present   _____
   ___ Religion in Gilbert   _____
   ___ The growth of Gilbert 1970 – present   _____
   ___ Other   _____

Teacher Survey
Gilbert Historical Museum
Page 2

3. Circle the room or area of the Museum that you like best for your students.

Town   Occupation   Families   Home Life   School   Old West   Military

Farm Equipment   Other_____

Why? _____

_____

_____

5. Please describe any displays, programs, or materials you would like to see added to the Museum.

_____

THANK YOU FOR YOUR HELP!

Please let us know if you would be interested in helping with future exhibit planning and evaluation projects.

Teacher's Trunk Activities Evaluation

SA=strongly agree   A=agree   N=neutral   D=disagree   SD=strongly disagree

G.I.F.T. Trunk Classroom Activities

Work & Play: Then & Now was age-appropriate for my students.	SA	A	N	D	SD
Work & Play: Then & Now supported my curricular goals.	SA	A	N	D	SD
Early Gilbert in Time and Space was age-appropriate for my students.	SA	A	N	D	SD
Early Gilbert in Time and Space supported my curricular goals.	SA	A	N	D	SD
From Alfalfa to Butter was age-appropriate for my students.	SA	A	N	D	SD
From Alfalfa to Butter supported my curricular goals.	SA	A	N	D	SD

Comments or suggestions: _____

_____

_____

1. Which activity was most useful for teaching students about Gilbert history and geography?

    _____

    _____

2. Which activity was least useful for teaching students about Gilbert history and geography?

    _____

    _____

3. What grade do you teach? _____

4. What suggestions or recommendations do you have for improving the Gilbert Historical Museum's educational program?

    _____

    _____

**Thank you for taking the time to complete this survey.
We appreciate your feedback.**

Sample Form 7.3

Student Evaluation
My Trip to the Gilbert Historical Museum

My favorite part of the visit was: _____

_____

I was surprised to find out that: _____

_____

I would like to learn more about: _____

*Draw a picture or write a story or poem about your
favorite part of the Museum.*

Name_____Grade_____School_____Date_____

"Design Your Own Program" Proposal Worksheet
An Outreach Program

Objective:

Have trained parents _____ "kits" to their child's class and present one
45–60 minute hands-on lesson about _____ based on _____themes.

Goals – Students will.

How –

Example – Sample kit

Benefits –
-
-
-
-
-
-
-
-
-
-

Process –
-
-
-
-
-

Conclusion –

Other Outreach KIT ideas –

Program Design Pyramid

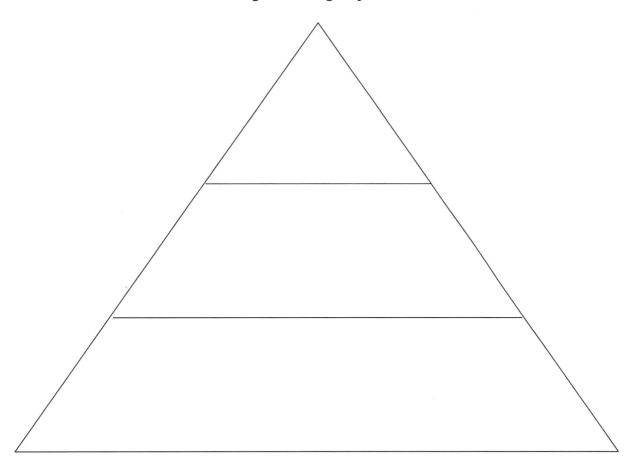

Use this pyramid example to design your own program format. Draw vertical lines to divide the 3 sections to represent the components of your programming. If you need more sections, add them to the pyramid, or make a rectangle. This is merely a sample way to look at the bigger picture and also indicate a ranking or relative importance for each part of your program.

Event Planning Time Line/Checklist for Programs and Special Events

Event Name _____ Event date(s) _____

Event hours _____ Admission fee _____

Event address _____

Event sponsors _____

Target audience _____ Estimated Attendance _____

Brief event description

Event goals and objectives

(Date) _____ 1 Year before event
- ☐ Establish event committee or hire event planner
- ☐ Establish event goals and objectives – visualize what your successful event will look like
- ☐ Review previous years' evaluations and reports if applicable
- ☐ Finalize date
- ☐ Get event on community calendar
- ☐ Establish budget
- ☐ Seek partners or sponsors
- ☐ Start event notebook
- ☐ Select the event manager and assistant manager
- ☐ Review and modify this event timeline
- ☐ Contact key speaker, performer or celebrity
- ☐
- ☐

Sample Form 8.2 Continued

(Date)_____ 9 Months before event

- ☐ Develop event program
- ☐ Select, contact and confirm speakers or entertainers
- ☐ Prepare promotional plan, and logos; begin early promotion
- ☐ Confirm site and apply for appropriate permits
- ☐ Secure street closures or relevant facility logistics
- ☐ Secure necessary insurance
- ☐ Establish guidelines for choosing booths, bands, performers, etc.
- ☐ Seek and secure sponsors or program partners
- ☐
- ☐

(Date)_____ 6 Months before event

- ☐ Review and revise budget and financial plan
- ☐ Contact vendors and suppliers
- ☐ Prepare information packets for vendors
- ☐ Order supplies
- ☐ Send announcements/invitations/press release
- ☐ Address staffing needs
- ☐ Develop logistic plan and map
- ☐ Review event goals and revise if necessary
- ☐ Produce PSA
- ☐
- ☐

(Date)_____ 3 Months before event

- ☐ Review and revise budget and financial plan
- ☐ Confirm audio/visual needs
- ☐ Prepare registration/access system
- ☐ Recruit volunteers
- ☐ Secure event materials (t-shirts, brochures, fliers, etc.)
- ☐ Send information to printers
- ☐ Order signs, flags, booths
- ☐ Establish menu or confirm food and drink vendors (check on food licenses)
- ☐ Hire security
- ☐ Hire set-up, take-down, clean-up help
- ☐ Order portable toilets
- ☐ Order garbage collection containers
- ☐ Develop instruction sheets/manual and send to printer
- ☐ Secure housing and transportation for out of town presenters
- ☐ Send some promotional materials
- ☐ Prepare evaluation forms
- ☐ Establish information and first aid booth(s) location, staff and supplies
- ☐ Order name tags/badges
- ☐
- ☐
- ☐

Sample Form 8.2 Continued

<u>(Date)</u>_____<u>1 Month before event</u>

- ☐ Review and revise budget and financial plan
- ☐ Prepare a daily activity calendar
- ☐ Send promotional materials
- ☐ Review entire event plan to verify all work accurate & complete
- ☐ Walk through event with event committee as if you are a participant, look for problems and needs
- ☐ Re-confirm with all speakers, vendors, staff and suppliers. Send necessary information such as maps, directions, instructions, etc.
- ☐ Prepare staff and volunteer training and scheduling
- ☐ Order golf cart, walkie talkies or other equipment needed to expedite communication/ transportation during the event
- ☐ Locate an area where staff and volunteers can eat and rest
- ☐ Prepare final site diagram
- ☐ Assign or hire someone to document the event
- ☐ Invite and notify neighboring businesses/residents of event (permit process may involve notification of event)
- ☐
- ☐

<u>(Date)</u>_____<u>2 Weeks before event</u>

- ☐ Review and revise budget and financial plan
- ☐ Set aside time for media interviews
- ☐ Collate event materials (programs, gift bags, etc.)
- ☐ Take all staff on-site and review event plan/logistics
- ☐
- ☐

<u>(Date)</u>_____<u>1 Week before event</u>

- ☐ Review and revise budget and general financial plan
- ☐ Train volunteers
- ☐
- ☐
- ☐
- ☐

<u>(Date)</u>_____<u>2-1 day(s) before event</u>

- ☐ Site set-up
- ☐
- ☐
- ☐
- ☐

<u>(Date)</u>_____<u>Event Day</u>

- ☐ Arrive early, manage event, leave late
- ☐ Acknowledge event partners, sponsors, participants and helpers
- ☐ Distribute evaluations

Sample Form 8.2 Continued

- ☐ Network with participants, vendors, visitors
- ☐
- ☐
- ☐
- ☐

(Date) _____ 1 Week after event

- ☐ Debrief with all staff and volunteers
- ☐ Send thank you letters
- ☐ Review bills and prepare invoice payments
- ☐ Prepare brief final report (including photos) and financial report
- ☐ Assess evaluations and determine if event will continue next year with the recommendations
- ☐ Repeat process for next year's event
- ☐ Send photos and write-up to appropriate media and newsletters
- ☐
- ☐
- ☐
- ☐

10 Questions to Ask After Your Special Event

1. Was the event fun? Nothing else really matters if you answer no to this question. The reason a special event exists is to provide the participants with a good time. If you fail to provide fun, then discontinue the event and plan something else.

2. Did the event achieve its financial goals? Your event should have a specific financial goal. Remember, the gross amount raised means very little -- it's the net amount, after expenses, which should be of vital concern to your organization and the event committee.

3. Did the event achieve its other goals? Did you have the attendance you planned for? Did you receive the media coverage you expected? Did you recruit new and dynamic volunteers?

4. What problems did we encounter? Every event, no matter how well managed, will have problems. All problems should be fully documented so they won't be repeated in the future.

5. Did we have enough volunteers? Special events often fail to achieve goals because of a lack of motivated and trained volunteers. Carefully evaluate each committee to make sure you have the people necessary for success.

6. Was the leadership adequate? The leadership ability of your event chairperson is the key to a successful event. If the results of your event were less than you hoped for, start your critique at the very top.

7. Have we recognized all supporters? You should have an established plan to recognize the leadership and the volunteers. Expressing sincere appreciation this year will insure voluntary support again next year.

8. What will improve the event next year? Ask yourself many questions. Will the event be improved if you change the venue? Will more people attend if you have the event at a different time of year? Was the fee too expensive? Was the entertainment ill-suited to the demographics of the crowd?

9. Is there any unfinished business? Was the dais returned to the hotel? Were the baskets used for flowers returned to the florist? Have all follow-up commitments with donors been satisfied? Have letters and gifts of appreciation been delivered to corporate sponsors?

10. Was the event fun? A redundant question? Not at all. It can never be stressed too much. Your ultimate goal is to have an event that is fun and draws people back year after year.

Courtesy of Bill J. Harrison, CFRE, author and trainer
www.iteachfundraising.com

Event Budget Information

Income	
Admissions	
Vendor fees	
% of sales	
Sponsors	
Parking fees	
Other	
Income Total	
Expenses	
Insurance	
Security	
Permits	
Licenses	
Public Service Announcement	
Publicity Materials	
Brochures and fliers	
Signs	
Maps	
Billboards	
Media advertising	
Design services	
Event program	
Banners	
Booths, tents and related rentals (tables and chairs)	
First Aid supplies	
Equipment/sound rental	
Electrical services and supplies	
Portable toilets	
Transportation expenses	
Temporary help	
Set-up/take-down services	
Trash	
Golf cart	
Photographer	
Walkie Talkies	
Performers and celebrity fees	
VIP reception	
Staff and volunteer refreshments	
Miscellaneous	
Expense Total	
Income – Expenses = Event Grand Total	

Sign / Exhibit Observation Tool

Sign/Exhibit: _____

Observer:_____**Day:**_____**Date:**_____

Time Start:_____**Time Finish:**_____**Weather Conditions:**_____

Instructions:

1. Observe first person to view either sign or exhibit. With two or more viewers, record the behavior of the person who reaches the exhibit first.

2. Start stopwatch. Continue stopwatch until person is no longer viewing exhibit. Then turn off stopwatch and record viewing time.
   - If the visitor does not stop, record a zero under total view time
   - If visitor ties shoes, tends child, or does something unrelated to the exhibit, silently count seconds and subtract that time from the total.

3. Record a 0, 1, 2, 3 for your perception of visitor's "involvement level."
   - 0 = no stop
   - 1 = casually looking at exhibit sign
   - 2 = reading the exhibit sign and casually looking at exhibit object
   - 3 = reading plus looking plus other behavior such as looking closely, pointing at exhibit or discussing exhibit with others

4. Under comments, record any other significant event (e.g. social interactions, questions related to exhibit, reading the exhibit aloud, pointing to the exhibit, etc.).

5. After visitor leaves, select the next visitor viewing the exhibit.

Visitor #	Sex	Age	Group Size	Total view time	Involve-ment level	Comments 1 = Brief read 3 = long read Note any comments or discussion
A						
B						
C						
D						
E						
F						
G						
H						

Sample Form 10.1 Continued

Page 2 - Sign / Exhibit Observation Tool

Visitor #	Sex	Age	Group Size	Total view time	Involve-ment level	Comments 1 = Brief read 3 = long read Note any comments or discussion
I						
J						
K						
L						
M						
N						
O						
P						
Q						
R						
S						
T						
U						
V						
W						
X						
Y						
Z						

Sample Form 10.2

OBSERVATION SUMMARY: Attracting / Holding / Involvement Power

Exhibit Area Observed: _____

Day:_____Date:_____ Time:_____

A   Number of minutes you observed visitors   _____

B   Total number of observations   _____

C   Total number of visitors that viewed   _____

D   Percentage of visitors that viewed $\dfrac{C}{B}$ _____ = _____ %

E   Range of view time of those that viewed
(ex: 2 seconds to 5 minutes)   _____

F   Involvement Scores of those that viewed:

$\dfrac{\text{\# of Level 1 Scores}}{C}$ =_____ =_____ %

$\dfrac{\text{\# of Level 2 Scores}}{C}$ =_____ =_____ %

$\dfrac{\text{\# of Level 3 Scores}}{C}$ =_____ =_____ %

G   Most interesting visitor comments and behaviors:

_____

_____

_____

_____

_____

H   Suggestions for revisions regarding design, content, location, etc.

_____

_____

_____

_____

_____

EXHIBIT COMMUNICATION POWER
Visitor Interviews Tool

Sign/Exhibit being evaluated: _____

Day:_____Date:_____ Time:_____

Evaluator: _____

"Hello. My name is _____ and I work here at the Desert Botanical Garden.
We are testing some new (signs, exhibits, etc.) about (saguaros, cacti, gardening, etc.)
Would you be willing to answer a few questions about your experience here?
It will take about 5 minutes. Thank you."

(The first few questions are meant to put visitors at ease;
they can be answered "yes" or "no" and are easy to answer.)

Is this your first visit to this are of the Garden?   Yes   No

Where are you from?_____

I noticed that you were looking at the sign about (saguaros, cacti, gardening, etc.)

Do you think the point of this exhibit is clear?   Yes   No

Explain: _____

_____

_____

How could we improve this exhibit so that visitors will understand and enjoy it more? _____

_____

_____

Do you have any special knowledge or training about (saguaros, cacti, gardening, etc.)?

Yes   No   Explain:_____

Do you have any other questions or comments about this or any other exhibits?

_____

_____

_____

Thank you very much. Enjoy your visit.

_____

<u>Visitor sex:</u>	M	F				<u>Age:</u>	20's	30's	40's	50's	60+
<u>Group size:</u>	1	2	3	4	5	6+		Adults only		Adults + kids	

Visitor Tour Survey

The _____ Museum is dedicated to presenting quality programs for our visitors. Your answers, comments and suggestions will be used to evaluate and improve our programs Please return the completed copy to your tour guide or the admissions booth. Thank you for your time and your opinions.

PLEASE circle a corresponding number to record your responses
5 = STRONGLY AGREE   4 = AGREE 3 = NEUTRAL   2 = DISAGREE   1 = STRONGLY DISAGREE

The introduction made me feel welcome and gave an overview of the museum.

                    5   4   3   2   1
Comments_____

The information presented was clear and interesting

                    5   4   3   2   1
Comments_____

The information was organized and understandable

                    5   4   3   2   1
Comments_____

Hands-on items—
Circle one
Enhanced the information   Hindered explanations   Did neither

Comments_____

Length of the tour was
Circle one
Too long   About right   Too short
Comments_____

Additional comments or suggestions

Optional—
Name
City, State, Zip
Are you a museum member?

Immediate School Program Evaluation by Docents

Program _____ **Date** _____

Docent _____

Did the students come prepared?

Was the teacher involved/helpful?

What was student behavior like?

Any particular thoughts about the group and what you saw and experienced today?

Guided Tours Evaluation / Feedback

Name of Guide_____ Date_____

TOUR BASICS   Mini-comments

| Yes / Sometimes / No |

Tour Introduction

___ ___ ___ Introduce yourself to the tour group
___ ___ ___ Introduce the Garden / Mission / How long in existence/ etc.
___ ___ ___ Tell length of time tour will take (and stick to it).
___ ___ ___ Eye Contact with visitors
___ ___ ___ State your theme and the goal of the tour

Communication of Information

___ ___ ___ Relate it to your theme
___ ___ ___ Keep it simple
___ ___ ___ Always be accurate - say "I don't know" rather than guessing

---

Tour Transitions

___ ___ ___ Carry the _theme_ and relate from one object to the next
___ ___ ___ Give visitor something to look forward to
___ ___ ___ Include a transition to the conclusion
                   (such as "The next stop will conclude our tour with ...")

Length of Tour

___ ___ ___ Time - 45 to 60 minutes
___ ___ ___ Stops - 6 to 9 approximately

Conclusion

___ ___ ___ Review your theme and tie it all together
___ ___ ___ Ask if there are any questions
___ ___ ___ Perhaps ask what was their favorite plant or a new thing they _discovered_

PRESENTATION
Eye Contact

___ ___ ___ Look at visitors and talk _TO_ them rather than talking _AT_ them

---

Vocal Presentation

___ ___ ___ Projecting
___ ___ ___ _Talk_ always _TO visitors_ - NOT to the plants/objects
___ ___ ___ Wait and gather your group together at the next stop before talking

---

Evaluator _____
Overall Comments

Sample Form 13.1

Keys to Successful Collaboration Checklist

DUTY	PERSON RESPONSIBLE	START DATE	END DATE
People:			
1. Seek supervisory and institutional support and approval for collaborative projects.			
2. Indentify strengths each partner brings to the collaboration.			
3. Identify decision-makers and get input from everyone who will be involved or has a stake in the outcome.			
4. Identify similar needs/audiences/problems.			
5. Select a Project Director.			
6. All partners must have specific roles and responsibilities. Put them in writing.			
7. Communication – Identify one contact person for each institution. Have all information relayed through this person.			
Principles:			
8. Be open to overlapping and creative solutions.			
9. Determine as a group how final decisions will be made and by whom.			
10. Determine as a group how disputes will be resolved and by whom.			
11. Define clear goals and record what success will look like.			
12. All partners must benefit.			
13. Use evaluation to assess the success of the program as well as partners' satisfaction.			
14. Evaluate the project, document the results, make modifications and repeat the process as necessary for long term projects/programs.			
15. Promote the success to the public, supervisors, funders and officials.			
16. Use the project as a model for other collaborative programs or projects.			
17. Consider additional future partners.			

Bibliography

INTRODUCTION

American Association of Museums. *Museums for a New Century: A Report of the Commission on Museums for a New Century.* Washington, D.C.: American Association of Museums, 1984.

American Association of Museums, and Ellen Cochran Hirzy. *Excellence and Equity: Education and the Public Dimension of Museums.* Washington, D.C.: American Association of Museums, 1992.

Stapp, Carol B. "Opening Up Professional Publishing." In *Writing for Professional Publications: Advancing the Museum Profession through Self-Development*, edited by Carol B. Stapp with Joanne S. Hirsch, 9. Washington, D.C.: American Association of Museums Technical Information Service, 1995.

CHAPTER 1

Bitgood, S. "The Role of Attention in Designing Effective Interpretive Labels." *Journal of Interpretation Research* 5, no. 2 (2003): 31–45.

Falk, John H., and Lynn D. Dierking. *Lessons without Limit: How Free-Choice Learning Is Transforming Education.* Walnut Creek, Calif.: AltaMira Press, 2002.

Grinder, Alison L., and E. Sue McCoy. *The Good Guide: A Sourcebook for Interpreters, Docents and Tour Guides.* Scottsdale, Ariz.: Ironwood Publishing, 1985.

Hein, George E. *Learning in the Museum.* New York: Routledge, 1998.

McLean, Kathleen. *Planning for People in Museum Exhibitions.* Washington, D.C.: Association of Science-Technology Centers, 1993. Reprinted 1996.

Moffat, Hazel, and Vicky Woollard. *Museum and Gallery Education: A Manual of Good Practice.* Walnut Creek, Calif.: AltaMira Press, 1999.

Roberts, Lisa C. *From Knowledge to Narrative: Educators and the Changing Museum.* Washington, D.C.: Smithsonian Institution Press, 1997.

Sachatello-Sawyer, Bonnie, Robert A. Fellenz, Hanly Burton, Laura Gittings-Carlson, Janet Lewis-Mahony, and Walter Woolbaugh. *Adult Museum Programs: Designing Meaningful Experiences.* Walnut Creek, Calif.: AltaMira Press, 2002.

Serrell, Beverly. *Exhibit Labels: An Interpretive Approach.* Walnut Creek, Calif.: AltaMira Press, 1996.

CHAPTER 2

American Association for Museum Volunteers (AAMV) www.ansp.org/hosted/aamv/

An affiliate of the American Association of Museums.

- Promotes professional standards of volunteerism
- Provides a forum for the exchange of ideas and information
- Offers opportunities for continuing education through panel discussions and workshops at local, regional, and national conferences
- Encourages volunteers and volunteer managers to become familiar with projects and programs both locally and nationally
- Informs and represents volunteers in advocacy for tax benefits and other legislation at local and national levels

Directors of Volunteers in Agencies (DOVIA) www.denverdovia.org/resources.html

Promotes professionalism in the field of volunteer management.

Risk Management

The National Recreation and Park Association website (www.nrpa.org/tlc2) offers guidelines it has developed for background screening as well as useful information on "Recommended Criteria for Exclusion."

Anderson, Kristin, and Ron Zemke. *Knock Your Socks Off Answers.* New York: American Management Association, 1995.

Bell, Chip. *Customers as Partners: Building Relationships That Last.* San Francisco: Berrett Koehler, 1994.

Brown-Fletcher, Kathleen. *The Nine Keys to Successful Volunteer Programs.* Rockville, Md.: The Taft Group, 1987.

Connellan, Thomas K. *Inside the Magic Kingdom: Seven Keys to Disney's Success.* Austin, Tex.: Bard Press, 1996.

Ellis, Susan J. *From the Top Down: The Executive Role in Volunteer Program Success.* Philadelphia: Energize, 1996.

———. *The Volunteer Recruitment (and Membership Development) Book.* 2nd ed. Philadelphia: Energize, 1996.

Graff, Linda. *Beyond Police Checks: The Definitive Volunteer and Employee Screening Guidebook.* Dundas, Ontario, Canada: Graff and Associates, 1994.

Lee, Jarene Frances. *What We Learned (the Hard Way) about Supervising Volunteers.* Philadelphia: Energize, Inc., 2004.

McCurley, Steve, and Rick Lynch. *Volunteer Management: Mobilizing All the Resources of the Community*. Downers Grove, Ill.: Heritage Arts Publishing, 1996.

Wilson, Marlene. *The Effective Management of Volunteer Programs*. Boulder, Colo.: Johnson, 1976.

Zemke, Ron. *The Service Edge: 101 Companies That Profit from Customer Care*. New York: New American Library, 1989.

———. *Generations at Work: Managing the Clash of Veterans, Boomers, Xers and Nexters in Your Workplace*. New York: AMACOM, 2000.

CHAPTER 3

Brochu, Lisa, and Tim Merriman. *Personal Interpretation: Connecting Your Audience to Heritage Resources*. Singapore: National Association for Interpretation, 2002.

Cunningham, Mary Kay. *The Interpreter's Training Manual for Museums*. Washington, D.C.: American Association of Museums, 2004.

Falk, John H., and Lynn D. Dierking. *Lessons without Limit: How Free-Choice Learning Is Transforming Education*. Walnut Creek, Calif.: AltaMira Press, 2002.

Gardner, Howard. *Frames of Mind: The Theory of Multiple Intelligences*. 10th ed. New York: Basic Books, 1993.

Gardner, James B., and Peter S. LaPaglia. *Public History: Essays from the Field*. Rev. ed. Malabar, Fla.: Krieger, 2004.

Gartenhaus, Alan. *Minds in Motion: Using Museums to Expand Creative Thinking*. Davis, Calif.: Caddo Gap, 1991.

Gartenhaus, Alan, ed. *The Docent Educator* 4, no. 4 (Summer 1995): 20.

Ham, Sam H. *Environmental Interpretation: A Practical Guide for People with Big Ideas and Small Budgets*. Golden, Colo.: North American Press, 1992.

Hooper-Greenhill, Eilean. *Museums and the Interpretation of Visual Culture*. New York: Routledge, 2002.

Rosenzweig, Roy, and David Thelen. *The Presence of the Past: Popular Uses of History in American Life*. New York: Columbia University Press, 1998.

Tilden, Freeman. *Interpreting Our Heritage*. 3rd ed. Chapel Hill: University of North Carolina Press, 1977.

CHAPTER 4

Brochu, Lisa, and Tim Merriman. *Personal Interpretation: Connecting Your Audience to Heritage Resources*. Singapore: National Association for Interpretation, 2002.

Falk, John H., and Lynn D. Dierking. *Learning from Museums: Visitor Experiences and the Making of Meaning*. Walnut Creek, Calif.: AltaMira Press, 2000.

Grinder, Alison L., and E. Sue McCoy. *The Good Guide: A Sourcebook for Interpreters Docents and Tour Guides*. Scottsdale, Ariz.: Ironwood Publishing, 1985.

Johnson, Anna. "Using Transitions to Teach Touring." *Docent Educator* 5, no. 1 (Autumn 1995): 14–15.

Levy, Barbara Abramoff, Sandra Mackenzie Lloyd, and Susan Porter Schreiber. *GreatTours! Thematic Tours and Guide Training for Historic Sites*. Walnut Creek, Calif.: AltaMira Press, 2001.

CHAPTER 5

Bloom, Benjamin S. *Taxonomy of Educational Objectives: Cognitive Domain*. New York: Longman, 1956.

Anderson, L. W., and D. R. Krathwohl, eds. *A Taxonomy for Learning, Teaching and Assessing: A Revision of Bloom's Taxonomy of Educational Objectives*. Complete ed. New York: Longman, 2001.

Kansas Professional Development Guidelines, 2006–2007. www.ksde.org (July 18, 2007).

Kowal, Penny H. "Vertical Teaming: Making Connections Across Levels." *Middle Ground* 6, no. 1 (August 2002). www.nmsa.org/portals/0/pdf/publications/On_Target/transitioning_hs/ (July 15, 2007).

Massachusetts Department of Education. "Recertification Guidelines for Massachusetts Educators." 2000. www.doe.mass.edu/recert/2000guidelines/ (July 16, 2007).

Munsart, Craig A. *Investigating Science with Dinosaurs*. Englewood, Colo.: Teachers Idea Press, 1993.

Munsart, Craig A., and Karen Alonzi VanGundy. *Primary Dinosaur Investigations: How We Know What We Know*. Englewood, Colo.: Teachers Idea Press, 1995.

Rosenzweig, Roy, and David Thelen. *The Presence of the Past: Popular Uses of History in American Life*. New York: Columbia University Press, 1998.

Smith, Shelly, Jeanne Moe, Kelly Letts, and Danielle Paterson. *Intrigue of the Past: A Teacher's Activity Guide for Fourth through Seventh Grades*. Washington, D.C.: U.S. Dept. of the Interior, Bureau of Land Management, 1993. Reprinted 1996.

CHAPTER 6

Adams, Melinda. "Optimizing Homeschoolers' Experiences in Museums." Master's thesis, John F. Kennedy University, 2005.

Borun, Minda, Jennifer Dritas, Julie I. Johnson, Nancy E. Peter, Kathleen F. Wagner, Kathleen Fadigan, Arlene Jangaard, Estelle Stroup, and Angela Wenger. *Family Learning in Museums: The PISEC Perspective*. Philadelphia: Philadelphia/Camden Informal Science Education Collaborative, The Franklin Institute, 1998.

Dierking, Lynn. "Families and Free-Choice Learning." Unpublished paper delivered at "Family Learning Roundtable: Successful Strategies for Engaging Families," June 14, 2005. www.familylearningforum.org/current/roundtable.html.

Egan, Kieran. "Accumulating History." *History and Theory* 22, no. 4, (Dec. 1983).

Falk, John, and Lynn D. Dierking. *Lessons without Limit: How Free-Choice Learning Is Transforming Education*. Walnut Creek, Calif.: AltaMira Press, 2002.

Family Learning Forum. www.familylearningforum.org/whatis/overview.html (Sept. 16, 2007).

Gardner, Howard. *Frames of Mind: The Theory of Multiple Intelligences*. 10th ed. New York: Basic Books, 1993.

Gatto, John Taylor. *Dumbing Us Down: The Hidden Curriculum in Compulsory Schooling*. 2nd ed. Gabriola Island: New Society Publishers, 2002.

Green, Wilma Prudhum. *Museums & Learning: A Guide for Family Visits*. Washington, D.C.: U.S. Department of Education, Office of Educational Research and Improvement, and Smithsonian Office of Education, 1998.

Grove, Tim. "I Never Knew History Could Be So Fun." *History News* (Autumn 1999): 18–20.

Hein, George, and Mary Alexander. *Museums: Places of Learning*. Washington, D.C.: American Association of Museums, 1998.

Holt, John, and Pat Farenga. *Teach Your Own: The John Holt Book of Homeschooling*. Cambridge: Persus Publishing, 2003.

Richardson, Joy. *Inside the Museum: A Children's Guide to the Metropolitan Museum of Art*. New York: Metropolitan Museum of Art, Abrams, 1993.

Richter, Katrina. "Homeschoolers Are Always Late: What Every Museum Needs to Know about Alternative Learners." *Museum News* (March/April 2007): 47–51.

Sheppard, Beverly. "The Learning Bond." Unpublished manuscript delivered at the "Family Learning Roundtable: Successful Strategies for Engaging Families" Boston, Mass., June 14, 2005. www.familylearningforum.org/current/roundtable.html.

CHAPTER 7

Google "Museum Outreach Programs" on the Web and you will find a vast array of possibilities.

CHAPTER 8

Devney, Darcy Campion. *Organizing Special Events and Conferences: A Practical Guide for Busy Volunteers and Staff*. Sarasota, Fla.: Pineapple Press, 1990.

Harrison, Bill J. *Ten Questions to Ask After your Special Event*. www.iteachfundraising.com/articles/10questions.html (June 13, 2007).

McNamara, Carter. "Basic Guide to Program Evaluation." Adapted from *The Field Guide to Nonprofit Program Design, Marketing and Evaluation*. 1997–2007. www.managementhelp.org/evaluatn/fnl_eval.htm (June 7, 2007).

CHAPTER 9

Din, Herminia, and Phyllis Hecht, eds. *The Digital Museum: A Think Guide*. Washington, D.C.: American Association of Museums, 2007.

Pew Internet and American Life Project. www.pewinternet.org/index.asp.

CHAPTER 10

Allen, Susan. "How Is Writing a Good Set of Questions Like Designing a Good Exhibit?" *Visitor Studies Today!* 3, no. 2 (Summer 2000): 17–18.

Bitgood, Stephen. "Designing Effective Exhibits: Criteria for Success, Exhibit Design Approaches and Research Strategies." *Visitor Behavior* 9, no. 4 (Winter 1994): 4–15.

Dierking, Lynne D., and John H. Falk. *The Museum Experience*. Washington D.C.: Whalesback Books, 1992.

Fink, Arlene, and Jacqueline Kosecoff. *How to Conduct Surveys: A Step by Step Guide*. 2nd ed. Thousand Oaks, Calif.: Sage, 1998.

Gartenhaus, Alan, publisher. *Minds in Motion: The Docent Educator; The Quarterly Journal for Dedicated Educators: Evaluation* 6, no. 4 (Summer 1997).

Harding, R., M. Kennedy, and L. Raphling. "Tour Evaluations: Taking a Collaborative Approach to Following Up." *Minds in Motion: The Docent Educator; The Quarterly Journal for Dedicated Educators* 10, no. 2 (Winter 2000/01): 14–16.

McNamara, Carter. "Basic Guide to Outcomes Based Evaluation for Non-Profit Organizations with Very Limited Resources," 1997. www.managementhelp.org/evaluatn/outcomes.htm (July 15, 2007).

Schneider, B., and N. Cheslock. *Measuring Results: Executive Summary*. San Francisco: Coevolution Institute, April 2003. www.coevolution.org.

Serrell, Beverly. *Exhibit Labels: An Interpretive Approach*. Walnut Creek, Calif.: AltaMira Press, 1996.

Weil, Stephen E. "A Glossary for Visitor Studies." *Visitor Behavior* 8, no. 4 (1993): 8–11.

———. "Beyond Big and Awesome: Outcome Based Evaluation." *Museum News* 82, no. 6 (Nov/Dec 2003): 40–53.

IMLS Grant Applications—Outcome Based Evaluation Overview, www.imls.gov/applicants/basics.shtm (April 20, 2007).

Visitor Studies Today! Access past issues, www.visitorstudiesarchives.org/vsa.

Committee on Audience Research and Evaluation (CARE). A standing professional committee with American Association of Museums, CARE provides a national forum for museum professionals dedicated to understanding, promoting, and representing the voice of the visitor in all aspects of museum planning and operations. CARE disseminates information about systematic research and evaluation about all museum publics through professional development programs at regional and national museum meetings and through publications. www.care-aam.org/ (Sept. 2007).

The Visitor Studies Association (VSA). Today's premier professional organization focusing on all facets of the visitor experience in museums, zoos, nature centers, visitor centers, historic sites, parks, and other informal learning settings, committed to understanding and enhancing visitor experiences in informal learning settings through research, evaluation, and dialogue. The Visitor Studies Association is all about the people you serve. www.visitorstudies.org/ (Sept. 2007).

Visitor Behavior. Published from 1986 to 1997, this journal was dedicated to the study of visitor behavior in exhibition-type facilities such as aquariums, museums, and zoos. Topics included visitor orientation and circulation, signs/labels/graphics, marketing and publicity, and visitor surveys. www.visitorstudiesarchives.org/vb.php (Sept. 2007).

CHAPTER 11

AAFRC Trust for Philanthropy. *Giving USA 2006: The Annual Report on Philanthropy.* Glenview, Ill.: Giving USA Foundation, 2007.

American Association of Museums. "Guidelines for Museums on Developing and Managing Business Support." AAM November 2001, www.aam-us.org/museumresources/ethics/bus_support.cfm (June 18, 2007).

———. "Guidelines for Museums on Developing and Managing Individual Donor Support." AAM November 2002, www.aam-us.org/museumresources/ethics/indiv_support.cfm (June 18, 2007).

———. "Mission & Institutional Planning." AAM 2007, www.aam-us.org/login.cfm (Jan. 21, 2008).

American Association of Museums and Ellen Cochran Hirzy. *Excellence and Equity: Education and the Public Dimension of Museums.* Washington, D.C.: American Association of Museums, 1992.

American Association for State and Local History. "AASLH Homepage: Technical Leaflet Bundles." AASLH 2007, www.aaslh.org/leaflets.htm (Jan. 21, 2008).

Foundation Center. "Foundation Center Homepage." Foundation Center 2008, www.foundationcenter.org (Jan. 21, 2008).

Institute of Museum and Library Services. "NLG Project Planning: A Tutorial." IMLS 2007, www.imls.gov/Project_Planning/index1.asp (Jan. 21, 2008).

CHAPTER 12

Bitgood, S. "The Role of Attention in Designing Effective Interpretive Labels." *Journal of Interpretation Research* 5, no. 2 (2003): 31–45.

McLean, Kathleen. *Planning for People in Museum Exhibitions.* Washington, D.C.: Association of Science-Technology Centers, 1993. Reprinted 1996.

Roberts, Lisa C. "Educator on Exhibit Teams: A New Role, A New Era." *Journal of Museum Education* (Fall 1994).

Serrell, Beverly. *Exhibit Labels: An Interpretive Approach.* Walnut Creek, Calif.: AltaMira Press, 1996.

Toohey, Jeannette M., and Inez S. Wolins. "Beyond the Turf Battles: Creating Effective Curator-Educator Partnerships." *Journal of Museum Education* 18, no. 3 (Winter 1993).

CHAPTER 13

American Association of Museums. *Museums for a New Century: A Report of the Commission on Museums for a New Century.* Washington, D.C.: American Association of Museums, 1984.

American Association of Museums and Ellen Cochran Hirzy. *Excellence and Equity: Education and the Public Dimension of Museums.* Washington, D.C.: American Association of Museums, 1992.

Hirzy, Ellen Cochran. *True Needs True Partners: Museums and Schools Transforming Education.* Washington D.C.: IMLS, 2001.

Huber, Kim. "Docent Training and Institutional Collaboration." *Museum Association of Arizona Newsletter* 9, no. 2 (Fall 1991): 4.

Huber, Kim, and Dale Steele. "Preserving Arizona, Providing Access." *Museum News* 78, no. 2 (March/April 1999): 40, 59–62.

International Council of Museums (ICOM). icom.museum/strat_plan_eng/intro.html#core (June 7, 2007).

True Needs True Partners: 1998 Survey Highlights. Washington, D.C.: IMLS, 1998.

About the Authors

Anna Johnson, MEd, has twenty-five years of experience working in museums as a director, curator/educator, and consultant. Johnson is a sought-after consultant, presenting special workshops on museum education, docent training, and transitions, and serves as a scholar for the Arizona Humanities Council in the Smithsonian's Museums on Main Street Project. Anna has coauthored a book on the history of coal mining in Colorado and has been active as an educator as well as a historian. Johnson took a struggling history museum in Colorado and developed it into a successful museum by building an effective organizational structure, recruiting and organizing volunteers, and developing strong programming. In addition, she served as the first curator of education at the Tempe Historical Museum, where she developed the focus and structure for the education department as well as establishing trainings and programming. All of her experience has been in history museums, and she has spent considerable time translating history into activities and programs that are interactive and interesting to visitors of all ages. Anna's time in the classroom included teaching American history. Anna has served as an adjunct professor at Arizona State University (ASU). In addition, she has been professionally active serving as president of both the Museum Association of Arizona and Coordinating Committee for History in Arizona, cochair of the Museum Educators' Council of Arizona, and as Arizona's representative to the American Association of Museums' EdCom committee. Johnson's experience has emphasized the value of organization and creative thinking as well as the importance of networking.

Kimberly A. Huber has an MA in anthropology and a museum studies certificate from ASU and a BA in anthropology from Purdue University. She has spent several years studying mediation at ASU and has done post-degree work in K-12 education at Northern Arizona University. She has been doing some form of teaching her whole life. Huber began her museum career in 1979 at the Museum of Northern Arizona. She has been a volunteer, intern, educator, curator, con-

sultant, administrator, and board member at a number of museums in Arizona including Mesa Southwest Museum, The Heard Museum, and Deer Valley Rock Art Center. Huber has been an officer and board member of museum organizations including the Central Arizona Museum Association and the Museum Association of Arizona, and she served as the chair of the Museum Educator's Council of Arizona. Throughout her career she has frequently written for museum newsletters and magazines, including *Museum News* (1999), and has been an oft-solicited presenter at local, state, regional, and national museum conferences. In 1998 Huber was hired by the Arizona State Library, Archives and Public Records Agency, where she served as liaison to the state's museum, library, and archives communities. She managed grants, programs, conferences, and workshops, which included ongoing training and educational programs for public, private, and American Indian arts and cultural institutions. She has written and received millions of dollars worth of grants and managed the $15 million federal LSTA grant program for Arizona. The Institute of Museum and Library Services recognized Arizona's success in building museum and library collaborations through LSTA funding. She was asked to report to colleagues and prepare white papers for Congress about the results of these programs. Although semiretired, she continues to do consulting work.

Nancy Cutler's museum career began in 1989 as a docent at the Desert Botanical Garden, where in 1992 she was hired as the interpretive coordinator. She principally managed oral interpretation, training docents and school tour guides, and also supported and developed other projects within the museum's education department. Cutler tripled the number of docents, to over 150, during her tenure. Many of her volunteers have remained with the Garden for over ten years. Cutler is a member of a number of professional organizations including the American Association of Museums (AAM), EdCom, the Committee on Audience Research and Evaluation (CARE); National Association for Interpretation; and the Western Museums Association. Cutler has been active on the local level as chair of the Museum Educators' Council of Arizona, and has served on the board and various committees (including chairing the conference planning committee) for the statewide Museum Association of Arizona. She also served on the Western Region Committee for an AAM study on "Best Practices in Museum Interpretation." She has published articles and given presentations on various topics relating to museum education, volunteer management, and the Desert Botanical Garden's successful National Science Foundation grant project that created a user-friendly outdoor learning environment for visitors of all ages, based on visitor evaluations of interpretive signage and supplementary materials. Cutler is currently a consultant in the field of museum education and interpretation and has worked on a variety of projects for local museums, including projects and trainings with the Desert Botanical Garden.

Melissa Bingmann, PhD, is presently assistant professor of history at Indiana University–Purdue University at Indianapolis (IUPUI) and teaches graduate-level classes in public history and museum studies. She has over eleven years of experience working at museums and historic houses in South Carolina, Illinois, Arizona, and Rhode Island and taught museum education at Tufts University in the graduate certificate program. Dr. Bingmann developed the program and grant proposal for four successful federal grants for professional development for teachers. She currently serves as the principal investigator on behalf of IUPUI for two Teaching American History grants. In addition to designing and implementing teacher training programs as both a museum educator and university faculty member, she has participated as an invited speaker for professional development workshops in Arkansas and Kentucky. She is a council member of the American Association for State and Local History, is active in National History Day, and has presented discussions at several conferences on the topic of university partnerships and professional development. Dr. Bingmann earned her MA in Applied History from the University of South Carolina and her PhD in History from Arizona State University.

Tim Grove is an education specialist and exhibition developer at the Smithsonian's National Air and Space Museum, where he oversees programming and educational publications and works on exhibition and Web development. Most recently he worked on America by Air, a 15,000-square-foot permanent exhibition about the history of commercial aviation. Prior to this position, he served as project educator for Lewis & Clark: The National Bicentennial Exhibition, which traveled the nation. He was involved in all aspects of the exhibition's development and guided the development of the exhibition's online presence, which won the Best Online Exhibition award at the 2004 Museums and the Web conference Best of the Web competition. He also directed the production of the exhibition's extensive curriculum, including two teams of teachers in St. Louis and Philadelphia. Before his work on Lewis and Clark, Grove spent six years at the National Museum of American History, where he managed the popular Hands on History Room, served as accessibility advocate, and worked on exhibitions and Web projects, including three educational Web activities and the online exhibition Within These Walls . . . . His career has also included presenting numerous teacher workshops, managing and training more than 200 docents, giving tours of the Smithsonian's National Portrait Gallery, and completing a graduate internship at the Colonial Williamsburg Foundation. He originated and currently authors the Web-focused History Bytes column in *History News*. He has also written articles about hands-on learning and docent management and served as an adjunct professor at Webster University in St. Louis. He holds a master's degree in history from George Mason University in Virginia. In 2008 Tim received the Smithsonian Education Achievement Award.